Love, Silk & Sand

Sissi Flegel

Love, Silk & Sand

Aus dem Deutschen
von Michael Turnbull

Thienemann

A Brand New Beginning

“We have to celebrate!” I shouted and danced around the kitchen table with my aunt Anne. “Three lots of good news in one hour!”

Aunt Lise put the kettle on. “She’ll be back in a month!”

She was talking about my sister Nicki, who had worked as an au pair in Hong Kong after taking her school-leaving exam and had been **hitch-hiking** through China for the last three months with her boyfriend Nick. And we had just got her message that she was coming home – at last! “And about time, too,” said Aunt Lise as she poured the water into the teapot.

“Nicki’s coming! And you’ve won a prize for your article!”

“Yes, and the **prospect** of a job!” My aunt spun me around left and right until we were **out of breath**. I plopped down onto the nearest chair and reached for the letter: *Dear Mimi, Your article about the Atacama Desert in Northern Chile was very well re-*

---

to hitch-hike – trampen;
prospect – Aussicht;
out of breath – außer Atem

*ceived by our readers. Because we are now planning a regular page for young readers of the Tagespost, we would be very interested in **gaining** your services as a permanent **freelance contributor**. And as you won't be giving up travelling in the near future, we can look forward to more exciting contributions …*

"Of course I won't give up travelling. After all, I want to become the most famous travel journalist of all time! Ouch! The tea's still hot!" I **spluttered**. "It's just a pity we don't have a journey planned at the moment. But perhaps Nicki will have an idea."

"Nicki? She'll have had enough of the **gypsy** life for a while," said Aunt Anne. "If I've been away for a long time, all I want to do is stay at home."

"Yes, *you*! But we're young, dynamic, full of energy and **eager for** adventure! Can't get enough of it – was that the doorbell?"

"I'll go," said Aunt Anne. "Oh, Carlos, how nice of you to visit us! Come in, you can celebrate, too!"

I flung my arms around Carlos's neck and told him straight away about the chance of becoming a "permanent freelance contributor".

"That's great! I've come just at the right time. I want to invite you to come travelling."

"No! Where to? And when? With you?" I had got to know Carlos on the trip to Chile the aunts had **prescribed** for me as a **cure** for lovesickness. At

---

to gain – gewinnen;
freelance – freiberuflich; contributor – *hier:* Mitarbeiter/in;
to splutter – sich verhaspeln, stammeln;
gypsy – Zigeuner-; to be eager for – begierig sein nach;
to prescribe – verordnen;
cure – Heilung

Easter I had planned to meet the love of my life in Paris – Rory, who I'd fallen **head over heels** in love with in Hong Kong. But just beforehand he sent me a mail: *Dear Mimi, it's over, we'll never see each other again.*

I had sworn to myself never to fall in love again. Never again! But Carlos was stronger than my **vow**. He was studying geology and geography and lived close by, so we saw each other several times a week. And even my aunts – who Nicki and I had lived with since our parents died in a car accident in Turkey – loved him. Differently from me, of course, but still! He was almost part of the family and had an exclusive right to our **spare room**.

"Mimi, I'm going on a field trip to Morocco. Perhaps you know about the heavy **earthquake** that happened there more than 50 years ago. It was in Agadir. And that's where our group is going to stay and **carry out investigations**. And I thought you could fly to Agadir afterwards – the field trip lasts two weeks and ends a week before **Whitsun**. We could travel around for a couple of days and spend some time in Marrakech. What do you think? It would fit in perfectly with your Whitsun break, wouldn't it?"

"Sure it would!" I cried enthusiastically. "And I'd

---

head over heels – Hals über Kopf;
vow – Schwur;
spare room – Gästezimmer;
earthquake – Erdbeben;
to carry out investigations – Untersuchungen durchführen;
Whitsun – Pfingsten

have enough material for my first Tagespost article!"

"Just a minute." Aunt Anne wrinkled her **forehead**. "You know we think travelling is a good thing, but this seems different to me. Carlos, you'll be with your **fellow** students for two weeks. If Mimi flies out she'll be the youngest, and only a schoolgirl, too. And the group will already have **gelled**. It certainly won't be easy for her."

"So what? I don't mind, Auntie Anne!" I assured her vehemently. "Just think, Morocco! Marrakech! The Thousand and One Nights!"

"I've **entrusted you with** Mimi once before," continued Aunt Anne, "but in Chile that was an emergency. You didn't disappoint us, Carlos, but now tell us quite specifically how and where you'll spend the nights. Mimi is only 17!"

Carlos looked down in embarrassment. "I haven't really thought it through in detail yet. I know we're meeting a student called Bahrim in Agadir. And he's going to organise all the travelling and **accommodation** for our group. I don't know exactly how many of us want to go on to Marrakech. But I give you my **solemn** promise that I'll look after Mimi. Nothing will happen to her!"

"That isn't the problem, Carlos," said Aunt Lise.

---

forehead – Stirn;
fellow – Mit-;
to gel – sich festigen;
to entrust s.o. with s.o./s.th. – jmdm. etwas/jmdn. anvertrauen;
accommodation – Unterkunft;
solemn – feierlich

"We know how much you like each other. *Now*. But in Morocco you'll be with girl students ..."

"I'm with them every day," interrupted Carlos.

"Yes, I know. But not in such close company as on a two-week excursion. Please understand us. We don't want Mimi to be disappointed. Have I made myself clear?"

Carlos nodded. "I won't disappoint Mimi."

"I know, Carlos. You and me! We love each other. Who could come between us? I'd like to get to know *that* girl," I said. "I'd **tear** her to pieces, really!"

We laughed.

In the end, and after a lot of **toing and froing**, my aunts agreed.

---

to tear – (zer)reißen;
toing and froing – Hin und Her

Left in the Lurch!

* ' * ' * ' * ' * ' * ' * ' * ' *

Now I know what a **nightmare** is!

I sank down onto my rucksack. Just don't cry, Mimi, it could be worse! No, I thought **in despair**, it couldn't! It's already bad enough. I'm stuck in a foreign country, in Morocco, in the arrivals hall at Agadir airport, I don't speak the language, I don't know where I can spend the night, I don't have very much money, I don't know anyone I can turn to ... so what's the message, just before ten p.m. local time? Damn! I looked at my watch for the millionth time. I'd been waiting for Carlos for over two hours. He wanted to collect me; he wanted to be on time – and he's left me in the lurch, the rat. The bandit, the **unreliable wretch**. Why did it have to happen to me?

I shook my head in disbelief and stood up. The hall was empty, **apart from** the two or three men

---

to leave s.o. in the lurch – jmdn. im Stich lassen;
nightmare – Albtraum;
in despair – verzweifelt;
unreliable – unzuverlässig;
wretch – Schuft;
apart from – außer

who had checked the arriving passengers' passports. They didn't have anything left to do now. Everyone had been **processed** ages ago, had collected their luggage and been **hugged** and kissed and met by loving friends and family.

Everyone except me! I was still standing here, waiting. I was thirsty. And hungry. And I was tired. And nervous. I felt so sorry for myself.

I wiped the palms of my hands on my jeans – and suddenly remembered my tour of Canada. Out there in the wilderness I had learnt something fundamentally important to me, that courage is **largely** a matter of training.

Okay, I thought, so I'll do a bit of courage training. What can you do, Mimi? Look for a hotel? Yes. But if Carlos has had an accident or been held up in some other way, how will he know where to find me? Perhaps I should spend the night here on my rucksack?

Out of the question. Nobody would let a girl sleep here all on her own.

So, what to do? I wiped my hands dry once again, then I took my mobile out of my pocket, pressed **redial** and heard for the thousandth time that Carlos wasn't available at the moment. I almost **hurled** the thing across the hall, but I stopped myself at the last moment because I had a **brainwave**. If some-

---

to process – abfertigen;
to hug – umarmen;
largely – im Wesentlichen;
redial – Wahlwiederholung;
to hurl – schleudern;
brainwave – Gedankenblitz

thing had really happened to Carlos, he wouldn't be able to help me right now. But later, as soon as he was able to, he'd ring me, and then I could tell him where to find me. So I had to make sure my mobile was charged.

So far, so good. And now? I decided to wait another ten minutes. Then I'd **hail a taxi** and get myself to a hotel. Tomorrow was tomorrow. I'd make my next plan then.

I yawned and shook my water bottle. Empty. Like the hall. There was a **bin** two metres away from me. I aimed and threw – and missed. Damn. Even simple things were going wrong, not to mention the journey. Yet everything had gone so well up to now. We wanted to meet up in Agadir today, and then travel around with four others from the study trip and spend the rest of the week in Marrakech.

I stood up and flung the empty water bottle into the bin. "Leaving me in the lurch like this! *That* wasn't the plan."

I looked at my watch again and saw that the ten minutes were already up. So I **hitched** my rucksack onto my shoulders, grabbed my old travelling bag and **strode off**. Towards the exit. Towards the taxis. I grinned. In a film the hero would come **dashing in** now and snatch the heroine into his powerful arms, murmuring something about an "unfortunate **delay**" into her hair. And immediately everything would be all right.

---

to hail a taxi – ein Taxi anhalten;
bin – Mülleimer; to hitch – *hier:* schwingen;
to stride off – wegstiefeln; to dash in – hereinstürzen;
delay – Verzögerung

I looked around. No hero, no Carlos came running up. So I **gulped bravely**, and then I was standing by a taxi, the first in the rank. The driver was asleep. I knocked on the window, opened the door and said, "Please take me to a **plain** hotel in town."

"Hotel?" the man repeated **in a doze**. "Name?"

"I've no idea. I need ..." A bicycle bell rang. Some idiot was riding without lights and coming straight towards the taxi. You could see it was an ancient model right away, even in the dark.

All **at once** the taxi driver was wide awake and pressed the **horn** in horror. But the cyclist kept on ringing and was on collision course for the taxi. At the last moment he jumped of the bike, letting it clatter to the ground, took a **daring leap** and snatched me into his arms. I was gasping for breath in shock, the driver was yelling – and then I realised: "Hey, Carlos!"

We were standing inside a ring of taxi drivers. One of them grabbed Carlos angrily by the collar; two others went towards him with raised fists; someone **shielded** me protectively. It took us quite a while to calm everyone down and explain what was going on in French and English.

---

to gulp – schlucken;
brave – tapfer;
plain – einfach;
in a doze – verschlafen;
at once – sofort;
horn – Hupe;
daring – waghalsig;
leap – Sprung;
to shield – abschirmen

Breathless and dripping with sweat, we all grinned at one another. The taxi driver put out his hand in **reconciliation** and loaded the bike into the **boot** – the fact that it stuck out a mile didn't seem to **bother** him in the least. We fell into the back seat and Carlos said, "Hotel Safir, please," and then we kissed. The kiss lasted almost as long as the drive.

We unloaded my luggage and the bike, paid and went up the steps leading to the hotel entrance. I sat on the top step and pulled Carlos down to me. "What happened? Why didn't you come to the airport on time? I almost died of **fright**!"

"I knew you would. That's why I borrowed the bike! It was like this: the five of us – you'll get to know everyone soon enough – left this morning from near Tafraoute in our **hired** van. Tafraoute's in the Antiatlas. We had planned to arrive at the Safir in the afternoon, and I would have **set out** again to pick you up from the airport. Everything went fine, but then ..."

"Then you had an accident, or the **petrol** ran out!" I said.

"No, it wasn't as bad as that. We only had a **puncture**. Left back wheel. It was about 20 or 30 kilometres outside Agadir."

---

reconciliation – Versöhnung;
boot – Kofferraum;
to bother – stören;
fright – Angst; hired – gemietet;
to set out – sich auf den Weg machen;
petrol – Benzin;
puncture – Reifenpanne

"So? All you needed to do was to stand by the road and stick out your **thumb**. Or don't they take hitchhikers here?"

"Slow down, wait. We were making such good time that nobody thought of that. It wasn't necessary either. We just had to change the tyre and then drive on. It would only take about ten minutes, we thought," explained Carlos, continuing. "We got out and fetched the **jack** and the **spanner** from the boot. The jack was okay, but not the spanner. Man, it was terrible! It bent so much on the first screw it was totally useless. So we did exactly what you said. We stood by the road and stuck out our thumbs. It was funny at first, but because we were on a tiny by-road, a sand track, there were absolutely no vehicles at first. In the end, two cars came by, but they just drove on. So the third time we stood in the middle of the road. The driver must have thought it was a **hold-up** because he **put his foot down** and **swerved** round us.

Suddenly, out of the blue, there was a man standing next to us. Bahrim – he's a student like us and has a side job as a driver – explained the situation to him.

The man hailed the next car that went by. It stopped, but the driver didn't have a spanner. And so it went on. In the end, the man went back to his

---

thumb – Daumen;
jack – Wagenheber;
spanner – Schraubenschlüssel;
hold-up – Überfall;
to put one's foot down – *hier:* Gas geben;
to swerve – ausweichen

house, which stood on its own in the middle of nowhere and couldn't be seen from the road. After a while he came back with hot peppermint tea and pita bread.

It was already starting to get dark. I couldn't ring you because you were still in the aeroplane. Finally I had the idea of asking the man through Bahrim whether he had a bicycle. He did, and he was prepared to lend it to me, but only if I left all my luggage with him for security."

"Heavens!" I exclaimed. "And you agreed?"

"Of course. It was my only way of getting to the airport today. So I left my luggage with him, forgetting about my mobile in the rush and excitement, and got the bike. Man, does it go! No lights, brakes don't work, no air in the **tyres**, no pump. But the bell works perfectly!

So I rode off, but because it was dark in the meantime and there were no signs, I badly lost my way twice. But still, I got there just in time!" Carlos finished his story and stood up.

I drew him back down. "And ... how are the others? I mean, you've been together for two weeks, and now I'm here on the scene ... and I'm much younger than the others as well." I swallowed. "I haven't suddenly become shy, Carlos. But I need to know what to expect. And don't forget, I'm still at school."

"You're my girlfriend and the best babe in the world," said Carlos and pulled me to him.

"But the others ..."

"You'll like them. Bahrim and Klaus are the best

---

tyre – Reifen

friends you can imagine. Always in a good **mood**, helpful, just good mates. Wolfi ..." Carlos hesitated. "Wolfi expects every girl to go crazy about him the minute he walks into the room."

"So?" I **screwed up** my nose. "Will he expect that from me?"

"I should hope not!" exclaimed Carlos, **genuinely appalled**. "He knows you're my girlfriend!"

"Good. And who else is there?"

"Wanda. There are no difficulties with Wanda. I got on well with her. Actually, I've just realised that we were together most of the time," said Carlos. "She's really nice. You'll like her."

"I hope so." I decided to take things slowly and give everyone a close look first.

"Now, come on!" Carlos jumped up.

We went to reception and were given our key. Then we heard a vehicle driving **hell for leather** into the car park. It stopped, doors slammed and a group of suntanned people stormed laughing and **whooping** into the foyer.

"Hey, Speedy Gonzales is already here! And is this the girl who's followed him?"

---

mood – Laune;
to screw up – *hier:* kräuseln;
genuinely – echt;
appalled – entsetzt;
hell for leather – mit einem Affenzahn;
to whoop – schreien

Testing the Water

* ' * ' * ' * ' * ' * ' * ' * ' *

Carlos **grinned** from ear to ear. "The tall one is Wolfi, the short blond is Klaus. Next to him is Wanda; that's Bahrim. And this ..." Carlos put his arm around me. "This is my Mimi."

"Hello!" Bahrim was as small as me and **wiry**. He had short, dark curly hair and a cheerful smile. I liked him immediately. I wasn't so sure about Wolfi. He was a typical macho, looked me up and down, took me in his arms, **felt me up** quickly and **expertly** and then nodded **appreciatively**. "Great girl. I like *you!*"

Fantastic. I **unhooked myself** and said hello to Klaus and then to Wanda. I caught my breath. Wanda had **plaited** her dark, red-streaked hair and some coloured ribbons into a thick **braid**. Her black

---

to test the water – die Lage sondieren/checken;
to grin – grinsen;
wiry – drahtig;
to feel s.o. up – jmdn. begrapschen;
expertly – fachmännisch;
appreciative – anerkennend;
to unhook oneself – sich losmachen;
to plait – flechten; braid – Zopf

eyes were highlighted with a dark purple eyeshadow and there was a matching **stud** on her chin. But her jeans and shirt were **filthy** and dusty, her hands were black and there was a big **smudge** on her face. "What happened to you?"

"I only fell into a **ditch**," she answered cheerfully. "Oh Carlos, it's great you're back. I've missed you. Nobody helped me when I ..."

"I'm dying of hunger," interrupted Bahrim. "What about meeting up in ten minutes in the restaurant?"

Everyone agreed. We went upstairs. Carlos shut the door, stared silently at the bed, then went over to the window and looked out into the night.

I was surprised. "Something wrong?"

"Yes," he said quietly. "It's Wolfi. He ..."

"I know. He **comes on to** every girl, whether she has a boyfriend or not, right?"

Carlos nodded.

"That's a pain." I fell onto the bed. "Does it bother you?"

"What kind of a question is that?" snapped Carlos.

I laughed. "Nice to know. Forget the idiot, Carlos. I can **deal with** him all right."

"I hope so."

---

stud – Piercing;
filthy – dreckig;
smudge – Schmierfleck;
ditch – Graben;
to come on to s.o. – jmdn. anmachen;
to deal with s.o./s.th. – mit jmdm. umgehen

"Don't worry. Have you got a toothbrush with you?"

"I haven't got a thing. No razor, no toothbrush."

"I always have a reserve toothbrush with me," I said proudly. "You can have it with pleasure."

"Nothing else?"

"What more do you want? I haven't got a razor, I'm afraid."

"I can borrow Klaus's, but ..."

He lay down next to me – with the result that we went down to the restaurant **pretty** late.

"There were only sandwiches left," Klaus called out to us. "We ordered for you."

Wanda had washed, changed and put on new make-up. She pointed to the chair next to her. "For you, Carlos!"

Wolfi moved up close to me. "Oh Mimi, you really missed something!" he **exclaimed** dramatically. "No one, but no one, could help us. The cars either drove past or they didn't have a spanner. In the end, the old guy – he only had two black **stumps** in his mouth and smelt dreadfully of **garlic** – remembered that the next village wasn't very far away and even had a garage. It **occurred to** him an hour after Carlos had left!"

Wolfi never took his eyes off me. He kept putting his hand on my arm. "So Bahrim drove the van **at a crawl** into the village and we trotted behind him,

---

pretty – ziemlich;
to exclaim – ausrufen;
stump – *hier:* Zahnstumpf; garlic – Knoblauch;
to occur to s.o. – jmdm. einfallen;
at a crawl – im Schneckentempo

so as not to put too much weight on the tyres, and Wanda **tripped** and was suddenly lying decoratively in the ditch. I rescued her immediately."

Wanda gave a **mocking** laugh. "You didn't even put out your hand to me, you liar!"

"You didn't see it in the darkness," replied Wolfi. I laughed. The guy was **quick off the mark**!

"The village," continued Wolfi, "consisted of a few, very few, **clay** buildings, and the men were all sitting in the only café amusing themselves by not talking and getting drunk on peppermint tea.

But we saved their evening. We brought them an **invigorating** dose of the big, wide world, of excitement and adventure. Suddenly they all stood up and surrounded the van and before we could get a word out there was this bear of a man standing next to Bahrim **brandishing** a colossal spanner over his head."

I actually didn't want to laugh yet again, but this scene was too funny.

"Don't laugh, Mimi. That was just the beginning. The guy set to work – but nothing happened. Nothing. All the screws had completely **seized up**. The guy **growled**, applied the spanner again – and jumped on it. A jerk, a terrible **grinding** noise and

---

to trip – stolpern;
mocking – spottend;
to be quick off the mark – schnell reagieren;
clay – Lehm;
invigorating – belebend;
to brandish – schwingen;
to seize up – festrosten, festfressen;
to growl – knurren; grinding – reibend, schleifend

the screw is out. Bravo! everyone shouts and claps their hands. The man goes through the procedure again, the screws are out, and while he's about it he changes the tyre as well. But if you think we were able to drive away, you're wrong. No way. We had to drink loads of tea, three glasses each. And you know what, Mimi?" Wolfi bent forward **confidentially** and whispered, "I've been in a bad way since then. The stuff didn't agree with me."

"You poor thing!"

I shouldn't have said that. Carlos mumbled something unfriendly, but Klaus just said calmly, "Wolfi, that's enough. You've had your little show. We're here, too. Right, everyone, when do we leave tomorrow?"

"We should make an early start," Bahrim reminded us. "We have to get hold of a new **spare tyre**, return the bicycle and collect Carlos's luggage. It'll be dark by the time we arrive in Imouzzer. But hang on!" He waved to the waiter. "What time is breakfast?"

"At eight."

"So, it'll be half past."

Wanda yawned and laid her head on Carlos's shoulder. "My God, I'm tired!" She gave Carlos a little kiss on the **cheek**.

What on earth was wrong with the woman? I stood up. "I'm quite tired, too."

"I'll take you upstairs, baby," offered Wolfi at once, but Carlos had already put his arm around me. "Come on, Mimi."

---

confidential – vertraulich;
spare tyre – Ersatzrad; cheek – Wange

In our room we flashed at one another angrily. "What have you got into your head?" hissed Carlos.

"Have you slept with Wanda?" I **hissed** back.

"Me? No, of course not," he replied vehemently. "We get on well, we're just friends ..."

"Oh yeah? Just friends? So why does she lay her head on your shoulder and give you a kiss while I'm sitting next to you? Can you tell me that please?"

"Why shouldn't she? What's wrong with that?"

I was **flabbergasted**. "You don't find it pretty **matey**?"

"No, I don't. But how could you laugh at every single one of Wolfi's stupid jokes? You'll give him the wrong idea!"

"Oh will I? He can think what he likes for all I care. At least he didn't **cling to** me!"

I was so angry and disappointed I fell onto the bed in tears. "We never argued in Germany!" I sobbed. "But now we're seeing each other for the first time in two weeks, now of all times we have to **have a row**! I'm going to fly back home tomorrow! You amuse yourself with Wanda and leave me alone!"

"You want to fly back home because of Wanda? Because of Wanda? Mimi, she's **not an issue**."

"Yes, she is!"

---

to hiss – zischen;
flabbergasted – entgeistert;
matey – *hier:* vertraulich;
to cling to – hängen an;
to have a row – sich streiten;
to not be an issue – unwichtig sein

"No way! But Wolfi's driving me crazy."

"Idiot! What **harm** can Wolfi do? None! Try and understand me, Carlos. I just didn't want to get into an argument with him right on the first evening."

"And with me you did?"

"No, I don't want to argue with you," I defended myself. "But do you think I like the way Wanda's behaving? She doesn't miss a single opportunity to show everyone how **pally** the two of you are. She's acting as if I weren't there!"

"So? Just let her. You're here, and that's all that's important to me," said Carlos softly.

Well, we **made up** after that.

---

harm – Schaden;
to be pally – *hier:* sich gut verstehen;
to make up – *hier:* sich versöhnen

Friction, Friction, Friction

Next morning Wanda made her big entrance. She was wearing the shortest shorts I'd ever seen, a pink boob tube with a matching blouse she'd done up with only a single button – at least it wasn't *completely* open. There were pink, neon green and shiny yellow ribbons plaited into her hair. At the buffet she went and stood right next to Carlos and whispered, so I could hear it, "So, did you have a wild night?"

Carlos **blushed**. Wanda smiled at him. Boy, was she good at that! With half-closed eyes, as if she shared a million intimate secrets with Carlos. She **fiddled** with her purple stud and said confidentially, "You've made a great **conquest**, Mimi. Wolfi is over the moon about you. Although that doesn't mean much with someone like him. He **raves about** every girl."

"Oh yeah? And about you, too?"

---

friction – Reibung;
to blush – rot werden;
to fiddle – herumspielen;
conquest – Eroberung;
to rave about – schwärmen von

"He's not my type," she answered, shrugging her shoulders.

"So? What a pity. Are you hoping he's *my* type? I have to disappoint you there. But can you tell me what *your* type is?"

Wanda rolled her eyes. "Are you getting jealous now? How **dreary**. That stuff just **grates** on me. But still, you're very young."

Aha, I thought angrily. I knew it. Here's someone showing me her claws.

But what's with Carlos? Is he giving me any support? Not one bit! He's **pretending** not to notice! Just wait ...

I sat down. Damn, I thought, does there have to be a trouble-maker on every trip? On the trekking tour of Canada there was that liar Keko. In Hong Kong – oh Hong Kong! The disappointment came afterwards with that trip. Only in Chile did things really go okay. No, that's not right either. In Chile I wanted to **steer clear of** Carlos, but everything turned out differently ... I spluttered my orange juice. At any rate, Carlos and I belonged together and whether Wanda liked it or not, she'd have to accept it. And Wolfi? That was a tiny problem. I'd deal with that all right!

I realised we were all morning **grouches**. No one said a word, apart from "Is there still tea in the pot?" and "Please pass the jam."

---

dreary – langweilig;
to grate on s.o. – jmdn. nerven;
to pretend – tun, als ob;
to steer clear of s.o. – einen Bogen um jmdn. machen;
grouch – Muffel

I pulled off a piece of pita bread and **spread** it with honey. They both tasted completely different from back home. But that's what travelling is like. If you want everything to be just like it is at home, you shouldn't get on the train or plane. I wiped my mouth on a serviette and said to myself, Mimi, you're a woman of action. Remember that the first opportunity is usually the best one. So take it.

We stood up, fetched our luggage and loaded the van.

Bahrim was already behind the wheel and Carlos was getting in when I put my hand on Wolfi's arm and pulled him behind the bus. "Hey, Wolfi, listen. Carlos and I are together and I don't want that to change. Got it?"

Wolfi widened his eyes. "What are you trying to say, Mimi? I know you're friends, but that doesn't mean you and I can't talk to each other, does it? Or are we in the Middle Ages? Have you been forbidden to speak? Has he got you **under his thumb** that much? I'd never have thought that, the way you look."

"My God, don't you understand what I'm trying to say?"

"To be honest, no, Mimi. I don't understand a thing."

"You're impossible."

"So I've been told, often," replied Wolfi coolly. "And it was always the start of a beautiful friendship."

---

to spread – bestreichen;
under s.o.'s thumb – unter jmds. Fuchtel

"Whaaat?" I stared at him **aghast**.

Wolfi grinned. "By the way, have you asked yourself what's going on between Carlos and Wanda?"

"Nothing," I hissed.

"Oh? Who says? Carlos? Ha ha! Who was with them for two weeks, you or me?"

I **clenched my fists**. "My God, you're horrible!"

I turned around, got in the van and saw that Wanda was sitting next to Carlos. That, too! This was going to be great. Great? It was going to be **tiring** and dangerous for Carlos and me. But I'd **put up a fight**, there was no question of that!

I **gnawed** at my lower lip. Mimi, I said to myself, don't forget: courage is a question of training. Only – this kind of training was new for me. But hadn't I always wanted to experience new things? Collect all kinds of impressions and become the best travel journalist of all time? I took a deep breath, counted to 20 and then smiled at Wanda and said, "Please, could we change places? Carlos and I have been separated for two weeks. We have a lot to catch up on, you know?"

I squeezed myself **ruthlessly** between the two of them.

Klaus had seen everything. He raised his thumb, grinned at me and said, "Bahrim has booked us rooms in a small hotel near Imouzzer. The village is

---

aghast – entsetzt;
to clench one's fists – die Hände zu Fäusten ballen;
tiring – ermüdend;
to put up a fight – sich zur Wehr setzen;
to gnaw – nagen;
ruthless – rücksichtslos

only about 80 kilometres from Agadir **as the crow flies**, but the journey will take a few hours because the road goes through a **gorge** and then zigzags up into the mountains."

This put us into a hectic rush. First we bought the new spare tyre, then we returned the bicycle and got Carlos's luggage back, and so it was early afternoon before we were finally on the road to Imouzzer.

The landscape was really cool. A rapidly flowing river bubbled through the **tight** gorge, which had **towering** sides and rocks everywhere. The road was narrow and **winding**. And then there were slow-moving **donkey** carts and huge trucks that made **overtaking** impossible. Bahrim was always braking, **accelerating** and changing **gear**, and we were getting worried that we wouldn't arrive before nightfall if he went on at such a crawl.

"It doesn't matter." Wanda yawned heartily. "We don't have anything else planned for today, do we, Carlos? All I want is to ..."

We all jumped, because Bahrim had given a sudden cry.

"What's wrong?"

---

as the crow flies – Luftlinie;
gorge – Schlucht;
tight – eng;
towering – hoch aufragend;
winding – kurvig;
donkey – Esel;
to overtake – überholen;
to accelerate – beschleunigen;
gear – Gang

"Nothing happens when I put down the **clutch**!"

"What do you mean?" asked Wolfi immediately.

"I can't change gear any more!"

"Oh great," I said. "I don't understand much about cars, but that doesn't sound very **reassuring**."

"It isn't either. I mean, it's not only not reassuring, it's a bloody **nuisance**! It means that the clutch is **bust**."

Now Klaus joined in. "We have two possibilities. Bahrim can either switch off the engine, we open the **bonnet**, make serious faces at the clutch, decide we can't do anything about it, push the van until the engine starts, hop in as quickly as we can ..."

"What? How are we supposed to push the van on such a steep **slope**? Can you tell us that?" asked Wolfi.

Klaus grinned at him. "I haven't finished. I've only told you the first possibility. The second one looks like this: because he can't change gear any more, Bahrim drives in second all the way to Imouzzer. We **keep our fingers crossed** that he doesn't have to brake suddenly and stop, that no one comes up behind and above all that there's enough petrol. Is there enough petrol, Bahrim?"

"Yes."

---

clutch – Kupplung;
reassuring – beruhigend;
nuisance – Ärgernis;
bust – kaputt;
bonnet – Motorhaube;
slope – Hang, Anstieg;
to keep one's fingers crossed – die Daumen drücken

"Well, that's something. So keep your fingers crossed and **pray** that no donkey cart or anything else blocks the road."

"What if one of us ran in front of the van shouting 'Out of the way, out of the way!'" suggested Wolfi.

"Good idea!" said Bahrim. "Especially because everyone here speaks your language!"

We sat in silence. The donkey cart in front of us suddenly turned into an almost invisible track across the fields. Bahrim **swore** and swerved to the left. The driver of the car that was overtaking us at that moment **sounded the horn** angrily and gestured angrily. Bahrim raised his hand in apology and wiped the sweat from his forehead.

"How far is it to Imouzzer?" asked Wanda.

Bahrim looked at the **mileage indicator**. "At this rate it'll take two hours at the most. No need to panic, as long as everything goes as well as it has up to now. Keep your fingers crossed, okay? And leave the rest to me."

And that was how we **joggled** uphill. It went surprisingly well – until just outside Imouzzer. Night began to fall – and our luck left us when a sheep hopped **merrily** onto the road and came **skipping** towards us **in curiosity**. "Oh no!" yelled Klaus, and

---

to pray – beten;
to swear – fluchen;
to sound the horn – hupen;
mileage indicator – Kilometerzähler;
to joggle – zuckeln; merry – fröhlich;
to skip – springen;
in curiosity – neugierig

Bahrim let out a stream of **curses**. He was only just able to swerve around the astonished animal, but that was it. The **flock** was **gathering** in the **stray**, **bleating** and watching Bahrim's breaking efforts in fascination.

"Well done, Bahrim, really!" Klaus gave him an admiring pat on the shoulder.

We got out, and a young boy holding his little sister by the hand greeted us politely and drove his animals happily on.

"And now?" The road sloped gently down to the village below. "Push," ordered Klaus **succinctly**.

"No," said Bahrim. "We'll leave the van here and go on foot to the hotel. Otherwise we'll have to push it uphill tomorrow."

That made sense. And so we arrived at the hotel about half an hour later with **all our gear** and pretty out of breath.

I let my rucksack slide off my shoulders and almost knocked over a moped that was leaning against the wall. I made a quick grab for it and stood it up straight again – and noticed that there were three red plastic roses draped around the **handlebar**. "Look, Carlos," I said appreciatively. "Someone has a sense of the romantic here, don't you think?"

---

curse – Fluch;
flock – Herde;
to gather in – einsammeln;
stray – Ausreißer;
to bleat – blöken;
succinct – *hier:* lapidar;
all our gear – unser ganzes Gepäck;
handlebar – Lenker

Rose Petals and Orange Blossom

* ‘ * ‘ * ‘ * ‘ * ‘ * ‘ * ‘ *

What a surprise! There was a fire burning in the **hearth** in the hall. Lamps **shaped** like stars **radiated** a warm light and upstairs in our room the bed was strewn with rose **petals**. And as if that wasn't enough, the branches of an orange tree hung over our balcony bearing sweetly smelling white **blossom** and **ripe** fruit.

Hunger drove us downstairs. The dining room was no less exotic. In the middle there was a grill upon which long **skewers** of meat were **sizzling**. Lamps of coloured glass bathed the room in a **dim** light. There were candles burning on the tables and the tablecloths were covered with flowers. The room was filled with an amazing, spicy aroma.

---

hearth – Kamin;
shaped – geformt;
to radiate – ausstrahlen;
petal – Blütenblatt;
blossom – Blüte;
ripe – reif;
skewer – Spieß;
to sizzle – brutzeln;
dim – dämmrig

"This is Bilal," Bahrim introduced the waiter. "Have you got anything nice for us?"

Bilal nodded and smiled and led us to a round table.

Captivated by the atmosphere, I sat down next to Carlos and noticed too late that Wolfi, quick as **lightening**, had moved his chair to my free side. Oh well, so what, I thought **serenely**. Apart from this morning he'd behaved normally all day.

Bilal placed a huge **platter** of different salads, hard-boiled eggs, olives and marinated chillies on the table.

"Thank you," said Klaus **with glee**. "That'll be fine for me. What are you lot going to have?"

The platter was empty in no time. The next course was a carrot soup spiced with **cinnamon**, **saffron** and coriander. I loved it and had a second **helping**.

"That's the way," said Klaus appreciatively. "Eat up, my girl, you're still growing."

Something was crawling up my leg. "Are there spiders here, or **beetles**?"

"There are spiders, snakes, scorpions and all kinds of other unpleasant creatures. But certainly not in Bilal's dining room," said Bahrim firmly.

---

captivated – verzaubert;
lightening – Blitz; serene – heiter;
platter – Platte;
with glee – fröhlich;
cinnamon – Zimt;
saffron – Safran;
helping – Portion;
beetle – Käfer

"That's a relief. It's gone anyway," I replied. But I'd hardly taken a second spoonful of soup when the tickling started again. I shook my head **indignantly** – and then I realised. A leg was moving cautiously up and down. Wolfi! I thought. This guy needs to be taught a lesson!

While I went on eating, I saw a serviette fall from Wolfi's knee. He bent down and his chair **tilted** to one side. My left leg shot out and Wolfi landed on the floor.

"Shaky ground?" I asked innocently.

"**Confident**, Mimi, confident," answered Wolfi coolly. But I could see he was **annoyed** and I got ready for the next round.

Bilal collected up the soup bowls. "Do you remember Mehdi?" he asked Bahrim.

"Of course! Have you heard from him?"

"He's fine, but you can ask him yourself. He's here."

"Mehdi is a friend of mine. We're studying together at the university – hi Mehdi, it's you!"

Grinning widely, Mehdi put a large round clay bowl on the table and raised its pointed **lid**. "Chicken **tajine** with honey, **almonds** and **raisins**. Enjoy it!" he said invitingly.

---

indignant – verärgert;
to tilt – kippen;
confident – sicher;
annoyed – verärgert;
lid – Deckel;
tajine – geschmort;
almond – Mandel;
raisin – Rosine

"Come and sit with us," said Bahrim. "There's enough space!"

Mehdi squeezed in between Wolfi and me. "Mehdi, you all need to know, is not only a fellow student, he's also a famous entertainer and magician," Bahrim explained.

"Really?" asked Wanda, putting a particularly large and **succulent** piece of chicken on Carlos's plate. "More, Carlos?"

"Yes, please. A few raisins and carrots."

"I'm still learning," Mehdi explained **modestly**. He reached for a glass of water, **drained** it in one, placed it in front of us on the table, covered it with my serviette, tapped it, removed the serviette – and the glass had vanished.

"Hey! Where's my glass?" I exclaimed.

"**Spirited away**," answered Mehdi.

We looked for it on the table; we looked under the table. The glass wasn't there! Then suddenly it was standing by my plate again.

"How did you do that? Do it again! But slowly, really slowly!" we all shouted in confusion.

Mehdi did as we asked. We watched his hands, we didn't take our eyes off him. But once again the glass vanished without a trace.

"There's something odd going on here," said Klaus.

"I bet it's just a cheap trick," said Wolfi **contemptuously**.

---

succulent – saftig;
modest – bescheiden; to drain – austrinken;
to spirit away – wegzaubern;
contemptuous – verächtlich

"Of course," confirmed Mehdi seriously. "**Conjuring** is all about cheap tricks." He reached into the air – and presented my glass.

"**Wicked**! Will you tell us how it's done?"

"No, it's a professional secret. Conjurers never reveal their tricks." Mehdi put the glass down by my plate, and I noticed that the nail on his first finger was blue. He must have squashed it recently. Of course, if you practice conjuring tricks, you can't avoid the **occasional** injury, I thought, filling my plate at last. "Hm ... this smells incredible!"

"It's a Moroccan speciality," Bahrim explained. "We need to change our plans for tomorrow because of the broken gears, **folks**. I suggest hiking to the Berber village of Irrerane. On the way we'll go past a geological sensation. I won't tell you what it is. Let it be a surprise!"

Mehdi nodded. "The surprise is worth the long hike. But to get there, you have to follow the river a bit before you can cross it. And you need to leave early; the weather won't hold."

"Even if it doesn't," said Klaus, "in our country the weather changes every day. We're used to it."

Bahrim and Mehdi looked at one another. "Will you come with us, Mehdi?"

"Me? Oh no, I ... I have other plans."

We laughed out loud.

Wanda leant over to Carlos. "This geological sensation – I think it has something to do with the **faults** ..."

---

to conjure – zaubern;
wicked – cool, toll; occasional – gelegentlich;
folks – Leute; fault – Verwerfung

"Oh Wanda," Carlos interrupted. "I'm really not interested in faults at the moment."

He laid his arm around my shoulders and whispered in my ear, "What do you think? Do you want to stay here?"

"Carlos," I whispered back. "We've been separated for two weeks! We've got a lot to catch up on!"

"I agree. What are we waiting for?"

Mehdi must have said something funny, because the others suddenly roared with laughter. When we stood up, the **merriment** disappeared from his face. "I **envy** you two," he said quietly.

"What? Yes, we're very happy," I replied just as quietly. "Good night!"

Wanda filled her glass and **winked** knowingly at Carlos.

"Don't forget to sleep!" said Wolfi **suggestively**.

"Thanks for the tip," I answered equally suggestively. "It's like this: we both …"

The others waited **eagerly**.

"… have a lot to tell each other."

"I really do have a lot to tell you," said Carlos on the stairs. "About all our experiences on the field trip. And then I want to know what you did without me. Oh Mimi, I missed you!"

"**Despite** Wanda? You know, I didn't miss *you* at all!"

---

merriment – Fröhlichkeit;
to envy – beneiden;
to wink – zwinkern;
suggestive – andeutungsvoll;
eager – begierig; despite – trotz

"Oh yeah? What a pity. But of course, you made a vow never to fall in love again," he mocked.

"You're right. But, unfortunately, I couldn't keep it. There was this guy who simply wouldn't believe I didn't want anything to do with him. He **got round me** somehow."

Wrapped in each other's arms, we went out onto the balcony. The oranges **swayed** in the evening breeze, the blossom smelled heavenly and the night sky was simply **breathtaking**.

We immediately forgot what we wanted to tell each other. But it didn't matter; we had plenty of time ahead of us.

And Wolfi? Wanda? They could both **take a running jump**!

---

to get round s.o. – jmdn. überzeugen;
wrapped in each other's arms – ineinander verschlungen;
to sway – schwingen;
breathtaking – atemberaubend;
They can take a running jump. – Sie können mir gestohlen bleiben.

The Storm

* ‘ * ‘ * ‘ * ‘ * ‘

What on earth had woken me up so early? It was hardly even **dawn** ... Who was singing? Ah, it must be a muezzin! I **leaped** onto the balcony. I couldn't see the minaret, but the wind **wafted** the call of the muezzin towards me.

I plucked an orange from a branch and while I was peeling it, I saw that the tree was **twined around** by a **creeper** with huge violet flowers, and the garden and terraced slopes **beyond** it were full of more orange trees, and lemon and **fig** trees, too. The sky was turning almost **imperceptibly** from a pearly silver to the brightest of blues and the Atlas Mountains were **emerging** in a soft brown. This is what paradise must look like, I thought, listening to the muezzin's final, extended tone.

---

dawn – Morgendämmerung;
to leap – springen;
to waft – wehen;
to twine around – herumwinden;
creeper – Rankengewächs;
beyond – jenseits; fig – Feige;
imperceptible – unmerklich;
to emerge – auftauchen

"Mimi! Where are you? Come to bed!"

"Come out to me instead!"

"What? Outside? Now? Are you mad?"

"I'm **entranced** ..."

"Oh!" Carlos came up behind me and put his arms around me.

"I've never seen anything so beautiful," I whispered. "Do you remember that morning in the Atacama Desert when it was so cold the engine wouldn't start? It was beautiful there, too, but it made you frightened."

"I know what you mean," replied Carlos softly. "Here the sky, the mountains, the flowers and fruit conjure up a very special atmosphere."

I nodded. "You smile without knowing it."

"Even if you're cold. I think we should warm ourselves up in bed."

And that's what we did, for a good long time, and arrived too late for breakfast.

The others **smirked**, of course.

Wolfi said to Wanda confidentially, "Can you see the love bite on Mimi's neck? I bet it's not the only one."

"Carlos, you **rascal**! Did you forget to watch out in the **rush**?" asked Wanda mockingly. I felt the blood rush to my face. Damn!

We heard that Bahrim had been to the mechanic. In all probability we could collect the van that evening.

---

entranced – verzaubert;
to smirk – feixen;
rascal – Lausebengel;
rush – Eile

So we packed our rucksacks and a quarter of an hour later off we went, supplied with Bilal's packed lunches and repeated warnings to pay careful attention to the weather. "It's much too hot for the time of year," he told us as we were leaving. "So there may be a storm. And don't forget, more people have **drowned** here than died of thirst. Be careful, do you hear?"

The moped with the roses had disappeared.

We walked through the village and followed a narrow path up into the mountains. At first there were all kinds of bushes and trees to our left and right. **Prickly gorse** shone out yellow between the greens and browns. There was a **fragrance** of wild thyme and rosemary, and the lavender bushes were so luxuriant they **dwarfed** those of Provence.

The landscape gradually became more **barren** until it consisted only of stone, rock and naked earth. It got very hot, too.

Dripping with sweat, we rested at midday under one of the very few **argan trees**. "Watch out where you sit," said Bahrim. "Check the ground for scorpions. They usually hide during the day, but once in a while they forget."

We didn't find anything dangerous, so we took out our food and water bottles and sat down on our rucksacks.

---

to drown – ertrinken;
prickly gorse – Stechginster;
fragrance – Duft;
to dwarf – in den Schatten stellen;
barren – karg; argan tree – Arganbaum

Before us lay a narrow, **scree** covered valley, behind which **foothills** and mountains stood out as far as the eye could see. The sky was a little **overcast**, the air was utterly still and even sitting down we were sweating buckets.

Nearby there was a clay-brown **dwelling** surrounded by a high wall. Its blue-painted door opened suddenly and a girl, my age at the most, came towards us carrying a tray, which she placed on the ground in front of us. We looked at the pita bread, the bowl of honey and the almonds **in amazement**.

"Is this for us?" we exclaimed in surprise. "Thank you so much!"

Bahrim exchanged a few words with the girl and then told us to **tuck in**. "That's how we do things in Morocco," he said proudly. "We look after strangers."

"In our country," said Wolfi, "we shut the door in their faces. Tell the girl she should come and sit with us." He patted the ground next to him invitingly.

The girl giggled and pulled her shawl over her head.

"Impossible," Bahrim protested. "Girls aren't allowed to sit with strangers."

Wanda fished a biro out of her bag. The girl

---

scree – Geröll;
foothill – Vorberg;
overcast – bedeckt;
dwelling – Wohnhaus;
in amazement – erstaunt;
to tuck in – zugreifen *(beim Essen)*

seemed to be pleased with it and thanked Wanda with a polite nod of her head. Then she spoke to Bahrim urgently.

"She says the weather's going to change. We should go back."

"Go back?" Klaus repeated. "Why? We all have waterproof anoraks and good hiking boots with us. We don't mind a bit of rain, Bahrim. Don't worry."

We stood up and hitched our rucksacks onto our shoulders. The girl reached for the tray – we hadn't left a single almond; they were fresher and sweeter than any we had ever tasted. She **gave a start** and quickly turned over a flat stone. We could see a large scorpion stretching its tail angrily into the air like a drawn bow before **scurrying** into hiding under the next stone.

"My first scorpion!" I exclaimed.

"Mine, too," said Wanda, shuddering a little. "That one certainly looked dangerous. I've got **goose pimples**, Carlos. Here, look!"

"No, thanks! But its huge **pincers** and **sting** were pretty impressive."

"Frightening, wasn't it," said Bahrim. "But a small creature like that is relatively harmless. And it'll only sting if it feels threatened. Still, no matter how small a scorpion is, its sting is always painful. Now come on. We've lost too much time already."

I reached for Carlos's hand and noticed that one

---

to give a start – zusammenzucken;
to scurry – huschen;
goose pimples – Gänsehaut;
pincer – Zange;
sting – Stachel

of his shoelaces had **come undone**. While he was doing it up again, I walked slowly on. "Hey, Mimi, what's Carlos doing back there?" Wolfi wanted to know. "Have you had an argument?"

"What gives you such a ridiculous idea?" I shook my head. "No chance, Wolfi. Carlos is just doing up his shoelaces."

"I see. Pity."

"Only for you." I gave him a provocative laugh. "Just get used to the fact that everything's okay between us. We've been through a lot together; we know we can **rely on** one another."

"Don't talk such crap, Mimi. No one knows how reliable another person is."

"Rubbish, Wolfi! You think that way because you're like that yourself." I looked back at Carlos. Klaus had joined him and the two of them were talking animatedly.

Wolfi **frowned**. "What did you just say? The two of you have been through a lot together?"

"Oh yes. We've tracked down a **tomb raider**, survived an earthquake and marched all alone through the highest desert in the world. Is that nothing?" I asked **challengingly**.

"Then it's about time to experience something *interesting* with a new partner," he answered.

I had to laugh. "Why should we split up if we're happy together? We love each other."

---

to come undone – *hier:* aufgehen, sich lösen;
to rely on s.o. – sich auf jmdn. verlassen;
to frown – die Stirn runzeln;
tomb raider – Grabräuber;
challenging – herausfordernd

"Don't tell me about love! It's soon over."

"You have no idea." A **gust** of wind blew up the dust. "At last a bit of fresh air," I said with relief and wiped a drop of sweat from my nose. "What's that?" I said **dumbfounded**, pointing in front of us. A brown wall was **hurtling** towards us. "Sand!" called Wolfi. "Dust and sand!"

Within seconds tiny, sharp-edged grains of sand were whirling about our faces. I took out a handkerchief and pressed it against my nose – the only way it was possible to breathe.

The dust cloud passed as quickly as it had come. Bahrim told us in a worried voice, "Listen, everyone. The storm is coming up. We all stay close together. No one stays behind or goes on ahead, all right?"

"How can a storm come out of the blue?" I asked Carlos.

"Not very blue any more. Can't you see those dark clouds? And listen – that sounds like thunder."

We had to go in single file because the path now led steeply down into the gorge. Loose **pebbles** rolled underfoot and we had to watch where we were going with every step.

At last we reached the bottom. The riverbed was completely dried out, and we crossed it, until Bahrim paused and pointed into the far distance. "Can you see those large rocks? Behind them is the only way out of the gorge. We need to hurry because – whoops! Now …"

---

gust – Böe;
dumbfounded – verblüfft;
to hurtle – rasen; pebble – Kieselstein

A gust of wind swept through the gorge; dust and pebbles whirled around us. We couldn't see anything any more; I could hardly breathe. I held on to Carlos, who screamed into my ear, "The storm! I heard the thunder!"

"I didn't!" But we unpacked our anoraks nevertheless, zipped them up tight and pulled the **hoods** over our heads. Not a moment too soon, for the first big drops of rain were falling.

"Let's get going! We have to get out of the gorge right away!" urged Bahrim.

"But why? The storm is miles away. The thunder was barely **audible**," Wanda protested. "You're not used to rain, Bahrim, so you're afraid of it. It's nothing special to us."

"No time to argue!" insisted Bahrim. "Come on! Stop standing around!"

"It's good the wind has gone down." I shook out my handkerchief. "Dust in the nose is much worse than rain."

A few seconds later the heavens opened and the rain came down in **torrents**. I **tucked in** my chin. The rain wasn't cold, but the stupid thing was how it interfered with my vision, like a grey curtain. All I could see of Wolfi, who was walking in front of me, was a vague outline with a red blot – that was his rucksack. I looked back; Carlos was hard on my heels.

As well as we could we balanced our way across

---

hood – Kapuze;
audible – hörbar;
torrent – Sturzflut;
to tuck in – *hier:* einziehen

the stones, because in no time at all masses of water were flowing through the gorge. Only a few minutes must have gone by when I slipped and found myself up to my **calves** in water. I noticed to my horror how high it had risen in the meantime, and I suddenly remembered Bilal's words: more people have drowned here than died of thirst!

Well, I thought, people don't drown *that* easily. But I don't understand why we're still wading through the damned riverbed rather than climbing up the slope. I wiped the rain from my face. **In vain**. It wasn't just pouring, it was **bucketing**. It was as if a giant pipeline had burst!

Carlos shouted something to me. I couldn't understand a single word, the **cascading** rain and the gurgling river were simply too loud, so I stood still. Carlos put his face close to mine and roared into my ear, "Mimi …" A whistle shrilled through the gorge.

"What was that?"

"That's Bahrim! I know that whistle! Something must have happened up front. Come on, Mimi, hurry up!"

By now the water was up to my knees. I clenched my teeth and worked my way step by step through the flood until I could make out Wolfi and Klaus and Bahrim. Wanda? Where was Wanda?

"Have you seen Wanda?" shouted Bahrim through the curtain of water. "No? She was between me and Klaus, then came Wolfi, then you, Mimi. And you were the last, Carlos. Didn't you see her?"

---

calf – Wade;
in vain – vergeblich; to bucket – wie aus Kübeln gießen; cascading – wasserfallartig

We shook our heads. The rain drummed down **incessantly**. Although the five of us were standing quite close together we could barely see each other, and the water was rising with every second. "Perhaps she wanted to try the slope. I mean, I thought about it myself," I shouted. "It would make sense, wouldn't it?"

"No way!" Bahrim shouted back. "The clay goes soapy in no time! The only **accessible** place is near the rocks I showed you!"

"Give another whistle, Bahrim. And we'll call. All together!" I said. "Wan-da! Wan-da!"

We listened. There was nothing except the roaring of the water. I thought feverishly. If Wanda had fallen into the water, we'd have noticed. Klaus and Bahrim couldn't have overtaken her, and neither could she have **vanished into thin air**.

So that only left the slope. If she'd been **sensible**, she would have chosen the right-hand side. So far, so good. Perhaps she was already at the top in safety and worrying if we'd all drown? So …

"Help! Help! Where are you?"

"That was Wanda's voice!"

"He-e-e …"

"That came from further up," I shouted and **trudged** off. The waves gurgled and **foamed** and I could hardly see, but then my leg struck against

---

incessant – unablässig;
accessible – erreichbar;
to vanish into thin air – sich in Luft auflösen;
sensible – vernünftig;
to trudge – stapfen;
to foam – schäumen

something soft. I bent down, reached into the water and felt cloth. I pulled … the cloth slipped out of my fingers … That must be Wanda's head … I made a grab for it, felt her long braid in my hand, let go, grabbed it again … That was her face … I held it above the water. Now the others arrived, and together we lifted, pulled and dragged her to the right-hand slope. We slithered and somebody shouted that the ground really was soapy. It was impossible to find a hold. We could only hope that the rain would ease off and that we could hold Wanda above water until then.

The level was still rising. It was well over my knees by now. My hands were getting stiff. I wouldn't be able to hold out for much longer … But then, as suddenly as it had started, the rain stopped. Someone must have been able to **mend** the pipeline. The brown waves foamed and swirled around us; a gap emerged in the clouds and a first ray of sunlight broke through. It was unbelievable!

I was still holding on to Wanda's face. Her eyeshadow and mascara were totally smudged; her eyes were closed. Was she breathing? I bent down to her. "Wanda! Hello, Wanda, can you hear me?"

No reaction. Now it had stopped raining we could see the rocks. We weren't all that far away from them. I pointed with my chin. "We have to go over there." "Right," said Wolfi eagerly. Those few metres were **incredibly** hard work. I'd never have thought a girl could be so heavy.

We leaned her upper body against a rock and stood up.

---

to mend – reparieren; incredible – unglaublich

"Wanda, do us a favour and say something," I **pleaded**, patting her cheeks. "Come on, say something! Can you hear me?"

"I've never seen anyone who's drowned," said Wolfi quietly. I flew into a rage. "Wanda hasn't drowned! She fell into the water; perhaps she hit her head. We have to lie her flat on the ground," I said decisively, and Bahrim was already pulling off her rucksack. Klaus lifted her legs and Carlos her upper body. Now she was lying stretched out behind the rock in safety and only had to open her eyes and say "What's going on?" and everything would be all right.

But it wasn't like that; it wasn't all right. "Put a rucksack under her legs." I thought hard. How were you supposed to do mouth-to-mouth **resuscitation**? I feverishly thought back to what I'd learned in my first-aid course. "Carlos, you have to place your hands on her chest and press when I say 'one' and let go when I say 'two', okay? But I'll try **artificial respiration** first. If that doesn't work it's your turn."

I held Wanda's nose closed and forced my breath into her. Without success. "Now you, Carlos!" I gasped. "One, two, one …"

Wanda's eyelids fluttered. "Go on, Carlos, go on," I screamed. "Now! You've done it!"

Wanda opened her eyes. She was breathing, she was coughing, she was spluttering water. Carlos held on to her. "Go on, Wanda, don't give up!"

---

to plead – flehen;
resuscitation – Wiederbelebung;
artificial respiration – künstliche Beatmung

Wanda took hold of Carlos's arm and whispered, "Carlos, you're here! Everything's all right now. I'm so happy ... I love you ..." Her eyes closed again and her arms dropped to her sides.

"That's not what we agreed!" I shouted angrily. I don't know to this day what I meant by it. I didn't want her to **faint** again, but even less did I want her to say "I love you" to Carlos. If she liked him, that was her business. But it was my business to make sure she kept her distance and accepted the relationship between Carlos and me. I was angry and I showed it. "Wanda!" I screamed and slapped her round the face left and right. That helped. No one was more surprised than me.

Her eyes became clear; she coughed a couple more times and then we helped her up.

"Right. And now tell us what happened," I snapped at her.

Wanda was in too much of a **muddle** to put up any resistance. "When the water began to rise and kept on rising, I wanted to go up the slope."

"Ha! I thought so."

"But it was so slippery I hardly made any **headway**. I did make it to a large stone, though, and I held on to it. But I had the feeling it wouldn't hold much longer, so I tried going on. Suddenly I slipped downwards. I can remember falling into the water, but that's all. I woke up and saw your face, Carlos. You saved me. Thank you, I ..."

"We all saved you," I interrupted her **roughly**.

---

to faint – ohnmächtig werden;
muddle – Wirrwarr; headway – Fortschritt;
rough – grob

"You could just as well have seen Bahrim's face, or Wolfi's or Klaus's."

"Most probably it would have been Mimi's," said Klaus objectively. "She brought you back to life with mouth-to-mouth resuscitation. Carlos only helped her. If you want to thank someone, thank Mimi. She was the only one who knew what to do, got it?"

"Is that true?" Wanda asked uncertainly. "But Carlos …"

"Everything Klaus said is true," Carlos confirmed.

"Oh …"

"Yup, that's how it was," said Klaus again. "So, can you walk? I'll carry your rucksack, okay?"

The Night

* ‘ * ‘ * ‘ * ‘ * ‘

It took almost half an hour, but then we made it out of the gorge to safety. We looked around for a last time. “Unbelievable!” called Wolfi. “Look! The water has risen even higher. How come?”

“The storm broke at a distance,” said Bahrim, “but it rained everywhere, and now the water is flowing off all the hills in the area. It collects in the gorge, and the more there is the higher it rises. If you’re in a deeper, narrower valley than this one, it can happen that you don’t see or hear the storm, but you’re suddenly surprised by torrents of water. So rule number one is that nothing is more dangerous than to walk through a dry riverbed, a wadi, during a storm. Rule number two: never spend the night in a wadi – you could be overcome in your sleep and drown. All right? And by the way, the water’s still rising, which is a damned nuisance.”

“So?” Wolfi shrugged his shoulders **casually**. “Thanks to our brave intervention, we’ve saved Wanda and we’re all in safety.”

“Have you wondered how we’re going to get back?” asked Bahrim.

---

casual – lässig

"There's **bound to** be a bridge somewhere."

Bahrim shook his head. "The only way back is through the wadi."

"That means that if the water level doesn't sink within one or two hours, we'll have to spend the night outdoors, even though we're **soaked** to the skin?" Wanda spoke for the first time since her rescue.

"That's right."

Carlos and I looked at each other. We grinned. "We're used to nights in the open air, aren't we, Mimi?" Carlos put his arm over my shoulders. "The water's still rising. We should look out for a comfortable place to spend the night. Perhaps there's a nice **cave** here. We'll collect some wood, light a fire, dry our clothes and play at being in the Stone Age."

"I don't think that's at all funny," complained Wanda.

"No? It doesn't sound bad to me," was Wolfi's comment. "All of us naked around the fire ... That would be fun, wouldn't it?"

"You're an idiot," said Klaus. "Bahrim, you know the area around here. Is there a café, a guesthouse, any kind of accommodation?"

"There's no café, no guesthouse, no accommodation – why are you laughing, Mimi?"

"Because when I was on the road with Carlos in Chile, I asked him exactly the same thing."

"Did you? And where did you spend the night?"

"In the car. It was freezing cold."

---

to be bound to – müssen;
soaked – durchnässt;
cave – Höhle

"Our car's in the **garage**. So, Bahrim, what are we going to do?"

"Bilal's family lives not far from here, in a kasbah."

We thought about this. "A kasbah? Isn't that an old clay castle where an entire clan lives, complete with their animals and everything?"

"It used to be like that. But Bilal's family kasbah is much simpler and not nearly so big as the famous old castles. I'm sure we can spend the night there."

"What are we waiting for?" asked Wolfi. "Why don't we just get going? And will we still go past the geological sensation?"

"**Achoo**, achoo, achoo!" sneezed Wanda.

"It'll still be there in the morning. Hurry up everyone, it's almost four! In two or three hours it'll be dark!"

We set off. My trainers squeaked, my jeans **chafed** at my legs, but Carlos and I walked hand in hand. That was all that mattered.

After a while we left that barren plateau and joined a narrow path winding through **stunted** vegetation. Then we saw the first grain fields, followed by an olive **grove** through which a little **stream** flowed. To one side there were some odd, cemented hollows in the ground. I couldn't **make head or tail of** them. "Bahrim, what's that?"

---

garage – Werkstatt;
achoo – Hatschi;
to chafe – reiben;
stunted – verkümmert;
grove – Hain; stream – Bach;
to make head or tail of s.th. – aus etwas klug werden

"That's the local **launderette**," he answered with a grin. "The women come here to do the washing in those **troughs**."

I had to take a closer look. Instead of going over the bridge with the others, I went down a few steps to the stream and on to the first trough – and couldn't believe my eyes. Right nearby, and well hidden by hanging branches, stood a moped. I wondered if it had three red roses on the handlebar, and laughed at myself – that would be an unbelievable **coincidence**! Things like that just don't happen – or do they? I whistled softly through my teeth. There was my coincidence! The roses on the handlebar! Who could the bike belong to? And how had it got here from our hotel? There must be a road after all, a road with a bridge. Or – or the driver had come through the wadi before the storm.

But why was the moped standing here? Well, perhaps its owner is a member of the family and lives in the kasbah.

But why was it standing hidden under the branches? Why not on the path or on the bridge?

I followed the others thoughtfully.

Bahrim was leaning against the trunk of an olive tree. "We're almost there. You need to know a couple of things before we arrive. We take our shoes off before entering the house; Bilal's father will give us something to eat and when he hears what happened, we'll be able to spend the night in his house. Those are the rules of **hospitality**. But don't speak

---

launderette – Waschsalon;
trough – Wanne; coincidence – Zufall;
hospitality – Gastfreundschaft

to the women, be polite and use the water sparingly. I think those are the most important things."

Before us rose a clay-brown, **multi-storeyed** square building with a tower at each corner. Its large gate was painted with mysterious colourful symbols and ornamentation. "They keep off the **evil eye** and only allow good to enter," Bahrim explained, banging an iron doorknocker.

We waited.

Wanda turned around to us. "If you knew how you all looked! Like **scarecrows**! I'd never let you into *my* house."

I still hadn't finished with Wanda, so I replied, "And if you're thinking about taking part in the Miss World contest, you haven't got much of a chance with that smudgy make-up. All I want is a roof over my head and a bite to eat."

"Pff," was Wanda's response as she turned her head away.

The door opened slowly and silently. An old man eyed us **quizzically** from one to the other. But he smiled when he recognized Bahrim.

Two little girls looked out in curiosity from behind their grandfather. They giggled and pointed to Wanda's long braid with its coloured ribbons.

Bahrim explained our **predicament** and the old man made a gesture of invitation.

We followed him into the inner courtyard. At

---

multi-storeyed – mehrstöckig;
evil eye – böser Blick;
scarecrow – Vogelscheuche;
quizzical – fragend;
predicament – missliche Lage

first I only saw the many flowerpots with roses, **marigolds** and mint. A brown goat bleated; a curtain was drawn hastily.

We went up a stairway. Along the building there was a covered veranda, from which doors and windows opened. The stairway lead to an area laid out with brightly coloured carpets and **cushions** where we sat down. I stretched out on my back and closed my eyes.

Klaus said, "It's a bit of a **cheek** for six people just to drop in and ask for food and a place to sleep. Shall we club together and pay for it? What do you think, Bahrim?"

"Out of the question," said Bahrim firmly. "That would be terribly **offensive**. You have to accept the hospitality as it's given."

The two little girls were sitting on the stairs, whispering to one another and giggling every now and then. Then a young man, Bilal's brother, came to serve us boiling hot, sweet peppermint tea.

"Do the brothers have a sister," inquired Wolfi.

"You never stop, do you?" said Bahrim. "Yes, they have a sister. But she lives in Marrakech most of the time."

"Pity."

Bahrim raised his eyebrows. "You're in Morocco, my **lad**!"

Wolfi laughed.

Later, when it had got quite dark, Ayoub – Bilal's

---

marigold – Ringelblume;
cushion – Kissen;
cheek – Frechheit; offensive – beleidigend;
lad – Junge

brother – brought us a huge bowl of couscous, meat and vegetables. As a **concession** to our eating habits, he handed each of us a wooden spoon.

"Where are the plates?" asked Wanda, screwing up her nose.

"There aren't any. We all eat from the same bowl."

Bahrim rapped Klaus on the hand with his spoon. "Keep to your side," he said with a laugh.

"But you've got more meat than me," Klaus protested.

"No way! It just looks like that!"

Our clothes had dried in the meantime, which was good because along with the darkness came the cold.

"Where will we sleep?" Wanda wanted to know.

"Here."

"And the bathroom? I want to have a shower and clean my teeth," Wanda demanded, taking a pocket mirror out of her bag.

"Without a toothbrush?" We all laughed at her.

I wrapped myself in a blanket, **shoved** a pillow under my head and snuggled up to Carlos. Slowly I warmed up. The stars shone much clearer and brighter than at home. They were the last thing I saw before falling asleep.

At some point I woke up. Someone was snoring. I rolled onto my back and felt for Carlos.

"Are you awake, too, Mimi?" he whispered.

"Yes. I don't know what woke me up."

---

concession – Entgegenkommen;
to shove – schieben

"It's nothing. Go back to sleep." Carlos put his arms around me. After a short while I could hear from his breathing that he was asleep.

I turned carefully onto my other side so as not to wake him. Someone was standing at the balustrade, a black form against the dark night sky. Wanda? It was Wanda.

I waited, but she didn't move. I gently unwrapped my blanket and tiptoed over to her.

"Can't you sleep?"

"No."

We were silent.

"Did you really pull me out of the water?" whispered Wanda.

"No. We pulled you out together. But I was the first one there and I held your head above water. And … I also gave you artificial respiration."

"Then … then I really … I really have a lot to thank you for."

I said nothing.

"You like Carlos, don't you?" I asked after a while.

"Yes."

"I'm sorry about that. But you must understand that we're more than just friends."

"We are, too. I thought our friendship would get even closer. But now you're here."

"But Carlos told you about me, didn't he?"

"Yes, but I thought you were … different."

"Did you? How? In what way different?"

"I … I thought you'd travel out to meet him, but get on his nerves. I didn't know – I couldn't know – that it was serious."

"No, you couldn't. But now you do."

"Yes."
"So?"
"What do you mean, so?"
"What are you going to do about it?"
Wanda **tilted** her head and giggled. "Me? You're a right one, girl. You've only been with us for a couple of days. At university Carlos and I are together the whole time."
I clenched my fists. "Oh yeah," I replied lightly. "Carlos, you and plenty of other girls. A lot of competition for you, Wanda."
She threw her head back. "For me – or for you?"
"No one can compete with me."
"You're very sure of yourself."
"Yes." I grinned at her cheekily. "Yes, I am. But one thing I'm not. I'm not stupid enough to run after a guy who already has a girlfriend." I put my hand on her arm. "All the best for you."
Wanda was so amazed she said, "Thanks."

---

to tilt – neigen

Shells in the Sand

* ʻ * ʻ * ʻ * ʻ * ʻ * ʻ * ʻ * ʻ *

The sun woke us in the morning.

After a breakfast of tea and little pancakes with honey and almond paste we thanked our host for his hospitality and **took our leave**. I needed to talk to Carlos about Wanda, but there hadn't been an opportunity up to now.

A few steps away from the house Wolfi said, "Did it also strike you that we didn't see a single woman? Who did the cooking?"

"Well, the women," replied Bahrim with a laugh. "Who else? But they never show themselves. It's a very traditional family. Women don't show themselves to strangers."

"Is it like that everywhere?"

"In a city like Marrakech men go out with their wives and daughters sometimes. But here in the countryside that would be unthinkable."

"It would be no life for me," I said.

"It isn't easy for daughters," Bahrim **confirmed**. "I could tell you a story ... but you'd never understand it."

---

shell – Muschel; to take one's leave – sich verabschieden; to confirm – bestätigen

"Tell us, please!"

"No. Perhaps later, on the day you leave. It would be far too dangerous now."

"For whom?" I asked **inquisitively**.

"For the people involved," was Bahrim's **brief** reply. I saw from the expression on his face that he wasn't going to say another word.

We had reached the bridge and the washing troughs.

I was curious to see whether the moped with the red roses on its handlebar was still standing under the branches. It had gone.

But someone had twined a rose around one of the branches. It looked funny, a rose in an olive tree.

"What about this geological sensation you promised us? There isn't one, is there?" Wolfi wanted to know.

Bahrim laughed mysteriously. "Have a little more patience. It won't be long now, and you'll wish you had a bigger rucksack with you."

It was a beautiful day, and not nearly so **swelteringly** hot as the day before. The plants smelled lovely; because we had taken a new route, we were walking between yellow-blossoming gorse bushes and blue lavender. But, unfortunately, I couldn't really enjoy anything; Wanda was ruining my day. She never left our side and was always pointing geological things out to Carlos – I couldn't keep up there, of course. That would have been bad enough,

---

inquisitive – neugierig;
brief – kurz;
sweltering – drückend heiß

but the way she kept on **gazing** adoringly at him and fluttering her eyelashes made me really angry.

All at once Carlos bent down. "This is extraordinary," he said in amazement. "Look, Mimi. There's a **fossil** shell just lying on the path ... and here, another one! And another one!"

"What did you say, Carlos? You've seen a fossil? My God, what sharp eyes you have!" Wanda was playing the **star-struck** admirer, and something clicked with me. Okay, I thought, if that's the way you want it. You have the advantage at the moment, but she who laughs last ...

We all knelt on the ground and collected fossil shells of all shapes and sizes: some **grooved**, some smooth, some looking like little **snail** shells.

Some had formed into clumps, but most of them were separate. It was incredible. In my enthusiasm and collecting fever I forgot about Wanda's flirting tactics and didn't hear Bahrim's explanation about how the "geological sensation" had come into being millions of years ago.

I collected and collected, and soon had so many fossils that I only packed the most special ones into my rucksack.

Wanda was sitting on the ground next to Carlos. "This is my most beautiful fossil," she was saying. "It's for you, Carlos. In memory of ... of some wonderful days and ..."

---

to gaze – anschauen;
fossil – versteinert;
star-struck – *hier:* hingerissen;
grooved – gerillt;
snail – Schnecke

"In memory of the field trip," said Carlos **curtly**. "Thank you."

"Have you got a most beautiful fossil for me?" asked Wolfi.

"For you? Why should I give *you* one?" Wanda threw back her braid and winked at Carlos. "Because I'm the only girl who isn't wild about you?"

"The only girl?" I repeated. "I know another one!"

From his place on the ground Klaus said, "Folks, for me this is – what do the reporters say on television? – for me this is a once-in-a-century event!"

In the early afternoon we saw the first houses of Imouzzer in front of us, and I still hadn't been able to talk to Carlos about the **bitch** Wanda. The van wasn't ready yet either, because the **spare part** had only arrived a few minutes ago.

"You know what? I'm going to **treat you all to** a Coke for rescuing me. Any objections?" Wanda stood in front of us with her legs wide apart and laughed. "Heavens, the way you look! A scarecrow would take offence at being compared to you lot!"

"You try sleeping in **damp** clothes!" complained Wolfi. "How elegant do you think *you* look?"

"Very. Thanks!" Wanda twirled around and disappeared into a shop. I whistled through my teeth. The woman wasn't going to give up, that much was clear. The only question was, did she love Carlos?

---

curt – knapp;
bitch – Miststück;
spare part – Ersatzteil;
to treat s.o. to s.th. – jmdn. zu etwas einladen;
damp – feucht

Or was it just that she couldn't stand **drawing the short straw**? Or was there a third reason?

And what was up with Carlos? Was he playing with us? Or was he really so naive and innocent as he was acting?

I gnawed at my lower lip. This, I decided, had to be cleared up today!

We sat down at the side of the road and waited.

"Right, folks, what shall we do tomorrow? Another hike? Or shall we drive to Marrakech and **immerse ourselves in** city life?" asked Klaus. "What do you think, Carlos?"

"Both are fine with me. What about you, Mimi?"

"Marrakech sounds very **tempting**."

"Okay. Bahrim?"

"Let me make a suggestion. Because the van will only be ready during the morning, we'll take in Imouzzer's main attraction, the weekly market. Then we'll leave, look at a saint's grave on the way and be in Marrakech by late evening."

I turned to Wolfi. "What's up? You're not saying anything."

"No. You know, I'm having a wonderful dream."

"Are you? And will you let us in on it?"

"Oh yes. I'm dreaming of life in full Technicolor. With me in the middle. And the best thing about it is that it starts tomorrow. Wicked. Cool. If only I were 24 hours older!"

We **roared with laughter**. "Dream on!"

---

to draw the short straw – den Kürzeren ziehen;
to immerse onself in – sich stürzen in;
tempting – verlockend;
to roar with laughter – brüllen vor Lachen

Wanda came back with the Coke cans. She wanted to go to Marrakech, too. "Do I have to wear a **veil**, or can I walk through the city like this? I mean, we've mainly been away from other people up to now."

"It's no problem," Bahrim assured her. "If you want to go out alone, you're safer in Marrakech than in Paris. Word of honour."

So that was that.

But not the thing with Wanda. "Listen, Carlos," I said when we got to our room. "What's up with Wanda? She told me she loves you."

"So? That's her business. It doesn't bother me."

I sighed. "But it bothers *me*. Why don't you tell her to go to the devil?"

Carlos laughed. "And then? Do you seriously think that would put her off? It would be quite the opposite."

"I don't agree!"

"Mimi, she'll give up some time or other. Just have a little patience."

"No! Can't you see you're risking our relationship? Wanda is a permanent source of friction. She has nothing to lose and she has no **pride**. She adores you and you love it. She bathes you in what you take to be admiration, she ..."

"Okay," Carlos interrupted impatiently. "Then tell me what to do."

"*I* should tell *you* what to do?" I shouted indignantly. "*You* should know what to do! You should know who means more to you: Wanda or me."

---

veil – Schleier;
pride – Stolz

"*You* should know that actually, Mimi "

I flashed at him. "Carlos, what do you think you'd do if I told you Klaus had fallen in love with me?"

"I'd say 'Bad luck, Klaus. Mimi and I are together.'"

"All right, so you can tell Wanda tomorrow 'Bad luck, Wanda. Mimi and I are together.' Okay?"

"Okay. I've already said it, but if you **insist,** I'll repeat myself. I'll do it. Are you happy now?"

"Yes ... We'll see."

---

to insist on s.th. – auf etwas bestehen

The Market and the Marabout

‘‘*‘*‘*‘*‘*‘*‘*‘*‘*‘*‘*‘*‘*

In the morning we went with all our bags to the mechanic. He assured us that the van would be ready in one or two hours and he'd keep an eye on our rucksacks during that time. So we wandered along the village street, avoiding donkeys and pedestrians, and admired the wares spread out on decorative cloths. I was particularly impressed by some buckets cut out of old truck tyres and **fitted with handles**.

The donkeys were **hitched** under the trees, and the women were gathered beside them on colourful blankets. They drank tea, made conversation and looked after the very young children. For the thousandth time I cursed the ban on taking photographs in Arab countries. I knew I'd get into a lot of trouble by ignoring it, but it really was a pity. Here, for example, was a car filled up to the roof with pita bread. Only the driving seat was empty. I sighed.

---

marabout – Grabstätte eines islamischen Heiligen;
fitted with – ausgestattet mit;
handle – Griff;
to hitch – anbinden

We went through a gateway into a narrow alleyway, and then we were in the middle of the action. "So, Wolfi, is this your idea of life in full Technicolor?"

"It's a modest beginning." He **screwed up** his nose. "What's that smell?"

"Hm ... it isn't fruit or vegetables. **Herbs** and **spices**? No ... it must be that over there! Look!"

On the ground lay some cleanly **severed** sheep's heads, and beside them the legs complete with hooves. Further on down the row there were bloody **chunks** of meat; it wasn't a sight for the **faint-hearted**.

We wandered on, looking at the old and new jewellery and the colourful dresses. "Carlos, where are the women? I haven't seen a single one on the market yet. Who buys the dresses and the jewellery? The men?"

"They must do."

We bought apples and oranges for the journey and met up a little later at the van.

Wanda sat next to Bahrim in the passenger seat. Wolfi squeezed in next to her singing, "We're driving to the city! Where all the girls are pretty!" until Bahrim had had enough. "Hey Wolfi, you'll get us into trouble! Choose your girls from the ones at home, okay?" He put his foot down and tore down the road so fast that we cried out in alarm.

---

to screw up – *hier:* rümpfen;
herbs (pl.) – Kräuter;
spice – Gewürz; severed – abgetrennt;
chunk – großes Stück;
fainthearted – *hier:* zartbesaitet

It wasn't a nice drive. Bahrim was angry with Wolfi, Wolfi was angry with Bahrim, Wanda stared out of the window lost in thought and then ... then **fate caught up with** us. We were on quite a straight road and could see a long way ahead, so Bahrim was able to brake slowly and approach the crowd of people safely. We got out.

It turned out that a truck had rammed into a boy on a bicycle and knocked him into the ditch. The boy was injured, not **fatally**, as we could see, but bad enough to need a doctor or hospital treatment.

The **enraged** villagers had taken hold of the driver and were waiting for the police. Chance had it that there was no other vehicle on the road apart from ours. The mother of the boy, **wailing** and gesticulating wildly, grabbed Bahrim by the collar and, in the end, we had to lay the boy in the van and Bahrim drove him, and as many women as could squeeze in, to the next doctor.

It was exactly five o'clock when he returned.

"Look," he said, "there's no way we'll make it to Marrakech today. I suggest we drive to the saint's grave and spend the night in the van – or in the open air, whatever you like – and drive on tomorrow. Why rush?"

We all agreed – except Wolfi, of course! – and we reached the marabout, the saint's grave, just before sunset.

---

fate – Schicksal;
to catch up with s.o. – jmdn. einholen;
fatal – tödlich;
enraged – aufgebracht;
to wail – jammern

Unfortunately, it was rather disappointing. In the middle of nowhere stood a little **green-tiled** hut that we couldn't even enter. The only good thing was a fountain with clear, cool water.

"Can you tell us why you've brought us here, of all places?" complained Wolfi.

"It's a holy place," Bahrim explained. "Can't you feel it? The atmosphere is different, and every dream you dream here will come true. And not only that – it'll **reveal** your future as well."

Great, I thought. What if I dreamed of a terrible future? I didn't want that at all. But the others weren't worried. Wanda was **electrified**. "Wow Bahrim! How did you know I always wanted to find out my future?" she cried.

We drove a few kilometres to the next village, where we ate couscous and **stew** in a roadside café and passed the time with lots of silly jokes.

Then, once we were tired enough, we drove back, washed at the fountain, folded down the seats and fought over the blankets. When we had almost fallen asleep, Wolfi decided our shoes smelled **musty**. "They've got to go," he said forcefully as he opened the door and shoved them all out.

"Before you put them on tomorrow morning, check if there's a scorpion inside," said Bahrim, which shut everyone up.

---

green-tiled – mit grünen Kacheln;
to reveal – enthüllen, offenbaren;
electrified – elektrisiert;
stew – Eintopf;
musty – muffig

The Scorpion

‘‘*‘*‘*‘*‘*

That night I didn’t have a single dream, nor did Carlos get a **glimpse** of the future. Wanda didn’t want to say anything, and the others also claimed to have only slept and not dreamed anything. “I knew it,” said Wolfi. He opened the door, jumped down, stretched out his arms and called out, “Marrakech, here I come!”

He sat down on the **running board**, reached out for his shoes and pulled them on.

“Hey!” shouted Bahrim. “Watch out. First you have to …”

Too late! There was a **bloodcurdling** scream. Wolfi **thrashed about**, flung off his shoe and began hopping around the van like a **maniac**.

We were out in no time. We sorted out our shoes, shook them out, pulled them on – and then saw to Wolfi.

“A scorpion!” he **bellowed**. “It stung me! It hurts! I can’t tell you how much it hurts!”

---

glimpse – flüchtiger Blick; running board – Trittbrett;
bloodcurdling – markerschütternd;
to thrash about – um sich hauen;
maniac – Verrückte/r; to bellow – brüllen

"Let's see!" I grabbed him and pushed him down onto the running board. He was right. His big toe was red and starting to swell up, and you could clearly see where the sting had gone in.

"Here it is!" called Wanda. "Quick! Has anyone got a tin?"

Carlos pulled his lunchbox out of his rucksack. Wanda **skilfully** slid the scorpion in and put the lid on. "What now?"

"I'm dying!" whimpered Wolfi. "How long do I have left to live, Bahrim?"

"It's a tiny scorpion, Wolfi. It's sting won't do you any harm!"

"You're just saying that! You're saying that to reassure me! I want to see a doctor. I'm telling you, drive me to a doctor! And anyway, why was the thing in *my* shoe?"

"How should we know that? Be **reasonable**, Wolfi. Calm down. If Bahrim says the sting isn't dangerous, then it isn't dangerous," said Carlos. "It's bound to be painful, but in a few hours you'll be as right as rain."

"Oh yeah?" Wolfi looked **mistrustfully** at Carlos. "To hear that from you of all people ... Did you put the scorpion in my shoe, perhaps? Has it been in your lunchbox since yesterday, when Mimi said you were tying your laces? Have you been waiting for a **convenient** moment to put it in my shoe? Admit it. It was you, Carlos."

---

skilful – geschickt;
reasonable – vernünftig;
mistrustful – misstrauisch;
convenient – geeignet

"Shut up, Wolfi," said Klaus sharply. "You're nuts. Why should anyone do a stupid thing like that?"

"Why? How should I know? Ask him yourself, him or his Mimi."

"That's enough!" Carlos pushed him back down onto the running board. I had wetted my headscarf to wrap it round Wolfi's toe. Perhaps the cold water would ease the pain a little.

"My father ..." said Klaus suddenly, "my father would say, 'Be a man. **Endure** the pain.'"

"You can talk, you and your father! You don't know how much it hurts. I need to see a doctor, really. I need to see a doctor right away!"

"You'll hold out until we get to Marrakech," said Bahrim. "Come on! Everyone in! We're off!"

---

to endure – aushalten, ertragen

Hotel Ayour

* ' * ' * ' * ' * ' * '

Bahrim drove. He drove so fast that more than once we gasped in horror. But he made it to Marrakech in record time. We knew he had booked rooms in Hotel Ayour, which belonged to an uncle of Bilal (most business in Morocco is done through relatives) and was supposed to be in the middle of the old city, so we would be able to explore the place easily on foot.

We kept on dampening the scarf with water from our bottles, and the toe stopped swelling up. Apart from the pain, Wolfi didn't seem to have any other complaints.

But we were still very glad when Bahrim – after a **nerve-wracking** drive through dark, curving alleyways – stopped the van in front of a rather unattractive building.

What a **dump**, I thought in disappointment. But still, we have hardly any money, what the hell. We're here for the experience, not to bathe in luxury ...

Never had I been so wrong in a first impression.

---

nerve-wracking – nervenaufreibend;
dump – *hier:* Absteige

But now Bahrim called out, "Hassan!" with **tremendous** relief in his voice and hugged a man in a long white shirt who looked almost exactly like the old man in the kasbah.

Hassan began a speech of welcome, but Bahrim interrupted him, unwrapped Wolfi's toe and explained what had happened.

Hassan **tut-tutted** in **sympathy**, waved a small boy over and sent him to fetch a doctor.

Wolfi **tottered** through the doorway, supported by Bahrim on his left and Klaus on his right.

Carlos was still angry with Wolfi and not prepared to exchange a single word with him. We fetched our rucksacks and bags from the van and waited until Wanda had all her things together. Then we followed Hassan – and found ourselves in a **courtyard** from the Thousand and One Nights.

The floor was a geometric **pattern** of brown and white tiles; the walls of the building were red and the **whitewashed** doorways had oriental **arches**. There were plants in tubs everywhere, and between them hung coloured lamps. A little fountain splashed lazily and ancient trees provided shade. I hardly dared to breathe and followed Carlos into our room, which was tiny – but even here the magic continued.

---

tremendous – enorm;
to tut-tut – mit der Zunge schnalzen;
sympathy – Mitleid;
to totter – taumeln;
courtyard – Innenhof;
pattern – Muster;
whitewashed – weiß gekalkt; arch – Bogen

A wide mattress lay on a **mortar pedestal**; the tiny windows were hung with **rugs**. A narrow, arched corridor led to a small, blue-and-green bathroom, and there were Moroccan lamps of **openwork** metal and coloured glass everywhere.

"Carlos! I'm in a dream!" We laughed, hugged and threw ourselves onto the bed, forgetting the whole ugly Wolfi-and-his-scorpion thing – until someone banged on our door.

"Where are you? Why aren't you coming?"

"Bahrim? We're coming!"

When we went downstairs, we discovered the inner courtyard where little white tables and chairs stood around a blue-tiled pool with palm trees. Wanda waved to us. "Where's Wolfi?" I asked.

"He'll be here soon. The doctor took a look at the sting and said it wasn't dangerous. And Wolfi is so fit he won't have any **circulatory** or heart problems. The only thing is that he'll hardly be able to walk for a day or two because his toe is still quite swollen. Well, all in all it's been a dramatic couple of days, hasn't it?"

"You can say that again. We've been through a lot. Hey, who's that? I mean, I'm not Wolfi, but that's a pretty good-looking girl …"

"This is my cousin Imane." Bahrim stood up and waved to the girl. "Come on, we're over here!"

The girl raised her hand. When she came closer,

---

mortar pedestal – Steinpodest;
rug – kleiner Teppich;
openwork – schmiedeeisern;
circulatory – Kreislauf

I saw that Klaus was right. She was amazingly good-looking. Tall, slim, long brown hair, oval face, almond eyes, a wonderful mouth – and brown! A really rich brown. The sun can't make such a **tan** in our part of the world.

I sighed. Sure, I wanted to look like that, too. But I don't look like that. I have **frizzy** blonde, boring hair, I'm not particularly tall – I'm just average. Not a bad average, I admit. But you can't have everything in life, and I'm usually quite satisfied with myself, with Carlos, with the fact that I want to become the most famous travel journalist of all time and am already on the way there.

"Hello, Imane," I said, holding out my hand. "I'm Mimi."

"Oh! Are you the great girl who's already seen half the world and writes for the newspaper and saves lives? You're so independent. I admire you. Bahrim has told me such a lot about you."

I blinked in disbelief. Was this Imane **pulling my leg**? Did she want to **creep up** to me for some reason I didn't yet know? She must have read my thoughts. "I mean it," she confirmed with a laugh. "I hope we'll have lots of time to talk because you're living the kind of life I dream of."

Carlos **cleared his throat**. "And the best thing about her is how casual she is about all her talents. I should know; she's my girlfriend."

---

tan – Bräune;
frizzy – kraus;
to pull s.o.'s leg – jmdn. auf den Arm nehmen;
to creep up to s.o. – sich bei jmdm. einschmeicheln;
to clear one's throat – sich räuspern

"**Flatterer**," I said.

After Imane had said hello to everyone, Bahrim said, "I hope you all don't mind if Imane comes with us. She knows the city well and apart from that ..." He looked at her encouragingly.

"Apart from that I asked him if I could come with you. This is my first opportunity to meet foreigners the same age as me. My father has given his permission because Bahrim will be with me the whole time. Do you understand? My father is very **progressive**. I'm still at school and I want to go to university later, but ... but ... it isn't certain yet."

"My friends aren't interested in that," interrupted Bahrim in obvious embarrassment.

"Yes, we are," I **contradicted** him. "But we can talk about it later, of course. What are we going to do now actually?"

"We're going to wait for Wolfi," said Klaus. "He's still one of us, even if he did behave like an idiot."

Carlos snarled and gave Klaus a black look. "I mean it," insisted Klaus.

"If only I hadn't taken you to the marabout ..." began Bahrim.

"Then he probably wouldn't have been stung by a scorpion. But you warned us all before we went to sleep. And anyway, it's no way to behave. Accusing me of **trapping** a scorpion and smuggling it into his shoe! The man's got a **sick mind**!"

---

flatterer – Schmeichler/in;
progressive – fortschrittlich;
to contradict – widersprechen;
to trap – fangen;
sick mind – krankes Hirn

I had never seen Carlos in such a fury, and now … along **limped** Wolfi!

Carlos leaped up towards him, but he hadn't **reckoned on** me or Klaus. We jumped up and held him back. "You're staying here!" warned Klaus.

"I'll get the bastard!" raged Carlos.

Wolfi had been watching Carlos as if **spellbound**, but now his gaze fell on Imane. He gave a start, looked questioningly from one of us to the other, then went up to Carlos with his hand out and … apologised.

"I'm sorry," he murmured **remorsefully**. "I don't know what I said any more. It must have been something really dumb to make you so angry with me. Really, Carlos, the poison must have affected my mind. I can't remember a thing. I'm terribly sorry!"

Carlos shook his head in amazement. We all knew that Wolfi was **lying through his teeth**, but what could Carlos do? He had no choice but to accept Wolfi's apology.

"Okay," he muttered.

Klaus patted him on the shoulder. "You're a good mate."

Carlos put his hand through his hair and threw himself onto a seat.

"Good," I said cheerfully. "Good you had no more than a shock, Wolfi. What did the doctor say? And when will you be able to walk again?"

---

to limp – hinken;
to reckon on s.o. – mit jmdm. rechnen;
spellbound – gebannt; remorseful – reumütig;
to lie through one's teeth – nach Strich und Faden lügen

"Oh, the day after tomorrow probably. By the way, I'm Wolfi."

Imane nodded. "I thought so."

Wolfi pulled up a chair next to her. Bahrim frowned. "Listen, Wolfi, Imane's my cousin, okay?"

"How nice for you to have such a lovely cousin!"

Imane stood up. "Is it all right if I come back tomorrow at ten?" She nodded to us and disappeared around a corner.

"Why didn't she stay?" Wolfi wanted to know.

"Let me tell you something, my friend," said Bahrim quietly. He stood up slowly and gave Wolfi a threatening look. "You keep your fingers off her, all right? If you behave badly even once, you'll pay for it. I'm telling you as a friend. And I'm telling you I mean it seriously. Very seriously. Got it?"

"Sure man," Wolfi replied in astonishment. "No need to be so uncool."

"I'll be the **judge** of that."

Wow, did that **hit home**!

---

judge – Beurteiler/in;
to hit home – sitzen

Place Djemaa el Fna

‘‘*‘*‘*‘*‘*‘*‘*‘*

At home I had read that Marrakech had been famous for almost a thousand years as one of the most exotic cities in the world. **Traders** from Europe and Africa came together here to do business with gold, spices, **ivory** and cloth. And Place Djemaa el Fna was supposed to be the most beautiful square in Marrakech.

And here we were! Carlos had put his arm around me and we were breathless with amazement at all the things that were going on!

A man was **squatting** on the ground with a long, colourful scarf around his neck, and at his feet a cobra was wriggling out of a basket.

A few steps away another man offered all kinds of medicine for sale: herbs, **roots**, pieces of **bark**, coloured oils and all kinds of other things. But the great thing about his stall was a **plaster** figure of a

---

trader – Händler/in;
ivory – Elfenbein;
to squat – hocken;
root – Wurzel;
bark – Baumrinde;
plaster – Gips

human being with an open **belly**, so you could see all the organs. Next to it lay a long stick with which the customer showed where it hurt and where the medicine was needed.

Two fantastically dressed men with **rattles** whirled about between the stalls like the famous dervishes. They **spun** their heads, and if you weren't careful their incredibly long **pointed** caps caught you in the face or on the arm.

Another trader was selling chains of huge balls of **amber**, pieces of coral and silver **beads**. There was jewellery made from **ebony** and ivory, **silver leaf**, shells and strange **seeds**, **kernels** and nuts.

There were cloths of damask, **silk** and cotton, and we discovered a trader offering silk veils in all the colours of the rainbow.

We had lost sight of the others ages ago.

Carlos **haggled** with all his might over an unusual fossil. I slid the **diaphanous** silk through my fingers and didn't know which colour to take. I'd like to have bought them all.

---

belly – Bauch;
rattle – Rassel;
to spin – wirbeln;
pointed – spitz;
amber – Bernstein;
bead – Perle;
ebony – Ebenholz;
silver leaf – Blattsilber;
seed – Saatkorn;
kernel – Kern;
silk – Seide;
to haggle – feilschen;
diaphanous – durchsichtig

"There you are!" called Bahrim.

"What's up?"

"We've been sitting in a café for hours waiting for you!"

"We're coming."

Carlos could **bargain** better than I, and he was gazing happily at his fossil. "I'm only going to pay half of what he wants for the veil," I said and folded my arms and followed Bahrim.

That really got the trader going! He ran after me, gesticulating wildly. I went back **reluctantly** and managed to get a dark pink veil for less than half.

I was very proud of myself – until Bahrim asked, "How much did you pay for it? What? So much? He took you for a ride!"

The café was on the first floor of a building at the edge of the square. The others had managed to find places at the front and waved at us enthusiastically. "It's like the theatre!" said Wanda **rapturously**. "You can see everything from up here!"

We ordered Cokes. It began to get dark. The traders packed up their wares, and then others came and put up tables and chairs, switched on cookers or lit up **charcoal** grills and in no time the bazaar had been turned into a huge outdoor restaurant.

"This I must see! I have to go down! Carlos, are you coming, too?"

We quickly arranged to meet at eleven in the hotel and then rushed down into the crowds again.

---

to bargain – handeln;
reluctant – widerstrebend;
rapturous – hingerissen;
charcoal – Holzkohle

"What shall we eat? Moroccan? African? Persian? Italian? They have everything – except sausage and **mustard**!"

We laughed and agreed on kebab on the **spit** with hot sauce.

When we were full, we wandered on and came upon a circle of people that was quickly attracting more onlookers. We joined them expectantly. An entertainer was fooling around, walking on his hands, **juggling** with three, four, five and then six balls. He was so good we were always bursting into applause.

He was a young man and he seemed **familiar**. "Mehdi ... It's Mehdi, Carlos!" I shouted. "Hello, Mehdi. Do you recognise us?"

He caught the juggling balls in his outstretched hand and came over to us. "Of course I recognise you! I saw you straight away. Good you're here!" A young boy went around the circle with a cap. Coins **tinkled** and Mehdi said, "I have to go on. This is my job. See you tomorrow, okay?"

Just before eleven we hurried back to Hotel Ayour. If Place Djemaa el Fna was something out of the Thousand and One Nights, here we entered another of Scheherazade's tales. Above the pool was an **elaborate arc** of turquoise tiles, and from its

---

mustard – Senf;
spit – Spieß;
to juggle – jonglieren;
familiar – bekannt;
to tinkle – klimpern;
elaborate – kunstvoll;
arc – Bogen

centre hung a large star of shimmering blue, a lamp that enveloped the water, the palms and the plants in a mysterious light.

I brought my silk scarf upstairs, washed my hands and hurried down again. Halfway down the stairs I heard voices. It was Carlos! What was he saying? I stood still, leaned over the **rail** and listened.

"But Carlos," I heard Wanda's voice, "she's much too young for you. She's still at school! What do you talk about? About homework, trouble with teachers and girlie arguments? Please! She hasn't got a **clue** about geology. You'll get bored with her in no time."

"You're completely wrong there, Wanda," replied Carlos.

"Am I? Carlos, I love you! Doesn't that mean anything to you?"

"To be honest, Wanda …"

"I'd do anything for you!" she **sobbed**.

That's it! I thought indignantly. That's more than enough! I ran down the last few stairs.

"Hey, Wanda, are you playing your big scene? Are you making a final **bid** to get hold of Carlos? You can't bear the fact that nobody wants you, not Klaus, not Wolfi, not Bahrim – and Carlos hasn't **succumbed** either. What could be the reason for that?"

"Carlos, she was listening!" cried Wanda angrily.

---

rail – Geländer;
clue – *hier:* Ahnung;
to sob – schluchzen;
bid – *hier:* Versuch;
to succumb – erliegen

No **trace** of heartbreak and tears. The bitch! I turned round and ran upstairs. Carlos followed slowly and closed the door.

"So!" I snapped. "What do we do now? Shall I pretend I didn't hear anything?"

He shrugged helplessly.

"If you think I'm going to put up a fight for you, you're much mistaken."

I tore off my clothes and pulled the bedcovers around me. He sat down on the edge of the pedestal. "Mimi ..."

"Save your breath. I've had enough. Go to hell!"

It was a **dreadful** night. Of course I couldn't sleep. I thought **frantically** about what I could do. Nothing very much at the moment, that was clear. If I was **in a huff** the next day, it would be an admission of **defeat**. If I pretended everything was fine, Wanda would emerge victorious. Great, I thought. Mimi, you're in a real **fix**. And what about Carlos? Well, if he had started to **waver** after only two weeks apart, I might as well give him up now. Actually, it was a good thing that I'd found out what a rat he was. From that point of view, I thought with a grimace, from that point of view the last few days hadn't been a complete **waste of time**.

---

trace – Spur;
dreadful – furchtbar;
frantic – wild;
to be in a huff – die beleidigte Leberwurst spielen;
defeat – Niederlage;
fix – Zwickmühle;
to waver – wanken;
waste of time – Zeitverschwendung

The Silent Girl

* ‘ * ‘ * ‘ * ‘ * ‘ * ‘ * ‘

The next day I felt completely done in. I went to the bathroom in silence, dressed in silence, packed my bag in silence and was leaving the room when Carlos held me back by my arm.

“Mimi! I can’t help it if Wanda … if Wanda is the way she is.”

“Oh yeah?” I hissed. “Who do you think you are? The **holy** innocent or the **top dog**? You loved her **showering you with praises** on your field trip, didn’t you? And now you’re surprised she’s exactly the way she was before I got here. That’s it. I’m through with you!”

Foaming with rage, I slammed the door behind me.

Imane was already there. “My best friend would like to get to know you all,” she said. “You know her father already, and her brothers Bilal and Ayoub. Malika designs and **sews** clothes, and her workshop is in a fondouk.”

---

holy – heilig; top dog – Platzhirsch;
to shower s.o. with praises – jmdn. mit Lob überschütten;
to sew – nähen

"She sews clothes? I'm not really interested in that kind of thing," said Klaus.

"We don't want to show you the clothes, but the fondouk."

"And what is a fondouk?"

"Oh!" Imane leaned forward eagerly. "40 or 50 years ago you would have ridden there on a camel. A fondouk is a **former** caravanserai, a business house and **inn** for traders and their camels. Wait and see. Fondouks and Marrakech go together like palms in an oasis!"

"Well then …" said Klaus a little sceptically. "Let's go! First to your fondouk, then to the old city and the souk, okay?"

"Everything all right with you two?" asked Klaus as we were setting off.

"Not one bit," I growled.

"Pity," said Klaus quietly and took my hand. "Can I help?"

I shook my head. "No, not now. Later maybe. **I dunno**."

Wanda was the heart and soul of our group. She played around with Wolfi, she linked arms with Imane, she wanted to know this, that and a thousand other things from Bahrim – and she flirted with Carlos. Well, I thought, why not? Goodbye and good luck! I'd get through the last three days. I had almost forgotten my goal of becoming the best travel journalist of all time. Good I'd realised my mistake in time. I pulled my shoulders back, got my

---

former – ehemalig;
inn – Gasthaus, Herberge;
I dunno. = I don't know.

camera out of my bag and started taking photographs like there was no tomorrow. Not of people, of course, but everything else that caught my interest.

I would never have found the way to the fondouk alone. The narrow alleyways were confusing, and the tall houses stood so close to one another that after a few minutes I'd lost all sense of left or right or straight ahead, although I wanted to remember the way.

"Here!" Imane rested her hand on a large double door. "It's double and triple locked every evening to keep the goods safe and let the **residents** sleep easily."

Then she pushed down the huge door handle, and the doors opened with a creak. We entered the courtyard – into another scene from the Thousand and One Nights.

I looked around in astonishment, then I took out my notebook and wrote: *A fondouk is a caravanserai, a high, square building around an inner courtyard. The walls are clay brown; there are camel stables and storerooms on the ground floor. On all four sides of the first floor there is a balcony, which is covered with climbing plants growing up from below. Washing hangs everywhere. The upper floors are* ***unadorned****; only the windows can be seen.*

There is a donkey standing in the courtyard, where an old man sits at a round table and –

"As I said," explained Imane, "fondouks were

---

resident – Bewohner;
unadorned – schlicht; schmucklos

and still are a world of their own. Artists have flats and studios here today."

A girl in a wide, flowing gown and a pink silk scarf around her head – just like the one I had bought – came over to us. "This is my friend Malika."

She was a little shorter and more **delicate** than Imane, but she had bigger eyes and a heart-shaped mouth. She was the prettiest girl I'd ever seen.

We stood there **awkwardly** until she said, "You've come to see my studio? Oh ..." Malika blushed a bright, deep red.

We turned around. A girl in a sand-coloured, formless cloak with rusty brown **edgings** was coming through the doorway. Her head and face were heavily veiled. You couldn't see her nose or mouth, only her **black-rimmed** eyes. In her hand she carried a bag of oranges.

"This is ... a friend," explained Malika hesitantly.

I screwed up my eyes. The scarf the girl had wrapped around her head was in the same rusty brown as the cloak's edgings and had a striking pattern of dancing monkeys.

The girl gave us her hand without a word, and in doing so dropped her bag of oranges. I bent down, and together we gathered up the fruit. I hesitated. There was something about her hand. Or was it her finger? Oh well, I thought, I'm probably mistaken. It can happen after all.

---

delicate – zierlich;
awkward – unbeholfen;
edging – Borte; black-rimmed – schwarz umrandet

"We don't want to disturb you any longer," said Imane quickly. "We'll come back tomorrow, okay?"

There it was again. Imane was behaving strangely, but the others didn't seem to notice. I'd ask Carlos later, I decided.

The new girl still hadn't said a word. Malika was looking at the ground awkwardly, and Imane broke into hectic rush. "Now I'll show you the souk and the man who sells the best kohl in Morocco."

"Kohl?" asked Carlos **blankly**.

Imane pointed to her eyes. "It's this black powder. We paint it around our eyes to protect them from sand and diseases, and to make them look larger and more beautiful."

"Great," said Wanda cheerfully. "I'll buy some, too."

We said, "Goodbye, see you tomorrow!"

At the door I turned round once more. Bahrim was giving the silent girl a sign – and she raised her fist, with the thumb up. It was the okay sign. But did it mean the same thing here as in our part of the world? I shook my head in confusion.

The souk was a labyrinth of hundreds of dark alleyways. In each one there was a different item on sale. There was an alley of pottery, an alley of rugs, of lamps, of leather goods, and so on. You saw men in long robes, called djellabas, and lots of children – but no women. Everything was confusing, breathtaking, mysterious. If you went round one corner, you found yourself in a **cul-de-sac**. If you went round another, you found wooden boxes on sale,

---

blank – verständnislos;
cul-de-sac – Sackgasse

around the next more wooden articles, around the next just cloth. We would have got hopelessly lost on our own, I was sure.

Led by Imane and Bahrim, and often stopping in amazement, we wandered to the famous kohl seller.

The alley was **uneven**, dusty and very dark. There was one tiny shop after another. I was sure we'd never have discovered the 'famous' one. From floor to ceiling its shelves were stuffed full of all kinds of bottles, pots, bags, packets and tins. Rolled-down sacks were full of powders in every shade from yellow to **vermilion**. Nets hung from the ceiling, and right next to the entrance there was a pile of plastic bowls, with a small, vase-shaped wooden container in each one. A little stick jutted out of the lid. "Kohl!" said Imane.

Disbelievingly, I took one of the **lathed** vases in my hand and pulled out the **stopper**. It was empty.

"What the …? Something's wrong here!"

"You have to fill it," said Imane **avidly** and handed me a tiny glass jar. Inside was a fine, slightly glittering black powder. "Kohl!" she repeated and showed us what to do.

She filled some of the powder into the little wooden vase, spat on it and **stirred** the mixture into a paste with the end of the stopper. Then she

---

uneven – uneben;
vermilion – zinnoberrot;
lathed – gedrechselt;
stopper – Stöpsel, Pfropfen;
avid – eifrig;
to stir – umrühren

outlined Carlos's eyes with it. "That's how you do it," she said proudly.

"We do that with eyeliner," I said.

"Do you?" asked Imane with interest. "Have you got some with you?"

"Sure, back at the hotel."

"Will you show me? And does it help against diseases and sand?"

"I don't think so," said Wanda. "Hey, is that rouge?" A little clay bowl, just the right shape and size to fit into the palm of your hand, held bright red powder.

Imane licked the tip of her **index finger** and **dabbed** a little onto the back of her hand.

"Hey, let me do it, okay?" Wanda wetted her index finger and painted Carlos's cheeks red.

"It really *is* rouge! All you need now is lipstick," Klaus **teased**.

"Lipstick?" Wanda dabbed Carlos's lips red, too. "Is it **kiss-proof**? Let's see!" She gave Carlos a great big kiss.

The others howled with delight, but I didn't find Wanda's fooling around at all funny. I'd written off Carlos, but I still meant to **settle my account with** this silly bitch. I'd **get my own back** at the first opportunity!

"Let's get going!" Klaus took Carlos's arm. "I want

---

index finger – Zeigefinger;
to dab – tupfen;
to tease – aufziehen;
kiss-proof – kussecht;
to settle one's account with s.o. – mit jmdm. abrechnen;
to get one's own back on s.o. – jmdm. eins auswischen

to show off my beautiful new girlfriend to everyone!"

The tradesman had been watching us **gleefully** and now sold Wanda kohl and rouge.

We were already two or three shops further on when I thought of something. "I have to go back," I said hurriedly. "Kohl and rouge are just the right presents for my sister Nicki! She's coming back from Hong Kong in a few weeks and she'd love it if I brought her something from Morocco."

Imane nodded. "We'll go on slowly."

"Shall I come with you?" asked Carlos.

"No need."

It didn't take long to choose and pay for the two items. The tradesman insisted on putting them in a bag. I thanked him, turned around – and couldn't believe my eyes. Malika's silent friend was coming down the alleyway. It was her without a doubt; the sand-coloured wrap with the rusty brown edgings, and above all the scarf with the dancing monkeys, were unmistakable.

I dashed into the next shop, hid behind a pile of baskets and **peeked** through a gap. People must have seen me, but what the hell! The silent girl was too **intriguing** for me to ignore. And hadn't I always had a nose for mysteries? In Hong Kong we'd tracked down a writer of anonymous e-mails, in Chile a tomb raider. And in Marrakech?

I held my breath and groaned quietly. Unfortunately, the silent girl had absolutely nothing to

---

gleeful – freudig;
to peek – spähen;
intriguing – faszinierend

hide. On the contrary, she was only doing what we had done. She carefully selected kohl and rouge, paid – and that was that.

Oh well, I thought in disappointment and hurried to catch up with the others. It would have been a huge coincidence if I had to play the detective again here!

After a little while we passed the **dyers**, who had hung **canes** from roof to roof across the lane to hang up their bundles of wool to dry. A row of yellow, a row of blue, a row of red; the colours stood out wonderfully against the glorious sky.

We turned into another alley, and there in this **medieval** environment was a sign saying CYBER INTERNET.

I whistled softly through my teeth. Not bad, I thought, and looked at the opening times pinned to the entrance. "Hey, what's this?" I asked in a low voice. "A plastic rose. Well, well." And then I laughed. Right next to the Internet café was a stall selling all kinds of plastic flowers.

"Do you want to go to the café?" asked Imane.

"Yes." I was already going up the dark stairway. Upstairs I came upon the utter contrast to the souk. Even at home you couldn't have found a more up-to-date Internet café. I quickly **took my bearings** and saw that the others had also followed me to send their mails. Then I typed out a message to my aunts: *Morocco and Marrakech are wonderful, but you*

---

dyer – Färber;
cane – Stock;
medieval – mittelalterlich;
to take one's bearings – sich orientieren

were right about Carlos. I'll get through the last few days, but it's a real mess-up. Please reply tomorrow. Lots of love, Mimi.

Okay. I went to the bar and asked for a coffee.

"And one for me, too," said Klaus. "I'll pay for both."

"Thank you! You're a good mate, Klaus." I really was grateful – not for the coffee, which I could easily have paid for myself, but for the **gesture**. He grinned at me. "You know," he said quietly, although the others were still at their terminals, "Wanda treats everyone like she's treating Carlos. She always has to be the queen bee. Don't let it get to you. It'll pass."

I said nothing.

He put sugar into his coffee and stirred it. "I'm talking from experience," he continued. "There are girls like Wanda, who are easy to see through. And there are girls who say, 'You can come to me any time. I'm always there for you. I don't want anything more than the occasional visit.' They're much more dangerous, and do you know why? Because they pretend to be the modest and **undemanding**. But it's pure calculation. It's all lies!"

"Man, you really seem to be talking from experience," I said with feeling. "But you know, your experiences are all very well, but what do *I* do?"

"To be honest … I've no idea."

I grinned. "Neither have I."

---

gesture – Geste;
undemanding – anspruchslos

Teeth Marks

‘‘*‘*‘*‘*‘

We arrived at the hotel very **worn out** in the late afternoon. "Will you show me your powders?" asked Imane immediately.

"Wanda has the bigger and better selection," I nodded at her. "You'll go and get them, won't you?"

"Of course!" She wasn't just silly, she was stupid, too, I thought and sat down with the sun in my face. And a few minutes later she really did come back with her make-up.

"Here, look! And here, and here!"

"Is that your kohl?"

"Eyeliner," Wanda corrected her and pulled out the brush.

"But it's blue!"

"It suits me better than black," explained Wanda.

"And how do you put the rouge on?"

"With this thick brush. And this is the lipstick."

The guys laughed themselves silly. Wolfi **hobbled up**, obviously annoyed. "Man, I'm so bored I don't know how to get through the day, and you're all in a good mood!" he complained.

---

worn out – erschöpft;
to hobble up – herbeihumpeln

"You shouldn't have let yourself get stung by a scorpion," said Klaus.

That annoyed Wolfi even more.

"Will you give me a guided tour alone tomorrow?" he asked Imane and laid his hand on her arm.

"Alone? That's impossible. I'm not allowed. I promised my father that ..."

"Forget your father!" cried Wolfi. "He doesn't need to know! And anyway, what's it got to do with him? Nothing."

Bahrim frowned. "Wolfi, I'm warning you."

"Oh, you're warning me, are you? What about? What's wrong with me going off with Imane alone?"

"You're in Morocco and not at home."

"Wolfi, behave yourself. You know the conditions under which Imane is allowed to be with us," said Klaus sharply. "Don't make things difficult for her, okay?"

"What would be difficult for her? I don't see any difficulties."

Now I got angry. "Wolfi, be reasonable, for heaven's sake."

"Reasonable? What does that mean?"

"Wolfi, you're getting on everyone's nerves," said Carlos. "When will you learn that not every girl you happen to meet wants to be your girlfriend?"

I raised my eyebrows.

"Pah!" said Wolfi.

But, luckily, we were **distracted**. Someone called,

---

distracted – abgelenkt

"Hello, hello! Where are you?" from a long way off.

"It's Mehdi!" said Imane. "We're here!"

"Hello!" he said, **bowing** low as he came over. "I'd like to invite you to a special performance, just for you – **no charge**. Would you come to the square?"

"Of course!" Suddenly we weren't tired any more. "When?"

"In two hours. I'll be waiting for you."

"What about me? Am I invited, too?" asked Wolfi.

"Of course, why not?"

"The others don't want me," he explained, looking accusingly at us.

"Why not?"

"You don't know him, Mehdi," said Bahrim. "He doesn't behave properly."

"That's bad." Mehdi scratched his chin.

"I can't walk either." Wolfi pointed to his foot, which was still in a thick bandage.

"That's the least of our problems. My moped's in the courtyard. You can ride on the back. But the other thing, the **improper** behaviour … that's really bad."

"Oh, **don't make such a fuss**! It's not what you think. And anyway, you try spending a whole day alone in a hotel in a foreign country!"

I remembered the two hours I had spent waiting

---

to bow – sich verbeugen;
no charge – kostenlos;
improper – unangemessen;
don't make such a fuss – mach kein Theater

in the airport at Agadir, and suddenly I could understand Wolfi's bad mood.

"Okay, Wolfi, you can come, too. Under one condition: you stay with me, all right?"

The others looked at me in astonishment. "With you?" asked Wolfi.

Wanda put her hand on Carlos's arm. "Yes, why not? Carlos wants to take me to the fossil seller, don't you, Carlos?"

"But ... but ... well, I mean, we could all go together, couldn't we?" Carlos stuttered.

We decided to **change** quickly and then go to the square together. Mehdi would drive alongside slowly with Wolfi on the back seat.

A little while later we met up at the front door. Mehdi pushed his moped into the street and gestured to Wolfi to get onto the back seat. Mehdi **straightened** his **headgear** – a mixture of cap and helmet – and took hold of the handlebar. It was – I opened my eyes wide – it was decorated with three plastic roses, red ones. I'd seen them before. So, I concluded with incredible **astuteness**, Mehdi had been on the road on the same day as us. Well, why not? What was so special about that? Mimi, I warned myself, don't start imagining things. Life is full of surprises, and a few roses on a handlebar don't mean anything, do they?

Wolfi's transport was perfect.

We promised Mehdi we'd be on time and went to

---

to change – *hier:* sich umziehen;
to straighten – zurechtrücken;
headgear – Kopfbedeckung;
astuteness – Scharfsinn

look for something to eat. This time it was an African dish, a kind of stew with meatballs, vegetables and potatoes, wonderfully tasty and incredibly spicy.

We washed it down with plenty of Coke, which only increased the burning sensation. "Heavens!" gasped Wanda. "How will I survive?"

She reached under her seat for her little rucksack.

"Hey, where is it?" She looked down – nothing. "My rucksack's gone!"

"Didn't Bahrim tell you to watch out for your things?" said Wolfi **derisively**. "This place is full of pickpockets and other **riff-raff**."

"Wolfi, shut your mouth!" said Klaus roughly. "Are you sure you brought your rucksack with you, Wanda?"

"Quite sure."

"And what was in it?"

"My comb and make-up case – I never go out without them. And my wallet, of course. No papers, no passport, no ticket. I left them in the hotel."

"What are you worried about then? I'll give you my comb," offered Wolfi.

"Along with the **lice**? Do me a favour! Of course I want my rucksack back!"

"All right, we'll look for it. Wolfi, you stay here, okay? You'll only get in our way."

It was dark and the square was full of people, and we knew we didn't have a chance in hell of finding Wanda's rucksack. But still, we began to look ... and

---

derisive – hämisch;
riff-raff – Gesindel;
louse, pl. lice – Laus

came back empty handed just before we had arranged to meet Mehdi.

"Hello! There you are at last! Look what I've got!"

"My rucksack!" cried Wanda in disbelief. "Did the thief bring it back?"

"Not exactly," replied Wolfi mysteriously. "But I kept my eyes open and found him out and grabbed your bag from his **prying** claws."

"Come on, Wolfi! Don't **show off**. Tell us what really happened."

"That's exactly what happened," he assured us. "The thief was a **stray** dog. I saw it playing with the rucksack as I sat here, so I **lured** him to the table and took the bag off him. That was all."

The story *might* be true, I thought. There were a lot of dogs – and cats, too – running around the square. On the other hand, you had to **take** everything Wolfi said **with a pinch of salt**. I decided to inspect Wanda's rucksack by daylight. If it had tooth marks on it, Wolfi would have been telling the truth. If it didn't ... then we had to be careful. We'd have to watch out for Wolfi and his jokes.

I took him by the hand.

Mehdi was surrounded by a big crowd of people. He was a real attraction.

We pushed and wriggled our way through and **marvelled at** the way he whirled first balls and

---

prying – räuberisch;
to show off – angeben;
stray – streunend; to lure – locken;
to take s.th. with a pinch of salt – etwas mit Vorsicht genießen;
to marvel – etwas bestaunen

then **clubs** through the air before beginning his conjuring tricks. First he pulled a **wand**, then a bird and finally a bag of oranges from his sleeve. "How on earth does he do it? Where did all those things come from?" I asked Wolfi, who only shrugged. "Ask me an easy question!"

"Imane ... what ... Malika, you're here, too!" I exclaimed. "You *are* Malika, aren't you?" The girl was heavily veiled, but she nodded, and I saw from her eyes she was laughing.

In no time at all, Wolfi had his arm over Malika's shoulder.

"Wolfi!" I hissed. "Behave yourself!"

He just laughed. Malika got herself free in a single movement. Behind her were two policemen. "Behave yourself, or I'll call the police!"

"Come off it!"

"They're already here. Turn round and you'll see them."

The bag of oranges bumped out of Mehdi's headgear onto the ground. The crowd laughed and applauded; they must have thought he had done it **on purpose**. But when the next trick went wrong, they began to mutter and quite a few people left without throwing any money into the boy's cap.

Malika said hello to a man, a woman and a younger girl. "Malika's family," Imane whispered into my ear. "I hope they didn't notice Wolfi!"

Luckily, they were acting normally. I gave a **sigh of relief**. But what was Mehdi doing? He bowed,

---

club – Keule;
wand – Zauberstab; on purpose – absichtlich;
sigh of relief – Seufzer der Erleichterung

threw the juggling balls and clubs and everything else into a box, which he closed with a slam and lifted onto his shoulders – and disappeared into the crowd.

Our cheerfulness **evaporated**. "Back to the hotel," ordered Bahrim.

"And how do I get back, huh?" whined Wolfi.

"On foot," answered Carlos roughly. "And don't make a fuss. You've caused enough trouble already."

We adjusted our **pace** to his hobble, but did we talk to him? No way.

In the hotel I held Wanda back. "Give me your rucksack for a moment."

"Why?" she asked in surprise.

I went over to reception, where there was more light, and breathed in audibly. "Look, there are teeth marks here, here and here. It looks like Wolfi was telling the truth."

"Mimi, you're a real detective! You're smart!"

"Rubbish. It was the obvious thing to check. Anyone could have thought of it."

A little while later I was in bed with the covers up to my chin. Okay, I was fed up with Carlos, but we had to get through the next few days somehow, so I said, "Wolfi wasn't lying. I found teeth marks on the rucksack. Did you notice the roses on Mehdi's handlebar?"

"No. Were there any?"

"I noticed them back in Imouzzer. And then I saw the moped near the kasbah. Do you remember? What was it doing there, I wonder?"

---

to evaporate – verfliegen;
pace – Tempo

"Mimi," exclaimed Carlos, "are you playing the detective again?"

"We caught the tomb raider in Chile," I reminded him. "You didn't believe me at first, but …"

"You're right. I had other things to think about. I had to convince a certain girl of my **affection**."

"Aha. Affection. What do you mean by that. Don't talk to me about affection. I can do without it."

"Mimi, I've told you a hundred times I don't want anything from Wanda."

I sat up. "I want to tell you something, Carlos. Wanda is being a total pain. If she *has* to break relationships apart, she can look for another victim. But why does it have to be you, of all people? Have you thought about that?"

"And why," **retorted** Carlos, "are you bringing *that* up again? I've told you it isn't an issue. You're getting on my nerves, Mimi."

"And Wanda isn't?"

"Of course she is. But you let her **wind you up**. And she notices, and probably enjoys it, so she does it even more. Just ignore her and things will take care of themselves. Believe me!"

"Hmm," I thought about this. "No, Carlos, girls are different," I said firmly.

"So what? I don't care how girls in general are. The main thing for me is how *you* are."

"Okay, okay. But open your eyes, Carlos. Wanda isn't the problem, *you* are. If you make it clear to her

---

affection – Zuneigung;
to retort – erwidern;
to wind s.o. up – jmdn. aufziehen

you can't stand her, she'll have to leave off. If you don't, she won't. You say I should just ignore her and things will take care of themselves. So how long do I have to look the other way? A day, a week, a month? Two or three years? Tell me, Carlos!"

"How should I know?"

"You see! And anyway, just suppose some fantastic guy turns up tomorrow and Wanda goes over the moon for him. She might leave us alone ..."

"That's what I mean ..."

"... but things will only be all right until the next 'Wanda' appears. Like I said, Wanda isn't the problem, *you* are!"

Alone in the Souk

* ' * ' * ' * ' * ' * ' * ' * ' *

That night I made a decision: I would spend the next day alone. I'd go and take photographs and gather material for my article.

I got up and dressed while Carlos was still asleep. When I went downstairs, I noticed to my great surprise that Klaus was already at breakfast.

"What are you doing here?"

"What about you? Why are you up so early?"

We smiled at one another. But I was **forearmed** and had decided not to tell anyone about my decision. "I couldn't sleep any longer," I said, and it wasn't even a lie.

"Me neither. But why did you come down with a bag?"

Klaus wasn't stupid; he saw more than I preferred. I shrugged. "Saves me running up- and downstairs."

"I see. And what about Carlos?"

"He's still asleep."

I had completely lost my appetite, but I pretended to eat as if I was hungry. When I had finished –

---

forearmed – gewappnet

thankfully there was still no sign of the others I said, "I'll be back in a second, okay?"

That really was a lie because instead of going to the loo, I ran across the courtyard and slipped out of the front door.

I had done it! I breathed a sigh of relief, swung my bag adventurously and walked along the alleyway. Because it was just after nine, I decided to go to the big square first and have a cup of coffee. Then I could see if my aunts had replied to my e-mail – and then? No idea. I'd just see what happened.

I was the first guest in the café. In the square down below the first tradesmen were setting out their wares. The snake charmer was putting his cobra basket into position and someone was decoratively arranging chains and bracelets on a piece of cloth. Then I saw an old man **shuffling** across the square with a cushion under his arm. He nodded to the snake charmer, lifted the lid of the basket and peered inside.

Both men laughed.

The old man carefully placed his cushion on the ground and sat down **laboriously**. Then his chin sank to his chest, and he appeared to be asleep. But a few minutes later at least ten or twelve men were squatting in front of him. The old man raised his head, extended his arms and began to talk and talk and talk ...

A story teller! I gulped down the rest of my coffee, paid, ran down and seated myself on my bag.

---

to shuffle – schlurfen;
laborious – umständlich

Of course I couldn't understand a word, but I was still fascinated by his face and gestures, and I almost – but not quite – made out a story. I forgot the **dreaded** Wanda and the idiotic Carlos! And I forgot my anger as well. But once the story teller had finished, I **slumped back** into my unhappiness. I shook myself and threw a few coins into a bowl. I looked at my watch. I hoped I'd be able to find the Internet café.

I remembered that there was a carpet seller's house at the entrance to the souk. You couldn't miss it because there were wonderful rugs hanging from the roofs and windows. I was soon standing in front of it, and I turned back to look at the square. It was filling with people **by the second**.

And then I **plunged** into the dark, mysterious world of the souk.

I wandered slowly through the first alleyway and stopped by the basketry to admire some **ornately** woven bags. In the next alley there were wooden items. A tradesman waved me into his shop. He was holding a box in his hand and gestured me to open it. But it was impossible.

I tried again and again, but I couldn't see the trick.

With a smile he took the box out of my hand and pushed a **slat** to one side, then another, then a

---

dreaded – gefürchtet;
to slump back – zurücksinken;
by the second – sekündlich;
to plunge – tauchen;
ornate – kunstvoll;
slat – Leiste

third – and then the lid sprang open. It was the perfect present for Aunt Anne! I had the man show me how to open it again, then I tried it myself, and when I was sure I'd got the **knack** of it I began to bargain.

Pleased with my **purchase**, I walked on.

In the next alleyway a **turner** was sitting on the ground operating a sort of violin bow with his toes and hands. In no time at all he had made a spindle out of an ordinary stick.

Around the next corner there were the **coppersmiths**, and then came **craftsmen** decorating mirrors with horn and **tin**. I wondered if Aunt Lise would like one, but I wasn't sure and wandered on.

I had lost all sense of direction ages ago. I was hungry and bought three oranges.

I ate two of them straight away and saved the third for later.

At some point I looked at my watch: half past eleven! I took my notebook out of my bag and wrote *CYBER INTERNET* on an empty page and held it out to a shopkeeper.

He nodded, waved and spoke to a little boy, who smiled at me and gestured me to follow him.

And after a few turnings left and right we did **indeed** arrive at the Internet café. The boy looked up

---

knack – Dreh, Kniff;
purchase – Einkauf;
turner – Drechsler;
coppersmith – Kupferschmied;
craftsman – Handwerker;
tin – Zinn;
indeed – tatsächlich

at me expectantly. I put a few coins in his hand and was opening the door when I glanced at the place were the rose had been yesterday.

It was there again today.

It was probably always there, I thought. But it looked too new for that; it looked as if it had been freshly picked, if you can say that about plastic!

I felt my way along the wall and **padded up** the dark stairway.

The café was full of people, and almost every place was taken, so I ordered a coffee first and waited. More and more people came in: two girls from Sweden, a German, an English guy who **turned out** to be Canadian and finally a handful of Japanese women. I tracked down a terminal.

You could always rely on the aunts. *Dear Mimi,* they wrote, *What a shame that our fears proved to be true! But we're with you and want to remind you about your* ***intention*** *to become the best travel journalist of all time. You don't need Carlos for that. And – although it's a* ***platitude*** *– you're still young and will get over him.*

Who is the other girl? Is she an intellectual ***poser*** *or the opposite, a* ***devious*** *witch? Or is she* ***merely*** *caring,* ***unassuming*** *and passive? Those are the worst.*

---

to pad up – hinauftappen;
to turn out – sich herausstellen;
intention – Absicht;
platitude – Binsenweisheit;
poser – Wichtigtuer;
devious – verschlagen, unaufrichtig;
merely – nur;
unassuming – bescheiden

But whatever the case may be, it's better to have your bad experiences early on.

You'll soon be home, and we look forward to seeing you and hearing about your adventures. Don't forget to write everything down and, where possible, take photographs. Take care of yourself. Your loving aunts.

I almost cried, but I fought back the tears and wrote: *Thanks for your reply. She's the devious witch type, combined with* **unstinting** *adoration. The idiot Carlos is too stupid to see through her and thinks she means it! But she only does it as long as she hasn't got anyone else. Oh well, haven't you always said men were a bit simple?*

I can only agree with you! Today I'm on my own in the souk. I'll write again tomorrow. Lots of love, Mimi. PS. Only two more days!!!

I clicked SEND and turned round with a sigh of relief. "Hey, Malika!" I said in amazement. "What are you doing here?"

I had never seen anyone so horrified by such a harmless question. Malika **winced** and hastily draped her silk scarf around her head and face. Then she turned and hurried to the door.

I sprang up and held her back by the arm. "It's me, Mimi! Don't you recognise me? We met yesterday in the fondouk."

"Oh, yes ..." she stuttered. "Yes, you're Mimi."

"Come and have a coffee with me, okay?"

Malika hesitated. I could see that she didn't really want to, but my curiosity had been **aroused**.

---

unstinting – uneingeschränkt;
to wince – zusammenzucken;
to arouse – wecken

We sat on two barstools and while I ordered, I noticed Malika continuously glancing sideways at the door.

We drank our coffee.

"Where are the others? Where's Imane?" she asked finally.

"No idea," I replied with a shrug. "I'm on my own today."

"On your own?" Her eyes widened. "Aren't you afraid? You don't know your way around!"

"No," I laughed, "of course not. But I'll find my way somehow."

"I hope so." She stirred her coffee. "How's your boyfriend?"

"I suppose he's all right," I replied **evasively**.

"And the girl? The one with the coloured ribbons in her hair?"

"She's even better!"

"Oh really? She ... she's ..." Malika hesitated. But I never heard her opinion of Wanda because she jumped up and wrapped her scarf around her face again. The little I could see of it went dark red.

Well, well, well, I thought. There's a mystery here. There was definitely something wrong. I turned my head. Malika's silent friend was looking through the room. Now she had seen Malika – and me. She hesitated.

I waved and called across the room, "Over here! There's a seat free!"

"I have to go," said Malika hastily.

"Wait, I'll come with you. It would be great if you

---

evasive – ausweichend

could show me the way back to the square. I just have to pay, okay?"

Malika had no choice; she had to stay. Her silent friend came over while I was waiting for my change. She nodded at me, whispered something in Malika's ear and rolled an orange across the **counter**.

Malika wasn't prepared for this, and the orange carried on rolling and fell to the floor. Then one of the Swedish girls, who was just getting up, kicked it accidentally and it **hurtled** on to the opposite wall. I ran after it like a shot. While I was down on my knees, I took out the orange I had in my bag and **swapped** it for the runaway one.

"Here!" I said, handing it to the silent friend, and as I did so, I noticed the nail of her index finger had gone blue in one place, as if she had recently **bruised** her finger.

Strange, I thought, I've seen the same bruise somewhere before! But where? I would have to think about it later.

"Shall we go?" I asked Malika.

"I can't," she answered. "I have to work. My friend, too. But we'll point you in the right direction. You'll find your way."

"If you say so. Pity you don't have time, but work's work, of course."

Outside they took me to the next corner. "Go in

---

counter – Theke, Tresen;
to hurtle – prallen;
to swap – tauschen;
to bruise – quetschen

that direction and you'll reach the square. Perhaps we'll see you this evening. Bye!"

I had intended to follow them, but I'd hardly shouldered my bag when I saw that they could have disappeared down at least three alleyways.

Lost in the souk, I thought, and grimaced. What now? First I had to take a closer look at the orange. Yesterday a bag of oranges, today only one – if it wasn't just a **craving**, they had to mean something.

I went back to CYBER INTERNET as a **precaution** because if there really *was* something going on, I didn't want people to connect me with the two girls.

I was sure about one thing, and that was how **secretive** and mysterious the souk was to me as an outsider.

Anyone who had grown up here would see it quite differently. They would know every street corner and every shopkeeper. And every outsider would look like ... like an apple in a bag of oranges.

And the souk traded in all kinds of possibilities and impossibilities – with the harmless and the forbidden.

I decided to go back to the café and use the toilet. Nothing could be more harmless than that. But when I opened the door, I caught my breath – the rose wasn't there!

---

craving – *hier:* Heißhunger;
precaution – Vorsichtsmaßnahme;
secretive – heimlichtuerisch

Lost in the Souk!

* ' * ' * ' * ' * ' * ' * ' * '

I locked the toilet and took the orange out of my bag. To the naked eye, it looked like any other orange, but I had been expecting that. So I ran my fingers over it carefully – and the blood rushed to my face. I could feel a point where the skin had been damaged and pushed back in place. I **peeled** it quickly and held my breath. I *knew* it! I gave a silent cheer and drew out a little glass tube from the fruit. It was one of those tubes you sometimes get as a free **sample** of perfume in department stores. I pulled out its plastic stopper, shook it – and a rolled-up piece of paper fell into my hand. I unrolled it and read *2*. Just the number 2. And next to it someone had drawn a rose. A rose and the number 2 …

Pensively, I rolled up the piece of paper again and put it back into the tube. I didn't eat anything of the orange – it might have been drugged or **poisoned** for all I knew. I washed my hands and went slowly into the alleyway.

---

to peel – schälen;
sample – Probe;
pensive – nachdenklich;
to poison – vergiften

I stopped in front of the stall with all the plastic flowers. The rose meant something, but what? And how could I find out? I chewed this over, and suddenly had a great idea. I chose a rose – there was only one kind, in red –, paid and, while the stallholder wasn't looking, stuck it in place. The next shop sold silver jewellery. I picked out a chain, put it around my neck and looked at myself in a mirror, keeping an eye on my red rose as I did so. The stallholder removed it and coolly put it back into the big pot with the others. I was **staggered**. What on earth was going on? What did it all mean? **The plot thickens**, I said to myself.

Now I urgently needed a quiet place to think things over. But there were no cafés or restaurants in any of the alleyways I walked through, so I looked for a **flight of steps** or the edge of a fountain instead – anything would do, but there was nothing. I walked on and on. I had lost all sense of direction long ago. Suddenly it dawned on me that I was hopelessly lost! Shopkeepers called out to me; there was a crowd of children at my heels, all eight of them begging non-stop, "Dirham! Miss! Dirham! Bonbon!"

The alleyways became narrower and darker, and I was continually getting into **dead ends** and having to turn back, trying to avoid the children as I did so. When I looked at my watch, I saw that it was already after five.

---

staggered – erstaunt;
the plot thickens – die Sache wird immer komplizierter;
flight of steps – Treppen;
dead end – Sackgasse

No wonder everything seems so dark, I thought **in dismay**. You have to get out of here, Mimi – **at the double**!

The problem was, how? And where did I want to go actually? Back to the hotel? No, first I had to think. And I certainly didn't want to see Wanda or Carlos at the moment. To the fondouk? Stupid idea. That only left the big square. Not bad. I could get something to eat there – I was already weak with hunger – and think about the number 2 plus rose plus orange plus girl – no, two girls!

But what was the square called, for heaven's sake? Djebel, or something. I tried writing this onto a page in my notebook and showing it to the children, but they just laughed and shook their heads.

"I got it wrong, didn't I?" I wrote *Hotel Ayour.*

More laughter and head-shaking.

Damn! What was I to do now? I wrote *CYBER INTERNET* – same result.

I was beginning to feel **queasy**. If only I had my guidebook, or at least a map! But I'd left both of them behind in my hurry this morning. And this was the result. What an **airhead**!

The word 'museum' would mean nothing to these children. So what was left? It had to be a square or a building where I could at least call a taxi. And then I had it!

---

in dismay – bestürzt;
at the double – schnell;
queasy – mulmig;
airhead – Hohlkopf

I wrote *mosque*. Once again, **raucous** laughter and **vigorous** shaking of heads.

"What? You don't know any mosques?" I asked in disbelief.

Then a boy with a huge gap between his teeth spoke up: "Mosque, Miss? Mosque?"

Now it was my turn to nod vigorously. I held my notebook up to him, but he pushed it impatiently aside and repeated, "Mosque?"

At last I realised that none of the children could read the Roman alphabet, so again I said, "Mosque!" I also reached into my bag for my wallet and fished out all my small change. "Mosque! Dirham, yes?" I said.

The children laughed and hopped up and down and shouted, "Dirham! Miss! Mosque!"

One little girl took my hand and another held on to my bag, and together we ran through the alleyways like a bunch of frightened rabbits. The children knew every corner, every dead end and every **short cut** in this labyrinth. It was their home and their playground, and at last they had found someone willing to pay for their knowledge in dirham! It was their lucky day – and mine, too!

We were joined by more and more other children, but the newcomers hadn't reckoned on the first group, who kept stopping and pushing the others away so they had no choice but to follow at a distance. What a **pecking order**! I marvelled.

---

raucous – laut;
vigorous – heftig, energisch;
short cut – Abkürzung;
pecking order – Hackordnung

They would even be able to stand up to the dreadful Wanda; a few **thumps** and bumps from them would certainly put *her* in her place. This thought made me laugh out loud. The children laughed, too, and pointed proudly forwards. "Miss! Mosque!"

And there in the twilight stood a mosque with a minaret on a large empty square. Home and dry! A weight – no, a heavy **burden** – fell from my shoulders.

"Miss? Dirham?" Eight expectant faces looked up at me. "Miss! Ben Youssef Mosque! Ben Youssef!"

"Ah, so that's what it's called. I'll try and remember."

"Miss! Dirham!"

"Sure, dirham! Mosque!" I said, laughing. "But how can I share out the money equally?" Of course they didn't understand my words, but they immediately **grasped** my problem. Seven little fists pushed a girl to the front. Her short, fluffy hair was all **matted** and she wore a dress of an **indeterminate** colour and worn-out plastic flip-flops that were far too small for her – but her eyes shone! She held out her hand confidently, and I gave her all my small change. "Here! And thank you! Thank you very much!"

The girl opened her eyes wide in astonishment and jumped for joy. Then she ran off, but only a few

---

thump – Schlag;
burden – Last;
to grasp – verstehen;
matted – verfilzt;
indeterminate – undefinierbar

metres, to the entrance to the souk. The children sat on the ground and eagerly put their heads together. In no time at all they had shared out the money between them, without any shouting or arguing. They waved at me, laughing and jumping up and down, and disappeared down a dark alleyway.

The Orange

‘‘*‘*‘*‘*

Luckily, there was a spot right nearby with several round tables under umbrellas that hadn't been folded away yet. I sat down at the first chair I could find and reached for the menu. There was pizza – surprise, surprise! – and sandwiches and salad and soup. I ordered the lot: tomato soup, pizza and salad, Coke with ice. It was fantastic! I hadn't been hungry in the morning, **what with** the Wanda-Carlos thing sitting heavily on my stomach. And although the two oranges had been good for me, they hadn't filled me up, so it was no wonder I **went for it** now!

I ate and ate and ate, and it was only after I had even chewed the ice cubes and ordered a second Coke that my brain was prepared to think about something other than eating.

The second Coke brought me back to the **puzzling** events. Two girls, the number (or rather the **figure**) 2, two oranges, the rose that was sometimes

---

what with – mit dem ganzen ...;
to go for it – zugreifen *(beim Essen)*;
puzzling – rätselhaft;
figure – Zahl

there, sometimes not. And then the stallholder who had had the nerve to steal my rose and resell it. How did he fit in to things? Was he part of the story, or was he simply a **shrewd** businessman?

I immediately **dismissed** this last possibility. Anyone living so close to the Internet café would notice people sticking up roses, as my case proved. So the plastic-flower salesman was somehow involved in the events.

The roses themselves had to be a sign. They could mean 'I'm here', or 'I'm waiting for you' or quite simply 'I love you; I'm thinking about you'.

Everyone in Europe knows that a red rose is a symbol of love. Was it the same in Morocco? I frowned. I didn't have a clue, but I **assumed** so.

Right, that explained the rose, but what did the oranges mean? It was a clever idea, even if it wasn't particularly original to hide a message in a piece of fruit. But it was a medieval strategy. Today everyone has a mobile – anyone can text a message without it being seen. At home ... aha, that was the key! Everyone has a mobile at home, but what about the less well-off people in Marrakech? I whistled through my teeth. The orange must have the same function here as a mobile; it fulfilled the same **purpose**. But there was a danger here that couldn't be **underestimated**: a mobile sends messages at the push of a button, but an orange would need direct

---

shrewd – schlau, klug;
to dismiss – aufgeben;
to assume – annehmen;
purpose – Zweck;
to underestimate – unterschätzen

participation or a **go between**. If Malika was one of the participants, was the silent girlfriend the other one or the go-between? And what role did the plastic-flower salesman play?

I **mulled** this **over** and came to the conclusion that Malika and her silent friend must be direct participants, because otherwise the message-bearing orange didn't make any sense in connection with the rose.

But what dangerous secret could **compel** the two girls to **resort to** such unusual tactics? Were they dealing drugs? What else was there? Two girls could meet anywhere for a gossip, even in Marrakech. Particularly in Marrakech! With a girl and a boy things would be different. *Then* I could understand the old-fashioned message delivery. But with two girls? No. Two girls … why was one always veiled, and silent, too? I took another sip of Coke and suddenly remembered our first meeting with Malika in the fondouk. Hadn't she gone all **self-conscious** when the silent girl arrived? Imane and Bahrim had **shepherded us out of** fondouk in no time, even though we'd hardly seen a thing! I was sure the silent veiled girl was the reason for their **conspiratorial turnaround**.

---

go-between – Vermittler/in;
to mull over – hin und her überlegen;
to compel – nötigen, zwingen;
to resort to s.th. – auf etwas zurückgreifen;
self-conscious – gehemmt;
to shepherd s.o. out of s.th. – jmdn. aus etwas herausbugsieren; conspiratorial – verschwörerisch;
turnaround – Kehrtwende

Now for the figure 2. It could mean anything: two roses, two oranges, two hours, two days, or … of course! The time! Two o'clock! The time in combination with the rose meant the rendezvous!

Not bad, Mimi, I congratulated myself. Despite heartache you can still think clearly!

I ordered a third Coke and considered one last point: how would I **proceed**? Because I knew for sure I wanted to solve the mystery.

If I assumed that the figure 2 didn't stand for the second meeting, but the time it was supposed to take place, then it seemed likely that the two of them wanted to meet tomorrow at two o'clock. And if there was a rose stuck in the boarding of the Internet café, I would almost have solved the case.

So I only had to … help! I jumped up from my chair in shock and dismay. *I* was the one with the orange and the message! I had disrupted the line of communication, and *one* of the two now knew for certain that someone was on to them! **Good grief**, the girl must **be scared stiff**! How could she know I was perfectly harmless and just enjoyed solving mysteries? I wasn't exactly harmless actually, but that was neither here nor there right now.

Okay, Mimi, what are you going to do tomorrow?

I thought for a moment about buying a djellaba, one of those long robes, and wrapping my pink silk veil around my head. In this disguise I could settle down in the Internet café and see how things developed.

---

to proceed – vorgehen;
good grief! – du meine Güte!;
to be scared stiff – eine Heidenangst haben

But I **ruled out** this idea straight away. It would have been a bit of exotic fun, but terribly uncomfortable because you tended to trip over and not get anywhere if you weren't used to wearing long robes. So I would stick to my jeans, but definitely be in CYBER INTERNET by two o'clock.

Once I had got this far, I was very pleased with myself. I paid and asked the young man who had served me where I could get a taxi.

He pointed in front of him. "Here, Miss. There's one here already."

Well, if this isn't my lucky day, I thought.

---

to rule out – ausschließen

Poolside Chit-chat

* ' * ' * ' * ' * ' * ' * ' * ' * '

After a few minutes the taxi pulled up in front of Hotel Ayour. I paid and opened the door with mixed feelings. The room key was hanging on the board, which meant that Carlos wasn't there, which was fine by me. I ran to our room, had a shower and changed because I was anything but clean after a day in the souk. Once I had blow-dried my hair and put on some mascara and lip gloss, I felt top fit again.

I hung my bag over my shoulder and decided to go to the square, but first I went to the pool. I don't really know why I did this. Perhaps I thought I'd see Carlos there. Or Klaus. I'd like to have talked to Klaus.

But I didn't see either Carlos or Klaus at the pool. Instead I heard some laughter that put me into a total **rage**; it was unmistakably Wanda.

I slipped behind a palm tree and peered around its trunk. The blue star in the **Moorish** archway was illuminating the water, palms and flowers with its

---

chit-chat – Geplauder;
rage – Wut;
Moorish – maurisch

mysterious light to create an atmosphere that couldn't have been more romantic. Wanda wouldn't have been Wanda if she hadn't used it to her own purposes. She was sitting by the pool in a bikini, dangling her legs in the water and flirting with the man at her side. He was wearing swimming trunks and avidly stroking her thigh.

The man? I scurried to the next palm. Who *was* the guy? I didn't know him; I'd never seen him before, I was sure of that. But boy, was he going for it! I grinned in respect. Now he stood up, laid a **deckchair** mattress by the tiled edge of the pool and settled Wanda onto it. Aha, I thought, and quickly took my camera out of my bag. I waited a little while, until I was sure the two of them only had eyes and ears for each other, and then I crept up closer and took three photographs.

What had I thought earlier on? It was my lucky day. And it wasn't over yet, I noted with satisfaction. Let's see what else it has in store!

I didn't have to wait long for my next lucky break. I went up to reception and said to the waiter hanging around there, "The couple by the pool would like something to drink."

"Right away," he said, hurrying outside.

To the doorman I said, "Excuse me, could you floodlight the courtyard? I must have lost my key in the water and I can't look for it very well in the **gloom**."

"Certainly, Miss."

---

deckchair – Liegestuhl;
gloom – Dunkelheit

So. Both schemes would seriously disturb their little **tête-à-tête**. She who laughs last …

Where would I meet the others? Probably on the terrace of the café. So I **strolled** in that direction, stopped for a short while in front of the snake charmer, laughed at a pantomime artist who was new to me … and then somebody grabbed my arm roughly. "Mimi! Where did you come from? Where the hell have you been?"

I could see that Carlos was really angry – angry, but relieved.

"Where have I been? It's none of your business, Carlos, but I'll tell you anyway. I was here in the square, in the souk, in the Internet café, by the Ben Youssef Mosque," I recited. "I've been getting around. I had a great day. I hope you did, too."

"It was an awful day," he said through his teeth. "Why did you **clear off** without saying a word? You must have known we'd be worried. It was really selfish of you, and uncooperative and …"

"That's enough," I interrupted him in a quiet, threatening tone. "If anyone here is selfish and uncooperative, it isn't me."

"What? We've been looking for you all day, everyone. We were …"

I interrupted him again. "Everyone? The darling Wanda, too?"

"Yes, even her."

"And were you looking for me just now?"

"Of course we were! Why else would I be running up and down the square?"

---

tête-à-tête – Stelldichein;
to stroll – schlendern; to clear off – abhauen

"Where are the others?"

"They're completely exhausted and they're having coffee up on the terrace!" He gestured in that direction with his thumb.

"But not you!" I said mockingly.

"No, not me."

"And the darling Wanda is bound to be with them, isn't she?"

"Wanda helped with the search until the afternoon," he explained hotly. "Then she had such a bad headache she had to lie down. The **anxiety** was too much for her."

"Whaaat? What 'anxiety' was she talking about?" I snorted with laughter. I laughed so loud that people stopped in amazement and looked **askance** at Carlos.

"Wanda and her headache! I saw her with her 'headache' by the pool. And if you come to the hotel, the doorman and the waiter will confirm the 'headache' with pleasure, my dear Carlos."

"What on earth are you talking about?"

"About the darling Wanda. She's acting just the way I thought she would. I've seen through her. And why? Because I'm a girl and I know what girls are like. But you didn't want to listen. *You*, of course, know *much* better how girls behave than I do, you oh-so-clever lady's man!"

"Would you please explain ..."

"Oh yes, Carlos, I'm doing just that! Do you remember the tomb raider in Chile? Do you remember the three photos I took of him as he was lifting

---

anxiety – Sorge, Angst;
askance – misstrauisch

a **find** out of the ground? Do you remember how your sister Bashi had them developed that night, and how they led to the tomb raider's capture in the end? Do you remember all that?"

Carlos nodded in obvious confusion. "Why are you telling me this?"

I took a deep breath. "Because I just happened to come upon Wanda and her 'headache' by the pool and I took three photos of them. I'll give you the prints as soon as they're ready."

Carlos still hadn't understood a thing. "How can you take three photos of her headache? Was she in that much pain?"

My **jaw** dropped. "Pain?" I hissed. "She was loving it – or rather, *him!* The photos prove how serious she is about you, you idiot! You totally **fell for** all her **drivel**; you were prepared to **jeopardise** our relationship! 'I love you, Mimi. Be patient with Wanda, don't take any notice of her,'" I **sneered**. "Isn't that what you said?"

Carlos winced. "Wanda is – she met up with someone else? By the pool?"

"Met? I wouldn't call it that. Fooling around, more like."

"I don't believe you."

I held the camera up to his face. "There's clear **proof** in here. Quite apart from the fact that, as I

---

find – Fund;
jaw – *hier:* Kinnlade;
to fall for s.th. – auf etwas hereinfallen;
drivel – Gefasel; to jeopardise – aufs Spiel setzen;
to sneer – höhnisch lächeln;
proof – Beweis

said, the waiter and the doorman can confirm my observations, because I sent them out to the two lovebirds. A girl's revenge is sweet. But you must know that already because you understand girls so well!" I had talked myself into an **almighty** rage.

Carlos was silent. What could he say anyway?

"Right. I'm finished with Wanda. I'm going to the café."

He crept alongside me with a **hangdog** expression on his face.

"Hey, here comes the runaway!" Wolfi took me theatrically into his arms and **smothered** me with kisses.

"Klaus, I have to apologise. But, you know, I couldn't tell you what I was going to do. You would have held me back and I ... I just needed to get away from things."

"I understand," was all he said. "The stupid thing is that a city like Marrakech, where people often disappear without trace, isn't exactly a quiet village in the Black Forest."

"I know. But I can look after myself."

"Yes, it seems you can, at least **in terms of** foreign countries."

I stared at him in surprise.

"You're still very young, Mimi."

"And how old are you, Klaus?"

"A year older than Carlos," he promptly replied. "I've already been through my Wanda experiences

---

almighty – mordsmäßig;
hangdog – beschämt;
to smother – bedecken;
in terms of – im Hinblick auf

and what they do to you. Thank God!" he added sincerely.

"Wanda," said Wolfi, "Wanda is an **inconsiderate** beast. I can tell because I can be a beast myself. But she can **disguise** it better than I can."

"So? How does she do it?" I asked innocently. "Pay attention, Carlos!"

Wolfi grinned at Carlos pityingly and placed a hand on his arm. "Listen and learn, mate. This'll be useful to you for the rest of your life. The Wandas of this world weave their webs out of admiration and noble-mindedness. You can come to me whenever you want! I'm always there for you!" he said in a **honeyed** voice. "You're the best, the greatest, the sexiest. And you know what, darling? Only *I* know how wonderful you are!" he **purred**.

We fell about laughing. I danced around my chair shouting, "Yes, yes! That's exactly what I meant, Carlos, but you didn't want to believe me. You ..."

"That's enough, Mimi," said Carlos softly.

It was a calm night. Carlos and I lay in our beds in silence. I was glad he didn't make any advances – that would have been too much for me. And I was also glad he didn't ask, "What about us?"

How could I have answered *that*? Am I **psychic**?

---

inconsiderate – rücksichtslos;
to disguise – sich verstellen;
honeyed – honigsüß;
to purr – säuseln;
to be psychic – übernatürliche Kräfte besitzen

The Bikini

* ' * ' * ' * ' * '

We were having breakfast when Wanda appeared. Today her hair was loose; the pink eye-shadow had been perfectly applied, as usual, and the rouge, too, but instead of the stud on her chin she had a little black **beauty patch**. She looked marvellous and sat down brightly.

"Boy, am I hungry!"

"Headache over, Wanda?" inquired Klaus.

"All over."

"It must have been terrible, the way you disappeared so quickly," Klaus continued.

"Yes, it was terrible. I was seeing double. But sleep is the best medicine. Ah, Mimi, you're back," she said in false surprise. "We were so worried about you running off that we combed half the city for you. The stress did me in so badly I got a migraine. God, it was terrible!"

If I hadn't got the photos **in the can**, I'm sure I would have fallen for her pack of lies. She was so convincing it was obvious to all of us she'd had years of practice!

---

beauty patch – Schönheitsfleck;
in the can – im Kasten

Klaus spread fig jam onto his bread. "And now you're feeling better, Wanda, what are you going to do today?"

I looked at Klaus sharply. Did he know something about Wanda's new boyfriend? Wait and see.

"Me?" She tossed her hair back. "Oh, Carlos, I need to take care of a few things on my own today. I spent the whole day yesterday looking for your little Mimi and didn't have time to look for presents for my mum and dad. My family's very important to me, you know. But you understand that, I'm sure. Of course I'd rather spend the time with you, but perhaps I'll find a present for you as well," she added **coyly** and winked at him in her inimitable Wanda way.

Carlos sat there like a **drowned rat**.

Klaus cleared his throat. "As we all know, Wolfi, you've given us a pretty hard time. It took ages for you to realise that in Morocco you can't behave the way you do back home. Now, unfortunately, Wanda has behaved so badly that it took all my **persuasiveness** and a lot of **slush money** to make sure we weren't all chucked out of the hotel yesterday evening."

Good grief! What had happened? Did it have to do with the rose and the message in the orange? Did it involve drugs after all? I waited **in suspense** for Klaus to continue.

---

coyly – kokett;
drowned rat – begossener Pudel;
persuasiveness – Überredungskunst;
slush money – Schmiergeld;
in suspense – gespannt

At first he said nothing at all. Instead he reached into his trouser pocket and pulled out a tiny piece of fabric.

I caught my breath. Wanda's bikini top!

"Wanda, the waiter *and* the doorman caught you and your friend playing around by the pool. You both ran away, but in the rush you left this behind. By Moroccan standards your behaviour was inexcusable."

Wanda opened her eyes wide. "My behaviour? What have I done? I was in bed sleeping off my migraine. There must be some mistake here. That thing doesn't belong to me."

I had had enough. I stood up slowly. "What if not only the waiter and the doorman can confirm that it's your bikini top? What if I had clear proof that you were wearing it – and took it off – yesterday evening by the pool?"

Wanda laughed. "Bring me your proof, sweetheart. I'll laugh myself to death when I see it!"

"Fine! You asked for it!"

"How dramatic! Our own little Ally McBeal!" Wanda rolled her eyes. She stuck a banana in her bag and stood up. "**So long**, my dears, be good. See you this evening, okay?"

She had given Carlos a nasty lesson, one he would have to think about for a long while to come. I was almost – but only almost – sorry for him.

Klaus sighed. "I don't know why some people enjoy lying so much. They must be really **screwed up**."

---

so long – bis bald;
screwed up – neurotisch

I suddenly remembered yesterday's story teller, and that made me think of a fairytale by the brothers Grimm. "Do you know Mother Holle?" I asked. "She gave each girl her proper **reward**. When the kind girl said something, a gold coin fell out of her mouth. When the unkind girl, who could tell lies as brilliantly as Wanda, said something, a **disgusting toad** hopped out. Imagine that with Wanda!"

The **spell** was broken. We had a laugh and then decided to spend the day doing what we wanted.

"Where's Bahrim?" I asked.

"Today's Saturday. That's like our Sunday, so he's with his family," replied Klaus. "Well, I'm going to the museum and perhaps to a mosque. As a man I'm allowed to. Do you want to come too, Wolfi?"

Wolfi yawned. "Museum? Mosque? I don't know … I think I'll stay by the pool for now."

"Watch it," I warned him.

"Don't worry, Mimi. I'll be as good as gold."

"I hope so."

We stood up.

"Shall we do something together?" asked Carlos.

I hesitated. "Why not? But only if you agree on going to the Internet café before two."

"Do you know how to get there?" he wanted to know.

"I know the way. Come on."

---

reward – Belohnung;
disgusting – ekelhaft;
toad – Kröte;
spell – Bann

The Fortune Teller

* ' * ' * ' * ' * ' * ' * ' * ' *

I asked the doorman to change a note into small coins, which I would need for the photos I wanted to take of the performers on the big square. No one on Place Djemaa el Fna – at last I had remembered its name! – would let you take their photograph for free.

We strolled off. I waved to the story teller, and he waved back. Had he really recognised me? I waited until he stretched out his arms and rolled his eyes dramatically. Then I **released the shutter** and threw a coin into his bowl.

My next victims were a snake charmer, a man whose trained monkeys did the most amazing tricks and, for their finale, pulled the hats off the men in the audience. Then I discovered a tooth **extractor**. He was sitting on a little wooden stool, and at his feet lay a tray full of pulled teeth arranged in **neat** rows. "Hey," I said to Carlos, "some of them are so big they could only belong to a camel, don't you think?"

---

to release the shutter – den Auslöser drücken;
extractor – Ausreißer/in;
neat – ordentlich

A smile appeared on his face for the first time since the Wanda shock.

I couldn't leave out the **faith healer**, nor the fire eater, and then – then I actually discovered a **scribe**.

He was sitting at a tiny little table, with a **fountain pen** and all kinds of **nibs** and paper within reach, listening **intently** to a customer. This man spoke slowly and steadily, and the scribe nodded and wrote everything down in beautiful Arabic script. Then he blew the ink dry, carefully rolled up the paper, named his price and gave his thanks. It was all incredibly **dignified**.

"Do you think he understands German? Or English, or French?" I asked Carlos.

"Why do you ask? Do you want to have a letter written? You wouldn't be able to read it, Mimi."

"So what?"

Carlos was **taken aback**. "Yes, so what, if you know what it says," he said thoughtfully.

The scribe had been watching us. Now he waved at his stools, smiled at us knowingly and asked in English, "You lovers? You want love letter? I can do!"

We looked at each other for a long moment, Carlos and I. In my mind's eye I saw the whole Rory business and my decision never to fall in love again.

---

faith healer – Gesundbeter/in;
scribe – Schreiber/in;
fountain pen – Füller;
nib – Schreibfeder;
intently – aufmerksam;
dignified – würdevoll;
to be taken aback – verblüfft sein

And then along came Carlos with his silly bet and the wonderful time we spent together. I saw the **Andean** dolls – and finally Wanda, the **cunning** little devil. All these experiences were now part of my life. But hadn't I always wanted to go through every high and low on offer? Too stupid of me. In future I would do without the lows, I swore to myself.

I awoke from my daydreaming, took a deep breath and heard Carlos saying, "Please write the most beautiful love letter for us."

The scribe carefully selected a particularly fine piece of paper – I only saw later that it was handmade. He reached for a black pen, collected himself, then **dashed out** the letter without interruption.

"How beautiful!" I said, spellbound. "I'm going to frame it and hang it in my room! Actually, you should have one, too. You know what, Carlos? I'll give you a high-quality photocopy, okay?"

"Okay."

We went on. I took a photograph of a fearless performer who was letting five scorpions crawl over his face. "How disgusting! Come on, Carlos," I **urged**. But, because I was always misplacing my bicycle keys back home, I bought a key ring with a nice, middle-sized scorpion in **resin**.

A man – everything about him was grey: his face, his headscarf, his djellaba, the neckline of his shirt, his shoes and socks – waved us over to him with

---

Andean – Anden-;
cunning – gerissen;
to dash out – *hier:* schnell niederschreiben;
to urge – drängen;
resin – Harz

such **urgency** that we obeyed as if we were under a spell. He pointed to a grey carpet, and we sat down. Then he gestured to the rolled-up piece of paper Carlos had in his left hand. "Love letter, yes?"

"Sorry?" I asked.

"He saw us with the scribe," Carlos whispered in my ear.

"No, no! I knowing!" he insisted. "Your hands, please."

We extended our hands **in bewilderment**. First he looked searchingly and with much concentration at the palms of my hands, then Carlos's. Then he took our right hands and put them together gently but firmly and said with a smile, "Love letter okay. Good."

We stood up awkwardly, and I put a few coins in his waiting, as yet empty, bowl. But the grey man shook his head. He carefully emptied the coins into his hand and passed them back to me. "Oh no, I can't," I insisted and held my hands behind my back.

But the old man was **unrelenting**, and I had to take back the money. I thanked him by giving him my hand and asking, "Why did you do that?"

To this day I don't know if he understood us or whether he simply guessed the meaning of my question, but he replied forcefully by pointing at Carlos and me. "You and you need help. Me, I help. Okay? Bye-bye."

My eyes suddenly filled with tears. I blinked and

---

urgency – Dringlichkeit;
in bewilderment – verwundert;
unrelenting – unnachgiebig

wiped them **surreptitiously** away and whispered – although the square was full of people and no one could have heard me – "What's wrong, Carlos? What on earth is wrong with us?"

He **blew his nose** for a suspiciously long time. "You know, if you sit here every day and watch the people all around you, you're bound to become a good judge of human nature."

"I suppose so ..."

We drifted to a stall selling freshly squeezed orange juice. I paid for a glass and pointed to myself and to the **palmist**, who was sitting motionlessly on his grey carpet a couple of metres away. Then I mimed carrying the drink over to him. "Okay?" I asked.

The juice presser nodded and handed me a small tray. "How nice!"

"I'll wait for you here," said Carlos.

The palmist was pleased with the juice, really. He emptied the glass in one go, put it back on the tray and said, "Thank you. You and ..." he turned round and pointed to Carlos, "you big travel. Wonderful, okay?"

"Th-th-thank you," I stuttered in confusion and hurried back to the juice stall. I reached for Carlos's hand for the first time since the Wanda thing.

"What's up with you? You're all **flustered**."

"You will be, too, when I tell you what the palmist said."

---

surreptitious – heimlich;
to blow one's nose – sich die Nase schnäuzen;
palmist – Handleser/in;
flustered – nervös

"So? What did he say?"

We **dodged** two **dwarves** who, to the great delight of the cheering crowd, were thrashing at each other with clubs, but missing at the last moment, or **toppling** to one side or **somersaulting** backwards out of reach.

"So, what did he say? Thank you for your kind donation? Please do me the honour of coming again?"

"Carlos, be serious for once," I exclaimed.

"Mimi, I've been serious for so long I'm still not in the mood for laughter, you know."

"Sure. But it serves you right. Why did you have to be so stupid as to ... Let's change the subject. For now anyway, all right?"

"All right." Carlos squeezed my hand. "So, how long are you going to keep me in suspense?"

"Until ... until ... What's the time?"

"Just after twelve. Time for lunch. Do we have enough time before you have to be at the Internet café?"

"If we only take an hour. Look, there's a little restaurant were we can get couscous. I love couscous!"

We ordered, and I leaned forward and said, "Carlos, after the man had finished his orange juice, he handed back the glass and said, by way of thanks, 'You and you' – by that he meant both of us – 'big travel. Wonderful!' What do you think of that?"

---

to dodge – ausweichen;
dwarf – Kleinwüchsige/r;
to topple – kippen;
to somersault – Salto schlagen

"He said that? Really? That's strange. Somebody **foretold** the same thing to me at home in Chile."

"Yes? What did they say?"

"That I . . . that I would go on long journeys with a girlfriend. Long and dangerous journeys, but we'd always return safely."

"Did they tell you your girlfriend was the most famous travel journalist of all time?"

"No, the woman couldn't see that far into the future."

"What a pity. That really is a pity. But never mind, the couscous at least is fantastic."

We enjoyed the meal. "Will you tell me what's going to happen at the Internet café?"

"I'd like to, but I don't know myself."

---

to foretell – vorhersagen

Missed!

* ' * ' * ' *

I looked at my watch. “We have to go, Carlos.” I knew the way so well by now that we got to the Internet café in record time without losing our way. A look at the **slatted** wall ... there was the rose! And upstairs the silent girl was sitting at the bar stirring her coffee. Hey, that was a surprise!

“Carlos, do you remember Malika’s silent girlfriend? She’s sitting at the bar, over there. Don’t let her out of your sight, and fetch me at once if she wants to go or if Malika arrives, okay? I just want to see if I’ve got a mail from the aunts.”

I sat down at a free terminal and typed in my password. Great! The aunts had replied:

Dear Mimi,

How are you?

*We’re very glad you’re not hanging your head although the ‘witch’ must be very trying for you. You’ll meet girls like that over and over again, but they have their good side: they separate the boys into the **wheat** and the **chaff**. Can you follow the comparison?*

---

slatted – Latten-;
wheat – Weizen;
chaff – Spreu

It's better to realise early on that someone is pretending to be wheat although he's only empty chaff. Then you won't spend so much time on hopeful feelings that will only be disappointed. But perhaps Carlos has also learned a thing or two? Don't rule this out and wait a little while before making a decision.
But despite everything you've gained some more experience, you've seen lots of lovely, interesting things, you've gathered material for your article and you've taken photographs. So the trip hasn't been a waste of time. And you'll be back tomorrow. We're looking forward so much to seeing you!

Your aunts.

PS: Aunt Lise is baking your favourite cake.

I thought for a moment and then typed:

Dear Aunts,

Yesterday the 'witch' fell headfirst into the ditch she'd **dug** *herself, hooray!*
I don't know for sure if Carlos is wheat or chaff. At the moment he's totally down, but we've just had a great time in the square – I'll tell you all about it.
By the way, I'm on the **scent** *of a mystery, but time is running out, and I'm not sure if I'll solve it. It has to do with roses and messages hidden in oranges!!! Keep your fingers crossed, okay?*

Lots and lots of love from

Mimi.

PS too: There must be loads of varieties of wheat. So I'm only going to be satisfied with an A-plus superior grade!!!

---

to dig – graben;
scent – Spur

There. I remembered a stupid advertising slogan: "Good to know what you want." How true! Because if you don't know what you want, you just **wobble** around the whole time like an idiot.

The Wanda business really did have its good side: I now knew what I wanted – top quality, that was what *I* wanted!

I looked around for Carlos. He was sitting on a barstool next to the silent girl, and he was bored. I pulled up another stool and ordered a coffee. The silent girl looked at the clock, at the door, at the clock, at the door. It was already after two, and Malika still hadn't arrived!

At half past two Carlos raised his eyebrows in **exasperation** and whispered, "Don't you think it's a pity to **fritter away** our precious time in Marrakech like this?"

"Sure I think it's a pity. But I don't think it'll take much longer."

I paid for our coffees just to be on the safe side. It was lucky I did so because suddenly the silent girl stood up and rushed out of the door so fast I could hardly catch my breath in amazement. How fast she could move! I hadn't noticed this up to now. We hurried after her, but, of course, once we were outside, she had disappeared and – the rose had vanished, too!

Aha. The flower quite clearly meant 'I'm here, waiting for you'.

---

to wobble – schwanken;
exasperation – Frust;
to fritter away – verplempern

"Would you please tell me what's going on?" asked Carlos. "And what you're going to do now?"

"I don't know what I'm going to do. We'll have to leave it to chance," I said **apologetically**.

"We …"

"Hallo! Miss! Mosque? Dirham? Miss!"

The children skipped around us, laughing. I counted six in all – but then the other two came running up.

"How do you know these children?"

"They helped me out of the souk yesterday. Without their help I'd still be wandering around in here."

"Miss!" They tugged at my trouser leg. "Miss! Mosque?"

"Dirham?" added the girl I had given the money to yesterday.

"What does that mean, 'mosque'? Do they mean a particular mosque?"

"It was like this, Carlos: when it got dark, I had to get out of the souk as quickly as possible. But I didn't know where to go. I didn't want to go back to the hotel, I couldn't remember the name of the big square, and the children couldn't read the Roman alphabet. So I just said 'mosque'. And they understood what I meant and led me to the Ben Youssef Mosque."

"Oh," said Carlos in astonishment. "You know it? Right next door is the Medersa Ben Youssef, a very famous former Koran school. The school was closed down, and today the building is open to everyone. I wanted to take a look at it actually …"

---

apologetic – entschuldigend

"So let's do it," I said. The children had been listening to us impatiently. Now they were dancing for joy. "Ben Youssef, Miss?"

"The stupid thing is, yesterday I gave them all my small change. I've no idea how much it was."

"Wait a second." Carlos took a few coins out of his wallet and showed them to the children. "Dirham okay? Mosque Ben Youssef, okay?"

The children bent over his hand and shook their heads. The clever girl said firmly, "Dirham!"

So Carlos added a few more coins. "Dirham okay?"

Now the children lit up again. "Okay! Mosque Ben Youssef!"

By now we were surrounded by even more children, but once again our friends defended their dirham **patch** with thumps and bumps.

Today the children chose a different route. We went past the silversmiths and the goldsmiths, past countless rug dealers, past the leather goods and the **fabrics** – and then the children came to a halt in avid discussion.

"What's wrong? Have you lost your way?"

"I'm sure they haven't," I assured Carlos.

"Miss!" Their spokesperson, the little girl with the worn-out flip-flops and the matted hair, tugged at my sleeve.

"Dirham?" I asked her **warily**.

She shook her head vigorously. "Dirham, mosque, okay."

---

patch – *hier:* Revier;
fabric – Stoff;
wary – vorsichtig

First she pointed to her stomach, then to her eyes – and then burst out with, "Supersupersuper!"

The others laughed gleefully and, dancing up and down the whole time, just pulled us along until we reached a **shady** courtyard, where the girl pushed open a door and we found ourselves in – well, what was it? A pharmacy? A storeroom for spices? Or both in one?

A fat man in a long white shirt, with a black **skullcap** on his **bald** head, put his fingers to his lips. The children fell silent immediately. The girl took my hand and pointed to the sacks full of cinnamon sticks, **nutmegs**, **cumin seeds**, **ginger** roots, dried rose petals, herbs whose names I hardly knew, pyramids of powder in all sorts of colours from light yellow to the deepest red. "Mmm, it smells so good! And the colours!"

"Mimi, you have to see this," said Carlos. He pointed to a row of jars containing only feathers, from tiny bits of fluff to brownish **down** to long chicken feathers.

"What are they used for?"

"Medicine," explained the man promptly.

"Medicine?"

The next row of jars contained little white bones, the one after that dried **talons**, the next one clumps

---

shady – schattig;
skullcap – Scheitelkäppchen;
bald – kahl;
nutmeg – Muskatnuss;
cumin seed – Kreuzkümmelsamen;
ginger – Ingwer; down – Daune;
talon – Kralle

of a yellow, waxy substance, the next white chunks of something or other.

"Miss! Supersupersuper?" The girl **beamed** at me expectantly.

"Yes, super*duper*super!" I agreed. "Great!"

The children **squealed** in delight and began shouting "great!" and "super*duper*super!"

At once the man said, "Shhh!"

Carlos tried in English, "Please tell us what that is!" He pointed to the jars with the yellow clumps.

"**Frankincense**," answered the man.

"And that? The milky chunks?"

"**Musk**!"

"Sorry? Is it really musk? It must be incredibly expensive!"

The man nodded, pointed to a glass, held up one finger and wrote down the price in dirham on a scrap of paper. We did some quick calculations and exclaimed, "What? Two hundred euros? For a chunk as big as a sugar **cube**?"

The man nodded again and raised his hands. "Very, very **precious**, musk!"

The frankincense wasn't quite as expensive, but still beyond our price range. What a shame. Incense and musk would have been a cool present for Aunt Lise. But the spices were definitely something for her because Aunt Lise was also a journalist, only she

---

to beam – strahlen;
to squeal – kreischen;
frankincense – Weihrauch;
musk – Moschus;
cube – Würfel;
precious – wertvoll

didn't write travel pieces, but articles about cooking and gardening.

So we bought a little bag of saffron because it was so expensive back home. I wasn't exactly satisfied, which the white-shirted man could see at once, because he pointed to a jar of ground herbs and **stalks**. "Ras el hanout," he said, writing the figure *27* under the price of the musk. "Typic Maroc," he explained. "Is 27 spices."

He rummaged in a box. "You German?" He shook his head when we nodded affirmatively. "English?"

"We can understand English."

"Good." He handed us a piece of paper with a recipe in English. "She'll love it!" I exclaimed and pointed to the ras el hanout.

The tradesman wrote down the price, and we were about to pay when the children started to jump up and down and shout, "Dirham, dirham!"

"Heavens, Carlos, we need to bargain!"

The tradesman was quite happy with half the price he asked for and handed us our change, accompanied by some agitated mumbling from the children. The man pushed his skullcap back and forth over his bald head; his eyes wandered across the jars, and he pulled one out. It contained some thin roots, about a finger in length. He took one out, broke it in half, tied each piece into a cord of red silk and hung them like chains around our necks.

"Love," he explained. "Good love."

---

stalk – Stängel

"Supersupersuper," said the children, very pleased with themselves, and dragged us out of yet another scene from the Thousand and One Nights.

In the alleyway Carlos burst out with, "Hey, Mimi, what did the shopkeeper mean by 'good love'? Did he mean 'strong love' or was he thinking about ... you know, **virility**?"

"I was asking myself that," I smirked. "But because he hung them around both our necks, I tend to think he meant 'strong love', don't you? And anyway, you're much too young to need any help with your virility."

"Who knows!"

The subject of love was still too explosive for us to be able – or want – to joke about it.

It wasn't long before we arrived at the Ben Youssef Mosque. Carlos put the coins into the little girl's hand, and the children immediately checked the amount and then nodded in satisfaction. I saw a flag with the words *Ice Cream* and shouted "Stop!"

The children looked up in astonishment. I bought eight chocolate cones and handed them to the children. "Miss!" they beamed and sat down on the ground to **savour** their **treat**.

I took a picture of them surreptitiously, over Carlos's shoulder. I would have it enlarged and hang it in a place of honour in my room.

---

virility – Männlichkeit;
to savour – genießen;
treat – Leckerei

The Dancing Monkey

* ' * ' * ' * ' * ' * ' * ' * ' * ' * '

The medersa, a combination of theological seminar and mosque, is surrounded by an unassuming, clay-coloured wall. But if you enter the gateway, you're **dazzled** by a courtyard **entirely** inlayed with brilliant white **marble**. In the middle there is a square pool, whose water reflects the blue sky and the walls covered with brightly **glazed** tiling. It is an unbelievably beautiful sight, and you could spend hours admiring the patterns on the tiles, the loveliness of the black **lettering** and the many different forms of the archways and windows.

On the upper floor are the **studies**: small cells with heavy **cedar beams** and tiny windows so high up that no matter how hard you try, you can only see the sky. "I can't imagine anything better for

---

dazzled – geblendet;
entirely – ganz;
marble – Marmor;
glazed – glasiert;
lettering – Schrift;
study – *hier:* Studierzimmer;
cedar – Zeder;
beam – Tragebalken

concentrated learning," I said, very impressed. "But you know what, Carlos? I'm slowly dying of hunger."

In the bistro I had discovered the previous day we ordered – what else? – pizza. I told Carlos about my **deliberations** on roses, oranges and the two girls, but the only thing that occurred to him was, "It doesn't make any sense. Why should two girls only be able to meet in secret?"

"That's exactly it!" I exclaimed. "I thought it might be some forbidden **racket**, like drugs perhaps, but I just can't imagine Malika being involved in anything like that."

"Me neither. But what else is there? Gold? Precious stones? The illegal ivory trade? Musk, perhaps, because it's so expensive? No, Mimi, it must be something completely different. We'll probably never find out what it is."

"I'm afraid you're right."

Carlos had brought a map with him, so we were able to find our way back to Place Djemaa el Fna. "The stupid thing is, most of the streets aren't named," I said.

"It doesn't matter. At least we know which direction to go in."

We set out, not through the souk but in an arc around it. The streets were very narrow, the houses very tall and close together. There were children skipping, or playing **hopscotch** or catch, and after

---

deliberation – Überlegung;
racket – Gaunerei;
hopscotch – Himmel und Hölle

we had turned one corner, we were standing in front of Malika's fondouk.

"Shall we go in and say hello?"

"Better not," I replied, screwing up my nose. "Whenever we meet, she always seems so embarrassed. God knows why."

We wandered on and realised we had missed a turning and had to go back to the previous street. We looked at the map again and as we looked up, I could see that the door to the fondouk was **ajar**, and a girl was slipping out to hurry along the street in front of us, keeping her pink-veiled head down.

"It's Malika! I know her pink veil and that dress! Hey, Carlos, perhaps we'll solve the mystery after all!"

"Don't make too much of it, Mimi. She's probably just going to the baker or the hairdresser."

"I don't think so," I contradicted him. "Just look how quickly she's walking! And without stopping or looking around." We didn't want to get too close, but we didn't want to lose her either, so we hurried after her as quickly as we could.

At one point we saw a sign with the name of the street. "Go on," said Carlos. "I'll find out where we are on the map."

"Be quick, okay?"

After a few moments I could hear Carlos's footsteps behind me. "She seems to be going to the same place as us: Place Djemaa el Fna. We're almost there."

"Oh no! We could lose sight of her in the crowd,"

---

ajar – angelehnt

I **moaned**. "How can we stop that from happening?"

"No problem," replied Carlos hastily. "It's just after five now. It doesn't matter if we stay together or not. The main thing is to stay on Malika's heels. If she shakes us off – which I don't think she will because she certainly hasn't noticed us – we'll meet up at seven at the latest in the café. I can't come up with a better idea **on the spur of the moment**."

Malika came to a halt at the edge of the square. She rearranged her long dress and adjusted her pink veil. With a piece of cloth from her bag she wiped the dust off her shoes, and finally she applied red paint to her lips with the help of a little mirror.

I giggled. "Perhaps she has a boyfriend and she's meeting him here?"

Carlos looked at me **in consternation**. "How come?"

"You must know that. After all, you're the expert on girls," I **jeered**. "If I'm meeting a boy, I do exactly the same as Malika here. I check that everything's in order: lipstick, mascara, hair, jeans, pullover – all the important things. I don't make such a fuss if I'm meeting a girlfriend."

"So?" asked Carlos.

"Just wait and see what happens!"

Malika was walking more slowly now, looking at this and that; she even chatted to a water seller and seemed to have all the time in the world. It was easy

---

to moan – stöhnen;
on the spur of the moment – spontan;
in consternation – betroffen;
to jeer – sticheln

to follow her because her pink scarf stood out in the multicoloured crowd. But then, quite suddenly, she stopped dead and looked around **unobtrusively**. She changed her direction and turned right …

"Carlos, there's the silent girl!" I whispered excitedly. "There! At the stall where we bought the orange juice this morning. Can you see her?"

"Yes, it's her. After all, I sat next to her for a whole hour!"

We stayed where we were.

The two girls went up to one another. They stayed very close together, whispering.

The silent girl wasn't silent at all, quite the opposite! Malika shook her head several times; the silent one kept on asking questions, but Malika just shook her head.

"It looks as if she's **reproaching** the silent girl **for** something," said Carlos. "They could be arguing, don't you think?"

In the end, Malika shrugged, turned around and left.

The silent girl hurried after her for a little while, then held her back by the shoulder … and the two of them walked on hand in hand.

"They've made up," said Carlos with a grin. "What shall we do now?"

"Follow them, of course!"

"As long as it's light enough."

"Okay."

They didn't seem to have any particular goal. Like us this morning, they watched the street per-

---

unobtrusive – unauffällig;
to reproach s.o. for s.th. – jmdm. etwas vorwerfen

formers and the dwarves, but, in the end, they stopped at a food stall, bought kebabs and couscous and sat down on a bench.

"The pizza," I said. "We shouldn't have eaten. I'm not hungry any more."

"I'm not either. What do you think, Mimi. Shall we give up the chase? I don't think it's getting us anywhere."

"You're right, Carlos. But just look at the tricks that monkey's doing. It's hopping from shoulder to shoulder – hey! It's run off!"

"Where?"

At that moment someone screamed, and the man with the cobra basket, who was sitting quite close to us, **roared** – it sounded like someone **swearing abominably**. The monkey scrambled around him, tore off his headgear and pushed over the basket, causing the cobra to **slither** out and make its escape. The people standing around **fled** in horror, and the monkey saw its chance and ran off with the **brass tray** onto which the spectators had thrown their coins.

"Carlos! The silent girl!"

Carlos didn't hear me any more. He ran off, chasing the monkey, and the silent girl **kept pace** just behind him. I stormed after them, avoiding one

---

to roar – brüllen;
to swear – fluchen;
abominable – entsetzlich;
to slither – gleiten;
to flee – fliehen;
brass tray – Messingtablett;
to keep pace (with) – Schritt halten (mit)

man here, bumping into another one there – but without losing sight of either Carlos or the silent girl.

The monkey definitely had the advantage. It scurried between people's legs, ran across a jeweller's wares and then appeared on the roof of a clothes stall. But it kept stopping to **bare its teeth** and **gibber** with excitement and look back at its **pursuers**. It seemed to be **having a ball**!

The banana-and-orange stall was almost its **downfall**. It sat down with delight in the middle of the fruit and threw down the tray – the coins had fallen to the ground long ago. Then it began hurling oranges into the laughing crowd and finally grabbed a **cluster** of bananas. It chose one, peeled it **in the twinkling of an eye** and stuffed it **greedily** into its mouth. It must have been waiting for the chance for ages!

Many hands reached for the monkey, but it skilfully avoided them all.

By now I had caught up with Carlos. "If only I had a rope," he **wheezed**.

"A lasso to **tame** the wild beast?" I **jibed**.

---

to bare one's teeth – die Zähne fletschen;
to gibber – schnattern;
pursuer – Verfolger/in;
to have a ball – viel Spaß haben;
downfall – Untergang;
cluster – *hier:* Staude;
in the twinkling of an eye – im Nu;
greedy – gierig; to wheeze – keuchen;
to tame – zähmen;
to jibe – zustimmen

Somebody wanted to grab the monkey from behind, but it was too clever. It turned round **in a trice**, slapped the rest of the banana right into the face of the dumbfounded man and **took to its heels** again.

The pursuit continued. Near our café there was a large car park, where the monkey jumped from roof to roof over the vehicles, or under them between the wheels, and was in a thousand places at once. The taxi drivers yelled, the spectators laughed and the monkey **jabbered** and enjoyed being the star of the evening.

Suddenly it took an enormous leap and landed right at my feet, but I drew back in surprise and bumped into a girl, no, a man. No, it *was* a girl. Rubbish, girls don't feel like that! Suddenly Carlos was at my side asking politely, "Haven't we met before somewhere today? Yes, of course, we sat next to each other for an hour in the Internet café, didn't we?"

The monkey was suddenly the most unimportant thing in the world. Judging by the yelling and cheering of the crowd it was still enjoying its freedom. I was more than happy to let him have it because now – now I was standing before the mystery in person. The long, colourless robe with the dark edging and the headscarf with the dancing monkeys – what a coincidence, too! – were being worn, without a doubt, by Malika's silent friend. But the face ... the kohl had run and smudged, and the

---

in a trice – im Nu;
to take to one's heels – wegrennen;
to jabber – plappern

scarf had loosened during the chase and fallen about the shoulders. At last I saw things clearly!

"Mehdi!" I cried. "Mehdi! *You're* the silent girl!"

My hand was up to my mouth in no time, and as quick as a flash he veiled his head with the dancing monkeys. His eyes flashed at me in warning. "Shhh!"

I reached for his hand. There! There it was – the bruised fingernail!

"Hello?" That was Malika. She looked uncertainly from one of us to the other. She had obviously just arrived and didn't know we had recognised her girlfriend as Mehdi the magician.

"I think you **owe** us an explanation," I said finally.

"Why?" asked Malika.

"Because – we might take things the wrong way."

Mehdi laughed. "What do we care? You're flying home tomorrow."

"You're right. It's just …" I cleared my throat. "I swapped my orange for yours in the Internet café yesterday. And in yours I found a glass tube with a piece of paper in it."

"So what?" Mehdi shrugged.

Now Malika took a step forward. "Is it true you're flying back tomorrow? Then I think we could tell them everything, Mehdi. I'd like to, actually, and perhaps – perhaps they could give us some advice?"

Mehdi **glowered** at the ground. You'd have to have been blind not to see that he was embarrassed

---

to owe – schulden;
to glower – finster blicken

by the whole thing and would rather have put a thousand miles between us!

"Is it about drugs, or something forbidden?" asked Carlos.

"Drugs?" They both widened their eyes in astonishment. "What gave you that idea?"

"Well, because your secret must be something terrible," Carlos explained.

Mehdi shook his head vigorously. "It's nothing terrible, but it is in fact forbidden. That is, in our country it's forbidden; in your country there wouldn't be a problem, would there, Malika?"

"Well, if that's how it is . . ." Carlos looked around in search of something. "It would be good if we could sit down somewhere. The café's out of the question, I suppose? And our hotel?"

"The park." Mehdi pointed behind him. "Right, then," said Carlos encouragingly. "How long have you got, Mehdi?"

"Until it's dark, more or less."

We went quite a long way into the park and found a place to sit down under a fig tree, far away from all the other people.

"So, what do you know?" asked Mehdi challengingly.

"What do *we* know?" replied Carlos. "Mimi had her eyes open. You'll have to ask her, not me."

"What did you see? Please tell us everything; it's very important," said Mehdi. "If you were able to find us out, other people could, too."

"It's very, very important," added Malika.

She looked at me in such fear and desperation that I knew that it meant everything to them.

I thought back, took a deep breath and began.

"The first thing I noticed were the three roses on your handlebar, Mehdi. That was in Imouzzer. Then I found your moped in the olive grove near the kasbah."

"What?" cried Mehdi in disbelief. "I thought I'd hidden it really well!"

"Of course it was well hidden, but not well enough. Don't you remember? That's where the washing troughs are. We don't have them in Europe, so I went to have a look …"

"… and you saw the moped," said Malika. "I … my family lives in the kasbah. I had a few days' holiday and was spending them there. Mehdi came to pick me up. Everyone thought I was going back to Marrakech by bus, but in fact Mehdi took me."

"Why do you have to meet in secret?" I asked, full of curiosity.

"There you have it," exclaimed Mehdi. "It's like this: you've met Malika's father. But did you get to know her mother or her sisters?"

Carlos and I shook our heads. "You see. That should tell you everything. Malika's father and mother – the whole family – think in very traditional ways. This means that the parents find a husband for their daughters."

We nodded.

"Okay, they haven't started looking for one for Malika yet, but they would never accept me. Their family isn't poor by our standards," Mehdi continued, "so they expect a man who wants to get married to have a house at least, and to earn enough money to be able to support his family. Which is right, because in this country there's no health in-

surance or life insurance like in Europe. If a poor person gets ill here …"

"You don't need to explain," I said quickly. "We know what you want to say."

Mehdi nodded. "I have no house and no money. I have a **grant** that enables me to study, and I can live off what I earn on the side with my conjuring tricks. *When* I've graduated and *when* I have a job, I might have a chance with her parents, but that will take quite a while, won't it, Malika?"

She nodded. I suddenly understood their predicament. "Ah, and that's why you need to meet secretly? That's why you thought up the thing with the roses and the oranges? That's why you disguise yourself as a girl, Mehdi?"

"Of course. We have relations all over the city. If they saw us together, Malika would have to return to the kasbah immediately."

I nodded. "What about the plastic-flower salesman?"

Mehdi laughed. "He's in on the secret, like Imane and Bahrim. He's a cousin of mine. The Internet café is run by a Swede who only cares about his business. That's why we meet there."

"Good grief! How long has this been going on?"

"That we've been meeting secretly? Over a year. And it will have to go on for a long time yet," he repeated.

"How do you … How can you keep going?" asked Carlos.

The couple looked at each other in surprise and

---

insurance – Versicherung;
grant – Stipendium

bewilderment. "We love each other," they replied **in unison**.

"You see," I said, almost adding, "you blockhead," but I suppressed it just in time.

Mehdi stood up. "I have to go."

"I'll come, too," said Malika, taking his hand. "Have you got any advice for us?"

"No," I replied. "All I can do is wish you all the best. But if you could come and visit us in Germany …"

"Yes, if the fire eater **spat** money! Or if you could buy flying carpets in the souk!" said Mehdi with a laugh – with a bitter laugh.

The couple disappeared into the darkness.

We were silent. Above us, through the leaves of the fig tree, I could see the stars. The noise of the square was only a murmur in the distance.

I fell back onto the grass and put my hands behind my head.

"Why did you say 'you see' just now?" asked Carlos quietly.

I had to think about this first. I couldn't answer this question in one simple sentence.

"You know," I said slowly, "we've experienced so many different kinds of 'love' in the past few days. Malika and Mehdi know they belong together, and they'll see it through. I can't imagine Mehdi even noticing his fellow female students. For him, there's only Malika, and for Malika only Mehdi. And then there's Wanda … For her, love means 'How can I get this man and that man and the other man, too?

---

in unison – einstimmig;
to spit – spucken

Which one has the most money? Who can I have the best time with? Who has the most on offer?' For her, love – or what she thinks of as love – can be **portioned out**. It isn't something that links her to one single person."

"Do you really mean that?"

"Oh yes. How else could she swap you for another guy from one minute to the next?"

Carlos winced, but I hadn't finished yet.

"And you, Carlos, you swing between both types. I mean a lot to you, but the time with Wanda wasn't bad either, was it? It was just a pity you couldn't shake her off so easily when I arrived. She loved being the nuisance factor; she did it **with gusto**, and she would have gone on with it even longer if the other guy hadn't turned up. I wonder where she met him?"

"No idea. It doesn't matter either."

"No, it doesn't matter *where*. But the *fact* that she met him does matter. Because if she hadn't met him, we wouldn't be sitting here, that much is clear."

"Don't say that ..."

"I'm saying it," I replied firmly. "I told you that Wanda – some Wanda or other – isn't the problem. *You're* the problem. We'll never have a minute's peace as long as you don't know what you want, as long as you go on **vacillating**. And as long as I don't know whether I'm the only girl for you, I can't **commit myself to** you." I stood up. "Got it?"

---

to portion out – verteilen;
with gusto – mit Vergnügen; to vacillate – schwanken;
to commit oneself to – sich festlegen auf

"No."

I slumped down in surprise.

"Why not?"

"I think you're making things too easy for yourself."

"How?"

"Firstly, you have to learn how to deal with girls like Wanda. Just play it cool and things won't be half as bad as you think they are. If they see you getting upset, they'll go on winding you up just for the fun of it. It's true that the Wandas of this world **ride roughshod over** other people, but you need to know that and take it into account.

Secondly, there was nothing between me and Wanda. You only had to think it and Wanda did everything to confirm you in your belief. But you didn't believe *me*. We flirted, okay, but that was all."

"Hm. I'll have to think about that." I turned onto my stomach and chewed my lower lip. In one way Carlos was right. I had to learn how to deal with girls like Wanda. On the other hand I knew Carlos was wrong in his second point. "Do you remember your silly bet in Chile?" I asked him. "That was when we said you can't play games with love. I still stand by that. Do you?"

He didn't reply.

"I'm not the only girl in the world, Carlos. You can take your pick. Some are prettier than me, some are cleverer, some are more athletic, some are … whatever. Every girl has her own special features.

---

to ride roughshod over s.o. – jmdn. mit Füßen treten

The same is true for boys; don't forget that, Carlos. Right, so just imagine if we ..."

"Okay, you don't have to go on, Mimi."

"And you don't have to say anything more about it this evening either. Let's go back to the square and watch Mehdi for a while, okay? Perhaps we'll meet the others."

In the Morning

* ' * ' * ' * ' * ' * ' * '

We didn't meet any of the others, neither on Place Djemaa el Fna nor at the hotel.

But in the morning Carlos discovered a note someone had pushed under the door of our room.

Hi you two!

You know I have to return the hired van. But tomorrow my father is lending us his ***carriage****, so I could show you all something of the surrounding area. If you want to come, we're meeting at breakfast at nine.*

All the best,

Bahrim.

"What do you think? Shall we go?" Carlos asked with a hearty **yawn**.

"Of course! We've got till this evening."

When we came down, Wolfi had just finished his breakfast. "Bye, you two, I'm off! I've met a lovely Swedish girl."

"In the Internet café, I suppose."

"How do you know that, Mimi?" he asked in astonishment. "Are you psychic?"

"You bet I am. Didn't you know?"

---

carriage – Wagen;
yawn – Gähnen

"I know now. See you this evening at the airport, okay? Bye." He jumped up. "Oh, just to let you know, Wanda isn't going either. She wants to show her new boyfriend around Marrakech – ha ha. I **suspect** the tour will be limited to her hotel room."

Bahrim actually arrived on a carriage drawn by a **jaunty** little horse, and our eyes almost popped out of our heads! "All aboard!" he cried, laughing out loud. "You weren't expecting this, were you?"

"Where are we going?"

"From one surprise to another," he promised.

I kept my camera at the ready on my lap. At first we travelled along a wide outward road in the direction of the airport and the Atlas Mountains. Most of the cars that overtook us **honked** their horns, and we waved cheerfully and felt sorry for all the poor folks who were having to spend such a wonderful day in an enclosed vehicle. After about an hour Bahrim turned left off the road, and after a short while we were driving through an exotic forest of palm trees, which had come about – so Bahrim said – through spat-out **date** kernels. "Come on," said Klaus, shaking his head. "You can tell us **fairytales** this evening!"

"I'm serious," insisted Bahrim. "About a thousand years ago, nomads wandered through this territory – really! They mainly lived on **nutritious**,

---

to suspect – *hier:* befürchten;
jaunty – lebhaft;
to honk – hupen;
date – Dattel;
fairytale – Märchen;
nutritious – nahrhaft

sweet dates, which keep well and are easy to transport. And the result you see before you: the largest palm forest in North Africa. If you cut down one of these trees, you have to pay a heavy fine."

I noticed some long, often rather **peculiar**, unexpectedly winding walls. "Yes, behind them live the super-rich. And if you want to know why they aren't straight, take a closer look, Mimi. When do they curve?"

"Ahhh! To avoid the trees!"

"Clever girl!"

I wished I had my silk scarf with me to cover my face. The road was getting dustier all the time and if a car overtook us, we saw nothing at all.

"It won't be long now," said Bahrim kindly.

But when he **pulled up**, we looked around blankly. "Why have you brought us here?" Carlos wanted to know. "Is there some kind of special structure here?" He pointed to a row of small hills – they began somewhere in the far distance and ended ... perhaps in Marrakech?

Klaus furrowed his brow. "I know what it is!" he exclaimed excitedly. "Hey Bahrim, great you're showing us this! Carlos, Mimi, they're khetteras!"

Carlos was electrified and sprang out of the carriage. "I have to see this!"

"Bahrim, what are khetteras?"

He pointed into the distance. "On the horizon you can see the mountains of the High Atlas. Water was **diverted** from there all the way to here – Mar-

---

peculiar – eigenartig;
to pull up – anhalten;
to divert – umleiten

rakech is an oasis city, you see. The underground canals are up to two metres high and they often lie 20 or 30 metres beneath the surface. And to prevent the water from going **stale**, **air shafts** were sunk at regular intervals. All this ..." he made a sweeping gesture "... is the work of slaves."

Carlos and Klaus had disappeared. "They must have crawled into a tunnel!"

"They aren't allowed to! It's strictly forbidden!" said Bahrim in alarm. "No water flows through them any more, so the **soil** has become dry and crumbly. The ceilings can collapse at any moment, and then we're in big trouble."

"Don't worry, Bahrim. We've had so many adventures this week we can really do without the chapter **headed** Buried Alive. I mean ..."

There! We heard a dull **thud**, a **stifled** scream – and then silence.

"So here we are," said Bahrim.

"What? Where?"

"In big trouble!"

I didn't take him seriously; Carlos and Klaus had only jumped out of the carriage a couple of minutes ago.

Bahrim shrugged and climbed down into the canal. I followed him, of course, avoiding the empty plastic bottles and the other rubbish lying

---

stale – schal;
air shaft – Luftschacht;
soil – Boden;
headed – *hier:* mit dem Titel;
thud – dumpfer Schlag;
stifled – unterdrückt

around – and then … then we were standing in front of a solid wall of earth and stone. The sun burned down from the bright blue sky; birds were singing; palm leaves **rocked** gently over our heads. I was in Morocco; our plane was leaving for Germany this evening – but Carlos and Klaus were trapped behind this wall!

I stroked back my hair. "Surely they'll climb up the next air shaft," I said and went on ahead.

"It's blocked, Mimi. You're minimising the danger, I'm afraid. The khetteras haven't been maintained for … for **decades**. I don't even want to imagine what it looks like down there, or who their companions might be."

"Come on, Bahrim, since when have you been such a pessimist?" For me the thud and the scream had been nothing more than a funny interruption to a lovely day. But this changed when we ran to the next air shaft and saw that it had almost completely **caved in** and was covered by a thick **layer** of dust. Now I began to feel queasy.

"I didn't bring a **shovel** with me, of course," thought Bahrim out loud.

"And palm trees don't have branches we could dig with," I added. "So what do we have?"

"Our hands," replied Bahrim dryly.

"For heaven's sake!" I exclaimed. "Are we **moles**?

---

to rock – wiegen;
decade – Jahrzehnt;
to cave in – zusammenbrechen;
layer – Schicht;
shovel – Schaufel;
mole – Maulwurf

Bahrim, you said there were houses behind the walls. Couldn't we ring the bell and ask to borrow a shovel?"

He just laughed. "They don't have doorbells. These houses aren't like the ones we know."

"What if we climbed over a wall?"

"We'd run into a watchman, for sure. Or a dog. And neither of them would ask questions before dealing with us. People who climb over walls are usually thieves."

"Hmm. Let's see what we've got in the carriage."

We ran back and found Bahrim's father's spare walking stick. "Now *that's* something."

We slid into the tunnel and began to work – **pok-ing**, **hauling away** lumps of clay with our hands, more poking. It was very slow work, and again and again we shouted, "Hello!"

No answer. No one answered, "Hey, hurry up, you two!" or "Well, well, well. Isn't that Mimi and Bahrim?"

I was sweating, and along with the sweat came the fear. If at least a car would come by, we could wave it down and ask the driver for help. But in this deserted area Bahrim had chosen the most deserted – and the most beautiful and **unspoiled** – spot imaginable!

But still, we were in luck, very good luck, because after an eternity we could hear Carlos' and Klaus' voices; then a hand appeared, and then it was easy.

"It's strictly forbidden to go down into the khet-

---

to poke – stochern;
to haul away – wegschleppen;
unspoiled – unberührt

teras," said Bahrim as the two of them came crawling through the gap.

"We didn't see the sign," Carlos said, sneezing the dust from his nose.

They each went behind a tree, tore off their clothes and **beat** the dust out of them. Once they were dressed again, they climbed back into the carriage, both pretty **sheepish**.

Bahrim passed me a large water bottle. I took a gulp and passed it on.

"Did you have a nice time?" Bahrim wanted to know. "A new experience for eager geologists?"

"I know we shouldn't have acted so **recklessly**, Bahrim," said Klaus. "Thank you for saving us."

"I hope you had a bad time down there," replied Bahrim angrily, which was very unusual for him.

Klaus was silent, but Carlos said, "At first we didn't realise we'd been buried. It was only when we couldn't hear you two any more and it was **pitch black** that we became alarmed. But the soil was loose and we could breathe, so we knew we'd get out sooner or later. Still – it's no fun being buried alive. Were you worried about us, Mimi?"

"It was the same for me – I didn't take it seriously at first."

"At first. And then?"

"Then we were just digging. Not exactly the ideal activity for thinking about things." I knew what Carlos wanted to hear. But no, at the moment I was-

---

to beat – *hier:* ausklopfen;
sheepish – kleinlaut;
reckless – unbesonnen;
pitch black – pechschwarz

n't capable. "Look, all my fingernails have broken. Awful, aren't they?"

"Apart from your nails, everything about you is beautiful, Mimi."

"Hey, was that a compliment?"

"A way of telling you I love you."

"Rubbish. More like the after-effect of a shock."

The bottle was empty. Bahrim took up the **reins**, clicked his tongue and the horse moved off. "To the olive groves around the Menara Basin – then we'll see how we're doing for time," replied Bahrim to our unasked question.

First the exotic palm forest, then an olive grove like the ones in Greece – you could hardly imagine a **starker** contrast. But it was even more surprising – the next place simply took our breath away.

We could see the High Atlas in the distance, the glittering, snow-capped mountains, and before them a **uniform**, brown plateau. But here, where we were standing, was a gigantic **rectangular** pool! It was yet another image from the Thousand and One Nights. I wouldn't have been surprised if the mighty **roc** or a flying carpet had landed in front of the picturesque building with the lightly coloured tiled walls, right between the two dark cypresses.

It was the **carp** that broke the spell. Nearby was a family with several young children, who were feed-

---

rein – Zügel;
stark – krass; uniform – eintönig;
rectangular – rechteckig;
roc – mythischer Raubvogel;
carp – Karpfen

ing the fish – they were big, fat carp – with lumps of bread. I had never heard such an **indecent**, unappetising **munching** and **gobbling**; and the wide mouths and the thick lips … disgusting, I can tell you.

"So," said Bahrim once we were back in the carriage, "what shall we do now? How much time do you have?"

"Time to see one last thing," I said quickly because I thought I knew what Carlos had in mind. But my plan didn't work out.

"There's a wonderfully exotic, very famous garden that was laid out by a fashion designer. It isn't far from here. Would you like to see it?"

"I'd like to go back to the hotel," said Klaus promptly. "All I want is a shower."

"I can shower later," replied Carlos just as promptly. "Bahrim, how would it be if you dropped us at the garden, and we came back to the hotel by taxi?"

"No problem. Is that all right with you, Mimi?"

I **dithered** for a moment, but because I probably wouldn't be returning to Marrakech for a while and didn't want to **miss out on** an experience, I said yes. "Fine. Let's go and look at the garden."

On the way, Bahrim explained that the French designer's house wasn't open to visitors, and the little museum he had built was closed for reno-

---

indecent – unanständig;
to munch – mampfen;
to gobble – hinunterschlingen;
to dither – zaudern;
to miss out on s.th. – sich etwas entgehen lassen

vations, but the garden was absolutely worth seeing.

He was right. From the very first moment we were **enchanted**. Palm trees grew in extravagant number, with dark green bushes beneath them. Between the trees stood pots full of red and pink geraniums. There were shiny silver head-high cactuses, and others with stiff rosette-shaped leaves, and still others with thousands of prickly branches. And a channel of water with bright blue painted edges **meandered** through the greenery.

In another part of the garden there were bushes and **climbers** covered in blossom of all shades from pink to deep violet.

"This is something for Aunt Lise," I said, taking one photograph after another, until Carlos pulled me impatiently onto a bench.

"Something wrong?" I asked innocently.

"Yes." He went silent – and then it burst out of him: "You can't imagine what I went through down there in the darkness!"

"Oh, you went through something, did you? On the quick? At least it didn't last long, though, because Bahrim and I got a move on!"

"Mimi!"

"That's my name," I confirmed.

Carlos had had enough. He stood up and disappeared round the next corner.

I had no idea why I was being so nasty to him. Mimi, I said to myself, be honest; you know exact-

---

enchanted – verzaubert;
to meander – schlängeln;
climber – Schlingpflanze

ly why. You flew **unsuspectingly** to Morocco and you **weren't up to** Wanda. Hang on! Hadn't Carlos given me the wrong information, or at least **insufficient** information? Yes, he had, I agreed, and now I was angry and afraid he might not be an A-plus grain of wheat. Oh sh… shoot, why does love have to be so complicated?

I stood up and followed him. Slowly, very slowly, but I did follow him …

There he was, sitting on a little blue bench, leaning on the armrest, staring at a pot of geraniums.

"All right," I said, sitting down next to him, "tell me what you went through."

"Only if you really want to know." Okay, Carlos could be **stubborn**, too.

I waited. Why should I make things easy for him when he'd spoiled some of my precious holiday time?

He'll start sighing now, I thought.

Carlos didn't sigh. "Look, yesterday the scribe wrote the love letter for us, the palmist foretold 'big love' and the herbalist hung amulets around our necks."

"True."

"When the earth and dust fell on top of me and it went pitch black, I was afraid the air would become **scarce**. It might have happened – and then Klaus and I would have **suffocated**."

---

unsuspecting – ahnungslos;
to be up to s.o./s.th. – jmdm./etwas gewachsen sein;
insufficient – ungenügend;
stubborn – dickköpfig; scarce – knapp;
to suffocate – ersticken

"Hardly. The soil was loose, and you had only gone a few metres," I **objected**.

"You're right. But, Mimi, if you're in a situation like that, you don't think very clearly – at least not as clearly as normal, know what I mean?"

I nodded because I was thinking about the earthquake in Chile. It had been a **titchy**, tiny earthquake, but oh boy had I been terrified!

"Yes, I know."

"Good. And while I was thinking we might suffocate, it suddenly seemed to me as if yesterday's three love **tokens** weren't a prospect of the future, but perhaps a … a view of the past. Can you follow me?"

"Not quite."

"Look, the first guy writes a love letter whose contents we don't understand. The second tells us about 'big love' and predicts long journeys together. The third hangs amulets around our necks. All in all it could mean we had loved each other very much and gone on long journeys together, namely to Chile and Morocco, but now it's over."

I rocked my head from side to side. "If you look at it that way, the three things could be a **succinct** summary of the past. But I think it's unlikely."

"You see!" he exclaimed. "Me, too! None of them had a sense of sadness or regret! But wait, Mimi, I wasn't thinking that quickly down there."

---

to object – entgegnen;
titchy – winzig;
token – *hier:* Zeichen, Pfand;
succinct – knapp, kurz

"Okay, what *were* you thinking at your snail's pace?"

Funny, Carlos didn't take any notice of my teasing. "I ..." he began and thought about his words carefully. "I ... no, it suddenly became clear to me how much I'd regret it if those three men had been showing me the past. No, I want to say it more exactly. It would have been absolutely terrible if they had shown me what I had lost."

I **pricked up my ears**. "Because of Wanda?" I asked expectantly. If he said, "Yes, because of Wanda," he'd be wheat of the lowest quality. I held my breath.

He shook his head. It could have meant all kinds of things. I had to know exactly what he was trying to say. "Because of Wanda?" I repeated.

"Rubbish," he said impatiently. "Not because of Wanda; you know that. Because of my stupidity!" He grinned. "As you said, for a **thicko** any old Wanda is a danger."

I went all warm inside, but I tried to stay as cool as possible.

"I see. Aha. And how long will this buried-alive realisation last?"

"Shall I say: for the rest of our lives?"

"Good grief!" I jumped up from the bench in shock. "That would be lying! That's far too long! We're much too young to know that, Carlos!"

"Well ... until neither of us believes in the amulets any more." He tapped the piece of root at his neck.

---

to prick up one's ears – die Ohren spitzen;
thicko – Dummkopf

"Okay." I was satisfied. "Then put it in resin, like my scorpion, Carlos."

"To keep it from losing its effect?"

"To make it less fragile."

"I see. And what about yours?"

"Mine, too."

I tell you, there couldn't have been a more beautiful place in the world for a reconciliation than that garden!

Farewell

* ‘ * ‘ * ‘ * ‘

We got back to the hotel very late. We had just enough time to stuff our things into our rucksacks, rush down, pay, hug Bahrim, promise to write, tell him to give our love to Malika, Mehdi and Imane, and clamber onto the bus to the airport.

"So, how are you two?" Klaus wanted to know. "**Hunky dory**?"

"Not quite. Carlos is bringing all the dirt home."

"Dirt?"

"He didn't have time to shower," I explained. "And we're getting onto a plane with him!"

"Why do we have to put up with it?"

"I'm asking myself the same question." Klaus and I grinned at each other. "Well *I* had a shower," he said.

"Really? Then perhaps I should seriously think about having *you* as my boyfriend. It would certainly be a clean break."

"Don't you dare!" raved Carlos. "You want to leave me just because of a bit of soap and water?"

Wanda looked uncomprehendingly from one of

---

farewell – Abschied;
hunky dory – alles in Butter

us to the other. "Can you tell me what's up with you two?"

"Tell *you?* You'd never understand," I replied.

"No, you really wouldn't," added Carlos and Klaus in unison.

Ebenfalls auf Englisch
bei Thienemann u. a. erschienen:

Sabine Both: *Move to Cloud Nine; Love in my Luggage*
Brinx/Kömmerling: *A Paul to Kiss*
Christamarie Fiedler: *Spaghetti Crime, Risotto Crime, Pumpkin Crime*
Sissi Flegel: *Forbidden to Love; Cool Kisses on the Beach*
Bianka Minte-König: *Mobile Phone Love; Schoolyard Flirt & Catwalk Dreams*
Hortense Ullrich: *Never Kiss a Witch; Love is Blonde*
Zimmermann & Zimmermann: *Maths, Stress and a Lovesick Heart; School, Trouble & True Love; Summer, Sun & Holiday Love, School Trip Love & Trouble*

Sissi Flegel freut sich über Leserpost: sissi.flegel@gmx.de
Sissi Flegel ist eine Autorin der AVA international GmbH
Autoren- und Verlagsagentur, Herrsching
(www.ava-international.de).

Flegel, Sissi:
Love, Silk & Sand
Aus dem Deutschen von Michael Turnbull
ISBN 978 3 522 18115 0

Reihengestaltung: Birgit Schössow
Einbandillustration: Birgit Schössow
Schrift: Stone Serif
Satz: KCS GmbH, Buchholz/Hamburg
Reproduktion: Medienfabrik, Möglingen
Druck und Bindung: Friedrich Pustet, Regensburg

5 4 3 2 1° 08 09 10 11

www.thienemann.de
www.frechemaedchen.de
www.sissi-flegel.de

Susanne Röckel

Chinesisches Alphabet

Ein Jahr in Shanghai

btb

Die Erstausgabe erschien 1999
in der Luchterhand Literaturverlag GmbH, München.

MIX
Papier aus verantwortungsvollen Quellen
FSC® C014496

Penguin Random House Verlagsgruppe FSC® N001967

1. Auflage
Neuauflage
Genehmigte Taschenbuchausgabe Oktober 2021
btb Verlag in der Penguin Random House Verlagsgruppe GmbH,
Neumarkter Straße 28, 81673 München

Umschlaggestaltung: semper smile, München
Covermotiv: © Shutterstock/sukiyaki; Kevin 5017
Satz: Uhl + Massopust, Aalen
Druck und Bindung: GGP Media GmbH, Pößneck
CP · Herstellung: sc
Printed in Germany
ISBN: 978-3-442-71993-8

www.btb-verlag.de
www.facebook.com/btbverlag

INHALT

»Wir besitzen alle Dinge.«

Kaiser Qianlong an König Georg III.

AUSLÄNDER

Als europäische Kriegsschiffe in der Mitte des 19. Jahrhunderts die Öffnung des riesigen Marktes und Arbeitskräftereservoirs China erzwangen, war es mit der stolzen Selbstgenügsamkeit der Qing-Kaiser ausländischen Handeltreibenden gegenüber endgültig vorbei. Die Kolonisten, die sich des sumpfigen Fleckens am Huangpu bemächtigten, dachten und handelten, wie es dem Geist der Zeit entsprach: Auch sie verachteten das Fremde – ohne den Nutzen zu verachten, der aus Fremdem und Fremden zu ziehen war. Bald blühte Shanghai, doch von der Ernte bekamen Chinesen kaum etwas ab.

Nachdem es den Kommunisten gelungen war, die De-facto-Kolonialherren mit ihren Verbündeten aus dem Land zu werfen, folgte eine neue Periode der Abschließung, die zwanzig Jahre dauerte. Die Weltstadt Shanghai wurde zu einem Dorf gemacht. Mao, der Bauernsohn, stellte sich vor, dass man aus eigener Kraft mit Schwierigkeiten fertigwerden könne, deren Gründe weit in die Jahrhunderte zurückreichten; das Scheitern dieser Politik hatte das Volk mit unermesslichen Opfern zu bezahlen.

Heute scheint die Zeit, da man Ausländern wie Hausierern die Tür wies, tausend Jahre weit weg.

Schon der oberflächlichste Eindruck zeigt den Einfluss des Westens auf die Stadt. Nicht nur dort, wo die Repräsentationsgebäude der ersten Besatzer stehen (die zum Teil wieder von ausländischen Banken und Versicherungen genutzt werden), auf dem Gebiet der Internationalen Konzession, oder in jenen ehemals französischen Vierteln westlich der Yan'an Lu, wo Kaufleute, Schiffseigner, Opiummagnaten, umgeben von Gärten und Dienstbotenheeren, ihre Mußestunden verbrachten, sondern überall in der inneren Stadt ist der Wohnungsbau des 19. und frühen 20. Jahrhunderts mehr als anderswo in China von westlicher Architektur geprägt. Die völlig heruntergekommenen Häuser und Siedlungen, in denen europäische Fassadengliederung, Fensterformen, Ornamentik mit chinesischen Wohnbedürfnissen harmonierten, werden nach und nach abgerissen, um Hochhäusern Platz zu machen, deren Architektur einen wichtigeren Zweck zu erfüllen scheint als den des Wohnens: Im Zeitalter der globalen Sachzwänge muss vor allem das Gefühl hervorgerufen werden, dass die Stadt in der Lage ist, sich im Wirtschaftswettlauf auf einem der vorderen Plätze zu behaupten.

Deshalb sind Ausländer, besonders Ausländer aus dem Westen, und nicht nur Investoren und Fußballtrainer, willkommener denn je.

Überall wird der westliche Ausländer von Leuten angesprochen, die sich mit ihm unterhalten wollen, um Englisch zu trainieren. Im Radio wird täglich eine halbe Stunde Dickens im Original vorgelesen. Im Fernsehen gibt es Benimmkurse, die in westliche Sitten und Gebräuche einführen. Reiche Leute suchen Ausländer als Klavierlehrer für ihre Töchter. Arme Leute suchen, wenn sie etwas zu verkaufen haben, Ausländer als Kunden, denn Ausländer lassen sich leicht übers Ohr hauen. Ausländer genießen Sonderrechte. Mehrmals habe ich es erlebt, dass man mir in vollgestopften

Bussen einen Sitzplatz anbot oder mir in einer Schlange den Vortritt ließ – nicht um meiner grauen Haare, sondern einzig um meiner langen Nase willen. Einmal saß ich irgendwo auf einer Bank, da trat mit strahlendem Lächeln ein Mann auf mich zu und ergriff meine Hand, um sie ausgiebig zu schütteln. »Hello! Hello! Goodbye!« Dann ging er weiter, nicht ohne mir aus der Ferne noch einmal herzlich zuzuwinken. Warum das alles? Offenbar vermutet man im Ausländer Qualitäten, die sonst nur Märchenfiguren besitzen.

Von Seiten der Behörden hat man als Ausländer weniger Freundlichkeiten zu erwarten. Bürokratische Schikanen sind an der Tagesordnung. Der private Briefverkehr wird vielerorts überwacht. Bis vor kurzem waren private Kontakte zwischen ausländischen Dozenten und chinesischen Studenten noch kaum möglich. Es liegt im Interesse der Behörden, dass Ausländer dort wohnen, wo sie unter sich bleiben. Das kommt den Wünschen vieler Ausländer entgegen.

Westliche Ausländer sind, unabhängig vom wirklichen Grad ihrer Kennerschaft, als »foreign experts« meist für chinesisch-ausländische Gemeinschaftsunternehmen tätig. Sie empfinden die Stadt als Erschwernis ihres Lebens, die ihnen neben der Arbeit zugemutet wird und für die sie von ihren Firmen entschädigt werden müssen. Oft leben sie jahrelang in luxuriösen Hotelghettos, ohne mit den alltäglichen Schwierigkeiten ihrer Umgebung, der Not, dem Dreck, der Enge je in nähere Berührung zu kommen. In dieser Hinsicht spart man chinesischerseits nicht an Aufwand, um es den Ausländern recht zu machen, das heißt, die Wirklichkeit von ihnen fernzuhalten. Ein schönes Bild dafür ist die lange Haube aus undurchsichtigem blauem Plastik, die man am seitlichen Eingang des Jinjiang-Towers den dort abgestellten

Fahrrädern der Angestellten überstülpt, um den Hotelgästen den Anblick von rostigem chinesischem Blech zu ersparen.

»Auch Singapur war früher ein Sumpf«, sagt ein durchreisender deutscher Professor, die neue Politik der Chinesen lobend, »und jetzt können Sie da von der Straße essen.«

Die Welt, von der er träumt, ist eine Welt, die es nicht mehr nötig hat, das Fremde zu verachten – das Fremde ist eingeebnet und verschluckt, auf dass nichts mehr davon uns erschrecke. Es wird eine kleine Welt sein! Was aber würde passieren, wenn es ihn einmal in eines der ganz anderen Viertel der Stadt verschlüge, wo vom Bann der boomenden City nichts mehr zu spüren ist, wo man ihn auf durchaus friedliche Weise begafft und seine außerirdische Erscheinung mit einem selbstvergessen gemurmelten *»Lao wai, lao wai«* (Ausländer) staunend zur Kenntnis nimmt? Könnte es geschehen, dass ihn eine Ahnung der unüberwindlichen Entfernung beschliche, die unseren Teil der Erde noch immer von dem großen China trennt? Stiege das ferne Bild einer Welt in ihm auf, die unseren gönnerhaften Erklärungen unweigerlich entgleitet? Dämmerte dem Ausländer das Bewusstsein der eigenen Fremdheit?

BAMBUS

Ich wähle den Bambus als Wappen.

Bambus ist stark. Sein Holz ist biegsam, Stürme können ihm nichts anhaben. Bambus ist nützlich. Bambus schmeckt, Bambus heilt. Bambus ist angenehm dem Auge und dem Ohr.

Bambus steht für Beharrlichkeit, Bescheidenheit, Langlebigkeit, freien und edlen Sinn. Doch das Symbol bliebe blass ohne das Spiel der Gestaltungen, denen der Bambus sein langes und reiches Leben verdankt.

Bambus wird geschrieben wie eine Kalligraphie, gelesen wie ein Gedicht. Bambusmalen kann jeder. Die Besten zeichnen sich aus durch höchste Subtilität der Pinselführung, der Aufteilung der Fläche. Aus den Kontrasten von Schwarz und Grau entsteht der Eindruck von Nähe und Ferne, Schatten und Licht. Sparsame Striche rufen Stimmungen von schneelastendem Winter oder windraschelndem Sommer hervor, Bilder von heilloser Verwirrung und dumpfer Qual, die sich in klare Ruhe wandelt.

Von der Malerei stammen die Bambusmuster ab, mit denen unzählige Gegenstände des täglichen Gebrauchs verziert sind, Stein und Glas, Porzellan und Seide, Baumwolle und Plastik. Der Pinsel, mit dem man malte und schrieb, hatte einen Bambusstiel. Das erste leichte und leicht handhabbare Material, das Schrift trug, waren Täfelchen aus Bambus. Auch

Papier wurde aus Bambus hergestellt, Musikinstrumente und Gegenstände des hochentwickelten Kunsthandwerks waren und sind aus Bambus, ebenso Tische, Stühle, Schränke. Die besten Kunstschreiner früherer Zeiten fertigten Möbel aus kostbaren Hölzern, deren Oberflächen Bambus imitierten, wie Porzellanmacher Schalen formten, die Gefäße aus Bambus nachahmten, um ihr Können unter Beweis zu stellen. Aus Bambus macht man Besen und Bürsten, Körbe und Matten, Jalousien und Zäune und Küchengerät. Bambushäuser und Bambusbrücken werden kaum noch gebaut; Betonpavillons und Betonbrücken in den Shanghaier Parks imitieren das frühere Material. Die wichtigste Branche der Stadt kommt weiterhin nicht ohne Bambus aus: Die Baugerüste bestehen aus Bambusstangen unterschiedlicher Länge, die von Arbeitern mit Draht und Schnur zusammengefügt und hochgezogen werden. Und die Bank of China wirbt im Fernsehen mit einem stillen Bambushain.

In Wolfgang Bauers großem Buch über die Glücksvorstellungen der Chinesen lese ich von den »fast rührend hausbackenen chinesischen Paradiesen« (im Gegensatz zu den ausschweifenden und schwülstigen frühen utopischen Phantasien Indiens). Diese Hausbackenheit zeigt sich auch in der Verehrung, die Chinesen von jeher dem Bambus entgegenbrachten, jener von Gestalt einfachen, bezüglich Boden und Klima anspruchslosen, schnellwachsenden, immergrünen tropischen Grasart. Ich nehme den Stift zur Hand, der auf dunkelgrünem Grund ein Muster aus hellgrünen Bambuszweigen zeigt, und hoffe, dass der schlichte und tiefe Geist des anmutigen Grases auch auf mich übergeht.

Ich wähle den Bambus als Wappen.

BAUARBEITER

»Yi-er-san, yi-er-san«, höre ich sie stundenlang vor dem Fenster. Ein langes Plastikrohr wird von einer riesigen hölzernen Kabelrolle abgezogen und in einem Graben verlegt. Stricke um die Brust gebunden wie Ochsen, mühen sie sich ab, kleine, grazile Männer mit dunkelfarbigen Gesichtern, ermuntern sich mit lautem »Eins-zwei-drei« im Chor zu immer neuer Anstrengung. Den Graben haben sie mit der Schaufel ausgehoben, es hat Tage gedauert, denn die Erde ist hart und steinig, und die Sonne brennt. Bagger gibt es nicht, nur einmal haben sie auf einem Handkarren einen vorsintflutlichen Pressluftbohrer dabeigehabt, um die Asphaltdecke der Zufahrt zu zertrümmern. Sie arbeiten von Sonnenaufgang bis spätabends, nach dem Dunkelwerden. Manchmal sehe ich sie auf dem Dach des Hotels gegenüber. Solange es im Umbau ist, gehört es ihnen. Vor dem grauen Himmel gleichen sie müden Wanderern, die von ihrem Gipfel aus die Welt betrachten, eine fremde Welt, der sie nichts hinzuzufügen, nichts wegzunehmen haben.

Den wandernden Arbeitern in der Stadt eignet eine seltsame Vagheit, Schattenhaftigkeit. Wie streunende Tiere bevölkern sie die Rohbauten, ihre geheimen Burgen und Festungen, zu denen Sesshafte keinen Zutritt haben. Manchmal sieht man sie auf der Ladefläche von Lastwagen sitzen, stumpf und erschöpft lehnen sie aneinander und lassen sich durchschütteln. Ein andermal sieht man sie irgendwo auf einem Haufen Bauschutt hocken und essen, schnell und gierig, mit krummem Rücken, als hätten sie Angst, dass man ihnen das bisschen Reis noch nimmt. An bestimmten Straßen stehen sie mit Pappschildern in Händen, auf denen steht, zu was sie taugen, Maurer-, Holz-, Zementarbeiten, in einem Beutel tragen sie ihr Werkzeug bei sich, Kellen und Sägen, alt und abgenutzt. Oft sind es junge Burschen, scheu, mit dickem, staubigem, grob geschnittenem Haar. Sie tragen Armeeturnschuhe und übergroße Jacketts, denen man ansieht, dass sie auch zum Schlafen nicht ausgezogen werden. Sie leben jahrelang in Behelfsunterkünften, grauen Waben mit dünnen Wänden, an den Rand des Baustellengeländes geklebt. Ab und zu erhascht man einen Blick in die winzigen, stickigen, mit Stockbetten und Hausrat vollgepfropften Räume, die an Ställe erinnern. Auf den Galerien hängt zerschlissene Kleidung, große Schilder fordern zur Umsicht auf den Gerüsten auf. Es wird im Schichtbetrieb gearbeitet, Ruhetage sind selten.

Einmal im Jahr, zum Frühlingsfest, fahren sie heim. Auf Züge wartend, die sie nach Anhui, Jiangxi, Hunan und in noch weiter entfernte Provinzen bringen, sieht man sie tagelang mit Kind und Kegel auf dem großen Platz vor dem Bahnhof. In Gruppen lagern sie zwischen Säcken und Kisten, Karten spielend, rauchend, schlafend, bei jedem Wetter. Plötzlich entsteht Bewegung unter ihnen, ein Zug ist aufgerufen worden, alles drängt zu den Eingängen. Doch so viele auch hinter den eisernen Absperrgittern verschwinden, so wenig scheint die Zahl der Lagernden und Wartenden je abzunehmen.

Wer weiß etwas von ihnen? Wer vertritt ihre Interessen? Wen gehen sie etwas an? Man scheint sich daran gewöhnt zu haben, die zu Hunderten entstehenden Hochhäuser als Hervorbringungen einer unerschöpflichen, quasi organischen Energie zu betrachten. Die Wanderarbeiter sind anderswo. Ihre Lebensgewohnheiten, die Modalitäten der Verträge, die sie binden, ihre Streitigkeiten, Unfälle, die Einzelheiten ihres Schicksals sind nirgends öffentlich verzeichnet und dringen nicht ins Bewusstsein. Mangelhafte medizinische Versorgung, Beschränkungen und Verbote, Schwierigkeiten bei der schulischen Eingliederung der Kinder – davon hört man gelegentlich, doch selten wird ein genaues Bild daraus. Scharenweise kommen sie, Millionen jedes Jahr, und die Stadt verleibt sich ihre Jugend ein, ihre Ausdauer, ihre Körperkraft, gibt ihnen Arbeit und wirft ihnen Pfennige dafür hin, und wenn sie genug von ihnen hat, spuckt sie sie aus wie bittere Kerne. Sie schaden dem Image, heißt es. Wie leicht fällt es, diese Ohnmächtigen und Hoffenden zu verleugnen, wie wenig scheint es zu gelingen, ihrer bedrohlichen Ströme Herr zu werden. Denn die Stadt selbst lebt ja von der Kraft jener Hoffnungen. Und die armen Bauern erkennen im täuschenden Glanz dieser falschen Perle, in ihrem Pomp und ihrer Hässlichkeit die eigenen rohen und naiven Träume wieder, die sie stets von neuem dazu treiben, das Land im Stich zu lassen, das karge Feld, die leere Kammer, das Dorf, das die Welt vergessen hat, und sich aufzumachen, um in der Stadt das Glück zu suchen.

BAUSTELLEN

Hohe Wände, mit Reklamebildern bemalt, umschließen das Gelände. Lastwagen stauen sich in der Einfahrt, beflaggte Maschinen bohren sich in den Boden, rostige Stangen ragen wie Stachelmähnen aus der befestigten Grube. Majestätisch schwenken Kräne ihre Gigantenarme, beflissen kriechen Außenaufzüge von Stockwerk zu Stockwerk, hektisch flappen zerrissene Planen über gähnenden Löchern. Wie wertvolles Pflanzgut von dichten Bambusmatten umhüllt, wie ein kostbarer Edelpilz von Scheinwerfern bestrahlt und von unermesslichen Mengen Beton begossen, wächst das Hochhaus Meter um Meter aus der Erde. Hinter verhängten Gerüsten hämmert und rattert es Tag und Nacht, blaue Schweißblitze erleuchten die trübe Luft. Und die Mauern dehnen sich und breiten sich aus und bilden schiefe Verwachsungen und strähnige Verschlingungen, bizarre Warzen, düstere Stümpfe. Und nach zwei, drei Jahren ist das pflanzliche Stadium überwunden, und der rohe Bau mit seinen tausend Augen steht linkisch da wie ein nackter Wilder unter lauter angezogenen Zaungästen. Zu diesem Zeitpunkt übt er, schattenhaft, phantastisch wie die unbewohnbaren Monumente der Träume in ihrer großartigen Vermessenheit, am meisten Faszination aus. Doch bald wird ihm das enge Kleid aus Glas und Marmor übergestreift, das ihn als zur Zivilisation gehörend aus-weist. Von Investoren und Offiziellen gehätschelt, bildet er noch eine Zeitlang den Mittelpunkt der Aufmerksamkeit, bis die Gewohnheit ihn seiner traumhaften Eigenschaften beraubt und das kritische Urteil nur noch Prunk und Hässlichkeit übriglässt.

BRONZEGEFÄSSE

Von Tierfüßen, Tierbeinen, Tiernacken, hin und wieder auch knienden menschlichen Figuren getragen, von Vögeln, Schlangen, Fischen und abstrahierten Tiergesichtern umfangen, runden und wölben sich Vorratsgefäße, Dampftöpfe, Wein- und Wasserkessel. Aus Reliefs und Halbreliefs werden ganzkörperliche Figuren, die die Formen erweitern und aufbrechen, große Augen, starrende Brustwarzen, Ohren, Zungen, Hörner, Schwänze, Tatzen. Tierfiguren und Tierköpfe krönen Deckel, bilden Henkel, Knäufe, Griffe. Die Gefäße zeigen, was sie enthalten und wozu sie bestimmt sind. Das harte, kühle, einst dunkel glänzende Metall hat Wellen wie Wasser, spiralige Auswüchse wie Dampf, Dornen und Schlingen wie Pflanzen, Maserungen und Schuppen wie Tierpanzer und Tierhäute. Überall ist Verwandlung. Form ruft Formlosigkeit ins Gedächtnis, der Gegenstand sein Material, das fest war und verflüssigt wurde, um wieder fest zu werden, kalt war und erhitzt wurde, um wieder kalt zu werden. Aus dem wandlungsfähigen Metall wurden Gefäße hergestellt, die der Verwandlung tierischer und pflanzlicher Lebewesen in menschliche Nahrung dienten. Die verschlungenen Muster bewegen sich im Rhythmus der schwimmenden, kriechenden, springenden, fließenden Wesen, Tier-Götter, deren überwältigendem und rätselhaftem Dasein die Menschen ihr Leben verdanken und denen sie sich entgegensetzen. Auch Inschriften finden sich, Hinweise auf Feste und rituelle Bankette, bei denen die Gefäße benutzt wurden. Historikern sind sie eine Hilfe bei der Datierung von Kriegen und Grenzverschiebungen. Die kleinen geritzten Zeichen scheinen Echos jener Muster und Figuren, skizzenhafte Versuche, in der Überfülle des Kosmos eine eigene, menschliche Ordnung festzuhalten.

Die Gewinnung der Nahrung ist prekär. Wer sagt, dass man morgen noch genug zu essen hat? Auf drei oder vier Beinen ruhend, wirken die wuchtigen Kessel, als verweilten sie nur vorläufig an ihrem Platz, erfüllten nur vorläufig ihren Zweck. Im Boden eines großen, pfannenartigen Topfes sind Bronzepüppchen jener Tiere versammelt, die hier gekocht und gebraten wurden, Fisch, Wild, Geflügel. Raubt man den Familien jener Tiere immer wieder Angehörige, um sie zu verzehren, so scheint man sie nun zu beschwören, sich davon in ihrem Dasein und Wachstum nicht beeinträchtigen zu lassen und Menschen weiterhin als lebensspendende Nahrung zu dienen. So wären die Tierbilder und Tiermasken Ausdruck eines Bewusstseins, dem ständig die Möglichkeit des Verlusts vor Augen steht, der überbordende Reichtum der Gestaltung entstammte der Erfahrung des Entblößtseins und des Mangels; dem Tod der gejagten, geschlachteten, geopferten Tiere entspränge die große Feier des Lebens, der man hier staunend beiwohnt.

Touristen mit Kopfhörern über den Ohren gehen zwischen den erleuchteten Vitrinen umher. Videorecorder zeigen Bilder und geben Erklärungen. Bronzeglocken klingen aus versteckten Lautsprechern. Die Bronzegefäße schimmern in allen Schattierungen von Grün. Wie jene Menschen den Stoff, dem sie ihre eigene, unvergleichliche Form gaben, haben wir sie aus der dunklen Erde ausgegraben, die sie dreitausend Jahre in sich barg, um sie durch unseren Blick erneut zu verwandeln.

BUSSE

Alles wird besser. Von diesem goldenen Versprechen eines unerforschlichen Gottes lebt die Stadt, leben wir alle. Eines Tages wird es den ganzen Dreck und Krach und Smog und das ganze fürchterliche Gewühl und Durcheinander nicht mehr geben, alle werden in stillen Villen mit Klimaanlage und elektronischem Whirlpool leben und auf Wolkenkratzer und Bambushaine mit herrlichen Steinen und Pavillons und Teiche mit ewig blühendem Lotus und melodisch quakenden schmackhaften Ochsenfröschen blicken und Fernseher mit Fernbedienung und Autos mit schwarzen Scheiben und nichtrostende Wasserkessel haben und jeden Tag Schildkröten und Schlangen und die Pfirsiche der Unsterblichkeit essen und tausendjährigen französischen Joint-Venture-Rotwein trinken und auf jadegrünem englischem Rasen mit Federbällen aus Kranichfedern Federball spielen und Handtaschen und Lederschuhe tragen, und nachts wird von Westen her ein Heer von Feen kommen, das den ganzen Abfall in fruchtbaren Boden verwandelt, auf dem duftender, total insektenresistenter Reis wächst. Auch Busse wird es dann nicht mehr geben. Natürlich wird es immer Fahrzeuge geben, die von fern irgendwie busähnlich aussehen, geheizte bzw. gekühlte Säle auf Rädern, in denen man, auf weichen Sesseln vor kristallenen Scheiben sitzend, die schöne Welt an sich vorüberziehen lässt, doch dass diese Fahrzeuge von den heutigen Bussen abstammen, werden nur noch die Historiker wissen. Geräuschlos und wohlgefedert bewegen sie sich vorwärts, geräuschlos halten sie an, wenn das gemütliche Häuschen erreicht ist, das dann Haltestelle genannt werden wird, und wie von Geisterhand öffnen sich die Türen. Niemand schiebt von hinten, drängelt von der Seite, stößt einem Ellbogen in den Magen, niemand tritt einem auf die Füße, und man selbst wird all das auch nicht tun, es besteht nämlich gar keine Notwendigkeit dazu! Fast ohne das Bein zu heben, steigt man mit einem einzigen leichten und tänzerischen Schritt ein, und wenn man drin ist, kann man seinen Körper mühelos in alle Himmelsrichtungen bewegen. Stabile, silbrig glänzende Haltestangen laden dazu ein, sich festzuhalten, obwohl man sich eigentlich überhaupt nicht festzuhalten braucht, und es gibt sogar manchmal Sitzplätze mit einem gänzlich unabgewetzten, unausgefransten, unekelhaften Polyesterbezug, und wenn man auf so einem Sitz sitzt, denkt man wegen der gänzlich ruck- und rumpellosen Fahrweise dieses Zukunftsgefährts oft, man sitze unbeweglich auf einem Kinosessel und ein Film rolle vor einem ab. Das Personal hat nur ein einziges Bestreben, nämlich den Fahrgast so wenig wie möglich zu belästigen und ihm die Fahrt so angenehm wie möglich zu machen. Keine Schaffnerin, die mit gellender Stimme die Stationen ausruft und saumseligen Passagieren rüde Befehle gibt! Kein Lautsprechergequäke! Keinerlei Ärger und Unbequemlichkeit, wenn die Schaffnerin die Mauer der zusammengepressten Menschen mit Hilfe ihrer eisernen Arme aufbricht, um die Zugestiegenen, die ja kaum noch so viel Platz haben, dass sie die Hand in die Tasche stecken könnten, im Kasernenton aufzufordern, den

Fahrpreis zu entrichten! Überhaupt keine Schaffnerin! Nur das leise Knacken und Klingeln einer stets funktionierenden Entwertungsmaschine, die eifrig und zuverlässig ihren Dienst versieht.

Und nun die Passagiere: Es wird keine von diesen ungekämmten und ungehobelten und gar nicht ins Stadtbild passenden Landleuten mit schmutzigen Hemdkrägen geben, die den ganzen Bus mit ihren Säcken und Bündeln und ihrer ganzen elenden Habe vollpfropfen, statt sich ein Taxi zu nehmen wie anständige Leute. Keine von diesen Ausflugsgesellschaften, deren Mitglieder sich laut schreiend um die Ehre des Bezahlendürfens streiten. Keine Arbeiter, die von der Schicht nach Hause fahren und die besten Sitzplätze besetzen, um mit wackelnden Köpfen auf ihnen zu schlafen. Es wird nicht einmal mehr solche Schnösel geben, in deren Jacken es plötzlich pfeift und die dann das Handy herausziehen und irgendwas hineinbrüllen, was keiner wissen will. Es wird nur noch diskret parfümierte weise Seniorinnen mit schön gelegten Locken und vielen Zähnen geben, die ganz leise sprechen oder einfach nur schweigend aus dem Fenster schauen, während ab und zu Erinnerungen an interessante Begebenheiten ihres Lebens in ihnen aufsteigen, und vielleicht zur Auflockerung der Atmosphäre hie und da ein paar fröhliche Schulkinder. Mehr nicht! Wer zweifelt noch daran, dass jede noch so kurze Fahrt in einem dieser Wundervehikel ein herrliches Erlebnis, ein wahrer und tiefer Genuss sein wird?

Wenden wir uns nun dem Fahrer zu. Er ist kein mürrischer Geselle mit schmutzigen weißen Handschuhen, kein abgebrühter, wortkarger Raubauz, der dauernd hupt und ohne jede Sensibilität die krachende Gangschaltung betätigt, kein abgehetzter Geringverdiener, der seinen Tee aus einer angestoßenen Emaildeckeltasse trinkt und an jeder Kreuzung aus dem Fenster spuckt, sondern ein gutaussehender, frischgewaschener, glattrasierter Mann in Uniform, der eine Aktentasche neben seinem Sitz stehen hat und sich lieber auf den Dienstplan verlässt als auf irgendwelche albernen Amulette, die von der Decke baumeln. Er hupt nie. Ein Druck mit dem kleinen Finger, und das schöne, große, saubere, lederbezogene Lenkrad dreht sich, wohin er will. Die Gänge werden auch nicht mittels rostiger Metallstangen eingelegt, sondern alles geht automatisch, so dass der Fahrer durch die kraftraubenden und rein technischen Aspekte seiner Arbeit nicht länger von der eigentlichen Aufgabe abgelenkt wird: den Passagier spüren zu lassen, dass er hier mit all seinen kleinen Sorgen und Kümmernissen ernst genommen wird und es nicht nur um einen profanen Personentransport von A nach B geht. Mit gänzlich unaufdringlicher Stimme sagt der Fahrer also ab und zu die Stationen an, sonst aber steht er mit seiner ganzen Freundlichkeit und Herzenswärme den Fahrgästen zur Verfügung, die ihn eventuell um Rat fragen könnten, obwohl an jeder Haltestelle eigentlich schon alles, was man über Stationen, Umsteigemöglichkeiten usw. wissen muss, auf die ordentlichste und übersichtlichste Weise angeschlagen ist. Schon aus Achtung vor der Schönheit und Nützlichkeit dessen, was wir dann Busse nennen werden, wird es nie jemandem einfallen, Haltestellen zum Wäscheaufhängen oder zum Lüften von Bettdecken zu missbrauchen! Die zukünftigen Menschentransportfahrzeuge tragen somit zur allgemeinen Zivilisierung bei. Für das Straßenbild der Stadt sind sie eine unschätzbare Bereicherung. Ihre Farben, ihr Glanz, ihre von keinem Staubkörnchen befleckten Scheiben! Ihre völlig unverbeulte, rostlose Glätte! Man wird sich anstrengen müssen, an ihrem Chassis irgendetwas zu finden, was auch nur entfernt an Dellen oder Dreck erinnert. Ferner die Tatsache, dass niemals die Achsen durchhängen oder der Auspuff locker oder schadhaft ist oder die Türen irgendwelche Mucken haben, so dass Hände und Füße oder Pferdeschwänze eingeklemmt und Schmerz und Unbill erzeugt werden. Es erübrigt sich hinzuzufügen, dass solche Fahrzeuge niemals mitten auf der Straße stehen bleiben, weil der Motor den Geist aufgibt. Nie ist es nötig, dass ein Fahrer die Fahrgäste zum Schieben auffordert, und wenn es sich um einen O-Bus handelt, muss der Fahrer kaum je einmal aussteigen, um die heruntergefallenen Stromabnehmer mittels einer mitgeführten Stange wieder mit der Oberleitung in Verbindung zu bringen. Natürlich verpesten solche Busse auch nicht mehr die Luft mit fettigem schwarzem Qualm, dessen Anblick allein schon Krebs erzeugt, sondern im Gegenteil! Durch ein raffiniertes japanisches Computerverfahren werden die Abgase mit echtem Sauerstoff angereichert, so dass der reine Äther des Hochgebirges aus dem Auspuff strömt! Steht man morgens wartend an der Haltestelle, wird man kaum noch unterscheiden können, ob man hier ist oder in St. Moritz!

Sollte dann noch jemand auf die Idee kommen, irgendwelchen alten Schrottmühlen nachzutrauern, die in unserem stets besser werdenden Leben überhaupt nichts verloren haben, so wird er mit mehrmonatigem täglichem Busfahren ohne Bewährung bestraft.

CHINESEN

Kennzeichen, allg.:
1. essen mit Stäbchen,
2. mögen keine Japaner,
3. knallen Türen.

COCA-COLA

可 口 可 乐	kěkǒu kělè	lecker, man kann sich freuen; so wohlschmeckend, dass man seine Freude hat; Wohlgeschmack und Spaß.

Endlich saß er im Flugzeug. Nach Deutschland! Der letzte Blick auf die grauen Flughafengebäude von Hongqiao, winzige Fahrzeuge und Männer in roten Arbeitsanzügen, verbrannter Boden, die lange Reihe der wartenden Flugzeuge, die mit großen Staubsaugerschläuchen Passagiere ansaugten – dann hoben sie ab, und nichts mehr war zu sehen, nur noch der wogende Dunst, der vom Meer aufstieg und die Stadt einhüllte, seine Vaterstadt.

Nach Deutschland!

Er hatte es also geschafft. Er würde also wirklich zu jenen Privilegierten gehören, die nicht nur ständig darüber redeten … Er würde wirklich dort ankommen, würde Briefe schreiben mit lateinischen Buchstaben auf dem Umschlag wie die vergilbten Briefe seines Urgroßvaters, die sein Vater spätabends Gästen zeigte, und sie würden seine Briefe mit derselben Ehrfurcht in die Hand nehmen und sie immer wieder lesen … Sie würden ihn beneiden, den traurigen Hund, weil er das weiße Schloss erreichte … Deutschland … Er saß also wirklich im Flugzeug …

Nach Deutschland!

In Deutschland hatten alle Autos. In Deutschland waren die Fernseher so groß wie Kinoleinwände. Auf den Dächern standen Hubschrauber. In den Straßen patrouillierten riesige grün-weiße Polizeimotorräder. Die Klos waren eingerichtet wie Wohnzimmer. Die Männer waren groß und hatten breite Schultern, sie aßen Ritter-Sport-Schokolade. Die Frauen hatten blonde Haare, ihre Augen waren grün und glänzten wie Edelsteine, sie hießen Tina und trugen keinen BH und waren so stark wie D. K. und Biff und Metalman. In Deutschland fiel nie der Strom aus. Es gab Bibliotheken und Labors und Computer, die jeder benutzen konnte. Im Winter gab es Heizung, sogar die Klassenräume waren geheizt, und im Sommer gab es Mücken, die nicht stachen. In den Parks liefen die Enten frei herum … Er hatte so lange auf das Visum gewartet, dass er schon fast die Hoffnung aufgegeben hatte wie das Männchen, das den Berg mit dem weißen Schloss erklimmen muss, rechts und links rollen eiserne Kugeln herunter und drohen ihn zu zermalmen, im Boden tun sich Risse auf, aus denen Feuer lodert, Untiere lauern hinter jeder Wegbiegung, und dann schafft er es doch, das weiße Schloss liegt vor ihm, das weiße Schloss mit den Fahnen und den Zinnen, auf denen Frauen stehen und mit Taschentüchern winken …

Nach Deutschland!

Er hatte Angst vor Deutschland. Auch das Männchen, das den Berg hochklettert, hat Angst. Wenn es die Wand mit dem Erdrutsch nicht schafft, ändert sich sein Gesichtsausdruck, die Mundwinkel ziehen sich nach unten, das Haar sieht struppig aus, die Ohren stehen vom Kopf ab, als hätte eine Teekanne zwei Henkel, es sieht aus wie ein Hund, ein trauriger kleiner Hund, das war es, was einem noch mehr Ansporn gab, sich zu konzentrieren und blitzschnell zu reagieren, man musste schneller sein als die anderen, geduldiger, entschlossener, besser, denn nach der Wand mit dem Erdrutsch kommt die Riesenechse von rechts, mit schillernden

Schuppen und Haifischgebiss … Er hatte Angst. Angst vor Käse und Butter und all den fürchterlichen Dingen, die die Deutschen aßen, vor dem hässlichen Klang der unnatürlich langen Wörter, dem komplizierten Regelwerk der Endungen, den r und dem Präteritum, Angst vor der Zimmersuche, den Polizisten auf ihren Motorrädern, den Frauen. Doch stärker als die Angst war die Sehnsucht, es mit der Fremde aufzunehmen, etwas von dem Wissen zu erwerben, das dieses Land groß und stark, seine Autos und Werkzeugmaschinen und Häfen und U-Bahnen berühmt gemacht hatte, ja, er wollte studieren, lernen, lesen, Tag und Nacht, davor hatte er keine Angst, er konnte arbeiten und fleißig sein, wenn er wollte, auch wenn sein Vater es nicht glaubte, und er würde nur das Allernötigste kaufen und nur Reis essen und Wasser trinken, in Deutschland kostete das Wasser nichts … Manche sagten, man brauche tausend Mark im Monat in Deutschland, aber er war entschlossen, mit fünfhundert auszukommen, er würde streng und asketisch leben wie Monk, und seine Kräfte würden in der Stille wachsen … Im Notfall gab es die Enten in den Parks … Und wenn er zurückkam, würde er seinen Eltern ein Haus kaufen, ein großes neues Haus auf Chongming, mit Garage und Balkon … Da würde sein Vater mit dem Fernglas beobachten, wie sie den Jangtse ausbaggern für die größten Tanker der Welt, das würde ihn für alles entschädigen, wenn er alt war … und nie mehr, nie mehr würde sein Vater zu ihm sagen können, er solle sich ein Beispiel nehmen an seinem Cousin Fangyu, der ihnen jedes Jahr aus Kanada gedruckte Karten mit Christbäumen und Weihnachtsmännern schickte, sein Cousin Fangyu, der schon fast fünf Jahre in Kanada studierte und immer noch keinen Master hatte, aber das machte seinem Vater nichts aus, weil Fangyu im Dezember Karten mit fetten glatzköpfigen weißbärtigen Männern in Kutschen schickte und zum Frühlingsfest ein paar kanadische Dollars und T-Shirts mit Michael Jordan … Kanada ist zu teuer für uns, hatte sein Vater gesagt … Also flog er nach Deutschland …

Nach Deutschland!

Die letzten Wochen des Wartens waren besonders schlimm gewesen. Nach der Semesterabschlussparty war er um ein Uhr nachts heimgekommen. Da hatte sein Vater mit Tränen des Zorns in den Augen zu ihm gesagt, er und seine sauberen Kameraden wüssten nicht mehr, was Arbeit ist und Fleiß und Treue und Wahrhaftigkeit. Und seine Mutter war gekommen in ihrem zerknitterten Nachthemd und den langen wollenen Hosen, die sie darunter trug, und hatte seinen Vater am Arm angefasst, wie er es noch nie gesehen hatte, und ihn ins Bett zurückgeführt, er hatte gezittert … Und dann hatte ihm jemand erzählt, die Deutschen würden sich mit zwanzigtausend nicht zufriedengeben, in vielen Städten verlangten sie jetzt vierzigtausend. Das wäre das Ende gewesen, von der schwankenden Hängebrücke direkt in den Wasserfall und zurück auf Position Null. Um diese unvorstellbare Summe aufzubringen, hätten seine Eltern noch ein weiteres Mal auf die größere Wohnung verzichten müssen, die ihnen seit langem zustand, noch weitere Monate und Jahre hätten sie auf Restaurantbesuche, neue Möbel, Schuhe, Kleider, Bücher und andere dringend benötigte Anschaffungen verzichten müssen, und seine Mutter hatte rechts und links fast keine Zähne mehr. Und dann wurde er ja auch älter und näherte sich unaufhaltsam den dreißig und hatte immer noch keine Freundin … Wie soll man eine Freundin haben, wenn man kein eigenes Zimmer hat, nirgends Platz, um allein zu sein, und kein Geld und keine Stelle, weil er auf das Visum wartete, während die anderen sich schon während des Semesters beworben hatten und angeben konnten mit ihren Aussichten bei Joint Ventures ... Aber jetzt hatte er sie überholt, es war nur der Nebel gewesen, wo es ein paar Sekunden rückwärts ging, und dann die Gletscherspalte, ein Sprung, geschafft ... Denn das kaum für möglich Gehaltene war doch noch eingetreten, das Visum war ausgestellt worden, und jetzt saß er im Flugzeug ...

Nach Deutschland!

Sein Urgroßvater war mit dem Schiff gefahren ... Das Bild seines Urgroßvaters hing über dem Schreibtisch seines Vaters. Von Anfang an hatten alle die frappierende Ähnlichkeit zwischen diesem Urgroßvater und ihm selbst festgestellt – dieselbe edle, längliche Gesichtsform, die schmale Nase, die weiße Haut. Sein Urgroßvater war Diplomat gewesen und hatte auf Chongming in einer Villa gelebt, er war in Europa gewesen, Berlin, Paris, der Vertrag von Versailles ... Sein Urgroßvater war in der Guomindang gewesen, aber das sagte sein Vater nicht, wenn er vor Gästen prahlte, er prahlte mit der Villa, in der der Urgroßvater seines Sohnes gelebt hatte, den Banketten, die es dort gegeben hatte, Käse und Butter und Champagner, weil er wusste, dass er damit alle beeindrucken konnte, obwohl ihm selbst nur Nachteile daraus erwachsen waren, obwohl dieser Urgroßvater seines Sohnes ihm das Leben zerstört hatte, weil er Grundbesitzer und Guomindangmitglied gewesen war ... Sein Vater war Ingenieur. Seine Eltern waren beide schon über fünfzig. Er schämte sich manchmal für sie und schämte sich dann dafür, dass er sich für sie schämte. Sein Vater färbte sich das Haar. Er hatte immer noch das braune Gesicht, die harten Hände des körperlich Arbeitenden, obwohl er heute nicht mehr körperlich arbeitete, sondern als Professor an der Universität. Seine Eltern hatten die ersten zwanzig Jahre ihrer Ehe nicht zusammenleben können. Seine Mutter hatte bei Bauern in Anhui gearbeitet, sein Vater war nach Dalian zur Fabrikarbeit abkommandiert worden. Über diese Zeit sprachen seine Eltern nie. Nur einmal, im Zorn, als er sich wieder einmal über ein Zeugnis aufregte, das sein Sohn nach Hause brachte, hatte sein Vater von der grausamen Kälte geredet, die dort oben im Norden herrschte, und dass morgens die Leichen der Verhungerten die Straßen gesäumt hätten und dass es sich damals keiner leisten konnte, im warmen Zimmer auf der faulen Haut zu liegen und darauf zu warten, dass einem die gebratenen Enten in den Mund fliegen ... Nachdem er die Zugangsprüfung für die Universität bestanden hatte – knapp bestanden, wie immer –, hatte sein Vater sein Studienfach bestimmt, Wirtschaft. Sein Vater hatte ihm das *Penguin Dictionary of Economics* gekauft mit den Dollarscheinen und Goldbarren auf dem Umschlag, heute muss man Wirtschaft studieren, hatte er gesagt, heute ist Wirtschaft das A und O. Aber er hatte nie etwas begriffen, und alles war ihm todlangweilig vorgekommen, was in den Lehrbüchern der Politökonomie stand, die sie benutzten, es gab Marxismus-Leninismus und Statistik, aber keine Computer. Du hast Glück, sagte sein Vater, wer die Zugangsprüfung schafft, schafft auch den Abgang. Ja, er hatte Glück ... Er flog nach Deutschland ...

Nach Deutschland!

Wenigstens hatte er nicht im Studentenheim wohnen müssen wie die anderen, die von außerhalb kamen, zu acht im Zimmer, in Stockbetten, mit einem dünnen Vorhang als einziger Begrenzung des persönlichen Bereichs, Hausaufgaben unter tropfender Wäsche oder im Freien, mit der Thermoskanne über den halben Campus, um heißes Wasser zu holen, weil Kocher auf dem Zimmer verboten sind, der Gestank der Klos und freitagabends duschen … Aber im Studentenheim hatten sie den großen Fernseher, die Mappen mit den Spiele-CDs … Und nur wenn er samstags mit der Steuerung in Händen vor dem Bildschirm saß, verloren sein Vater und das *Penguin Dictionary of Economics* und die Kälte und die Zahnputzbecher und Klopapierrollen, die auf dem Apparat aufgereiht waren, und der schmutzige löchrige Bretterboden zeitweilig an Bedeutung, und es blieb nur noch die reine Welt des nackten Kampfes übrig, Kampf um Tina, Sieg im Rennen, im Dschungelkrieg im Wüstenkrieg im allerletzten aller Weltkriege zwischen Panzern mit Insektenaugen und Panzern mit Flammenwerfern rechts und links wie Blumensträuße für Tina … Kampf um den Gipfel, das weiße Schloss, die Fahnen die Zinnen die Taschentücher … Japanische CDs, die besten, und sie hatten alle … Und dann kam er heim, und sein Vater saß mit Gästen auf dem Sofa in dem winzigen Wohnzimmer, das mit Bücherschränken, dem Schreibtisch, dem Sofa vollgestopft wirkte wie eine Rumpelkammer, und ging mit ihnen die Alben durch. Hafenanlagen, Wellenbrecher, Pumpstationen, der Flyover an der Nanpu-Brücke, die zweite U-Bahn nach Pudong – Baustellen, immer wieder Baustellen, und sein Vater mit dem Helm auf dem Kopf und seinem Fotogesicht im Vordergrund, sein Vater vor der Tafel im Hörsaal, und die Gäste gähnten, und die Mutter wusch das Geschirr in der Küche. Mit welch kindischem Stolz sein Vater redete und erklärte und Pläne glättete und Konstruktionszeichnungen entrollte, mit welch lächerlicher Ehrfurcht er die Einladungen zu Konferenzen über Hafenbau, sein Spezialgebiet, in Amerika, in Norwegen vorzeigte, die man ihm schickte und die er immer absagen musste, weil man ihm das Geld für das Flugticket nicht mitschickte... Die Ausländer lachten über ihn, aber davon merkte sein Vater nichts. Und er selbst, der Urenkel des Urgroßvaters, dieselbe edle Gesichtsform, dieselbe Blässe, er verstand nicht einmal, wie ein Auto funktionierte und interessierte sich auch nicht für Autos oder für Schiffe oder für Computer wie sein Cousin Fangyu, er wusste nicht, wofür er sich überhaupt interessierte, außer für Tina und D. K. und das Männchen, das ewig den Berg hochrennt, um das Schloss zu erreichen, das weiße Schloss mit den Teppichen den Goldbarren dem Champagner der Garage für die Kutschen, das war Deutschland, diese komischen Ritter ohne Gesicht, groß und breitschultrig, die plötzlich höhnisch ihre Zähne zeigten und das Männchen im letzten Moment in Stücke hauten mit ihren Armbrüsten ihren Steinschleudern, wenn man nicht aufpasste, das Seil ergriff, das die Prinzessin einem von oben zuwarf, und hochgeschleudert wurde in die Luft...

Nach Deutschland!

Er saß auf dem alten Hocker über seinen Büchern und versuchte vergeblich, sich zu konzentrieren, in dem winzigen fensterlosen Raum mit den gelben, jahrzehntelang nicht mehr gestrichenen Wänden, in dem sie abends zusammen aßen, im Erdgeschoss neben dem Fahrradabstellplatz, wo es durch die Türritzen zog, eisiger Wind, an dem Tisch mit Glasplatte, unter der ein Bild von Einstein steckte und ein Foto von seinen Eltern und ihm selbst als Acht- oder Zehnjährigem in einem Garten in Hangzhou und ein Foto von der verwitterten Fassade eines halb eingestürzten Hauses auf Chongming und ein Reklameprospekt von einer norwegischen Schifffahrtsgesellschaft mit Ausländern in Badeanzügen auf Liegestühlen, weil sein Vater einmal norwegischen Ingenieuren den Hafen gezeigt hatte, aber bei der Gegeneinladung hatten sie das Flugticket nicht mitgeschickt … Jetzt war er es, der flog, das Männchen, das den Berg bezwang, der Urenkel des Urgroßvaters …

Nach Deutschland!

Ein neues Leben begann, eine neue Zeit. Auf dem Bildschirm lag China vor ihm, ein Schmetterling, und Shanghai war nur noch ein winziger Punkt am Flügelrand. Die Stewardess hatte rote Lippen und ein Haarnetz, lächelnd fragte sie, was er zu trinken wünsche. Kaffee, sagte er, Kaffee, und sie beugte sich über ihn, und er roch das Parfüm, das an ihr klebte, und den Kaffee, er dachte an Tina, Tina mit ihren japanischen Muskeln und deutschen Brüsten, dem flatternden Taschentuch, und wusste plötzlich, dass Tina so riechen musste, genau so …

DIEBE

Wir waren aufgebrochen, um die Bahnhofsgegend zu erkunden. Eben noch waren wir am Seiteneingang des Bahnhofs, wo sich uralte staubige Überlandbusse mit Menschen füllten, Säcke und Kisten auf den Dächern verstaut und festgezurrt wurden. Jiaotong Lu, Datong Lu – wir waren kaum einen Kilometer vom Bahnhof weg. Das langgezogene Pfeifen einer Lokomotive ertönte. Wir haben die Orientierung verloren.

Um uns ist alles in Bewegung. Unsere Blicke finden keinen Halt mehr. Tausend armselige Dinge bieten sich dar, fordern Aufmerksamkeit. Überall wird gehämmert und gesägt, gehandelt und gestritten, gewaschen, geschleppt, gekocht. Straßenhändler halten vor den Fronten von Billigkaufhäusern noch billigere Waren feil, zwischen Schachteln voller Schrauben und Werkzeug und allen möglichen auf dem Bürgersteig verstreuten Utensilien werden Fahrräder repariert, Möbel gezimmert, Metallgitter zusammengeschweißt. Junge Frauen in zerschlissenen Pantoffeln hacken Gemüse. Alte Frauen sitzen unter trocknenden Unterhosen auf kleinen Stühlchen in der Sonne und stricken. Wir stoßen auf eingezäunte freie Plätze, wo Menschen in schmutzigen, abgewetzten gefütterten Baumwolljacken in den letzten Schuttresten nach irgendetwas Brauchbarem stochern, während schon die ersten Bagger ihre Zähne in die feuchte graue Erde stoßen.

Hier entstehen Hochhäuser. An vielen Häuserwänden steht mit weißer Farbe das Zeichen: Abriss. In ein paar Jahren wird das Viertel so, wie es jetzt ist, verschwunden sein.

Ohne es zu wollen, geraten wir immer tiefer in das Gewirr der alten, übervölkerten Gassen und Höfe hinein, die abgenutzt und heruntergewohnt sind bis zur Baufälligkeit. Und doch wollen die Menschen nicht weichen und leben mit einer Art von verzweifeltem Trotz ihr Leben wie eh und je. Die Miete für eine Wohnung in einem der neuen Hochhäuser kann sich keiner leisten. Ein mulmiges Gefühl steigt in uns auf. Wir haben hier nichts verloren. Wir sind Eindringlinge. Es ist, als würde es in unserer Nähe stiller, man starrt uns an und hört auf zu reden, wenn wir vorbeikommen, und auch wir hören auf, uns zu unterhalten. Jeder ist mit sich selbst beschäftigt.

Wie viele Menschen hausen in diesen dunklen, zugigen Höhlen? Womit verdienen sie ihren Lebensunterhalt? Wie halten sie sich warm? Was machen sie, wenn sie krank werden? Wie viele teilen sich einen Wasserhahn, eine Kochstelle, ein Bett? Mir ist kalt. Ich will weg hier. Das ganze Viertel kommt mir vor wie eine faule Frucht, die, von breiten Abrissschneisen aufgebrochen, ihr stinkendes Inneres herzeigt. Weg mit diesen geflickten Dächern, diesen feuchten Wänden, diesem Gerümpel, diesen Lumpen, diesem Dreck!

Automatisch streben wir den Hochhäusern zu, deren Silhouetten sich schwarz gegen den kalten roten Abendhimmel abzeichnen. Dort ist Ordnung und Sauberkeit, dort sind wir daheim. Aber das Viertel lässt uns gerade jetzt nicht los. Aus einem Fabriktor quellen Menschen. Und immer mehr Menschen stehen da, mit den Händen in den Taschen und hochgeschlagenen Krägen, rauchend, Mandarinen schälend,

Kerne spuckend, und starren uns an. Wir stellen fest, dass wir im Kreis gegangen sind. Ein Taxi! Aber hier scheint es nur Fahrräder und Busse zu geben, kein Auto ist in Sicht. Wir gehen weiter, fragen nach dem Bahnhof. Dort – links – die Unterführung ... Ich merke, dass sich jemand an mich herandrängt und der Reißverschluss meiner Handtasche aufgezogen wird. Hat uns nicht eben erst eine Verkäuferin in einer der armseligen Essensbuden freundlich vor Dieben gewarnt? Und doch kann ich nicht glauben, dass gerade ich es bin, die hier bestohlen werden soll. Der Schreck lähmt mich. Als ich mich, meinen ganzen Mut zusammennehmend, umdrehe, sehe ich ein Kind von höchstens zehn Jahren, schmächtig, schmutzig, das sich blitzschnell abwendet und wegläuft.

Erst im Taxi finde ich meine Ruhe wieder. Es ist geheizt. Mein Geld, mein Ausweis, alles ist noch da. Wir fangen wieder an zu reden, es sprudelt nur so aus uns heraus. Ich schaue zurück. Wie riesige Räumfahrzeuge haben sich die Hochhäuser in das Dickicht des alten Viertels hineingefressen. Nach getaner Arbeit stehen sie verlassen in der Dämmerung, tote Maschinen, vereinzelt von Funken hellen Lebens gesprenkelt. Ich denke an den Dieb, die Frostbeulen in seinem Gesicht, sein stumpfes, staubiges, lange nicht geschnittenes Haar. Plötzlich ergreift mich ein vages und drückendes Schuldgefühl, und es ist mir, als wäre ich es, die hier die Flucht ergreift.

DRACHEN

Die alte Kunst des Drachenmachens stirbt aus. Nur noch in Touristenläden oder in Büchern sind die farbenfrohen Schwalben und Schmetterlinge, Libellen, Krebse, Fische, Drachen und Phönixe zu bewundern, die, aus Seide oder hauchdünnem Papier auf Bambusrahmen aufgezogen und oft mit im Wind klingenden Saiten ausgestattet, in der warmen Luft tanzen. Die Drachen, die man heute in Shanghai zu kaufen bekommt, sind meist phantasielose Drei- oder Vierecke aus einem wie Regenschirme gemusterten Plastikgewebe. An einem schönen Sonntag im Volkspark, mitten in der Stadt, wimmelt es von Drachenverkäufern. Wenn es aber vom legendären Erfinder des Drachens, Meister Gongshu aus dem vierten vorchristlichen Jahrhundert, heißt, seine Drachen schwebten drei Tage am Himmel, ohne herunterzufallen, so ist Vergleichbares heute schon deshalb undenkbar, weil es nahezu unmöglich ist, einen Drachen in der Luft zu steuern und sich auf dem Boden gleichzeitig durch eine dichte Menschenmenge hindurchzukämpfen.

Lu Xun hat eine Geschichte über einen Drachen geschrieben, sie findet sich in seinem *Unkraut* betitelten Zyklus von Gedichten in Prosa. Der Erzähler berichtet darin von seinem kindlichen Hass auf Drachen, die er als dummes Spielzeug für Nichtsnutze betrachtete. Sein jüngerer Bruder hingegen, ein schwächliches, ängstliches Kind, liebt nichts mehr als ebendieses Spielzeug und macht sich heimlich daran, selbst einen Drachen zu basteln. Der Ältere spürt die Werkstatt des Bruders auf, und in einem Anfall rasender Wut nimmt er den Bambusrahmen, der ein Schmetterling hätte werden sollen, mit großen Augen aus rotem Papier, wirft ihn auf den Boden und trampelt auf ihm herum. Die dem Bruder angetane Gewalt kommt ihm erst über zwanzig Jahre später plötzlich zu Bewusstsein, beim Lesen eines ausländischen Buches über die Bedeutung von Spielzeug für die Entwicklung der kindlichen Seele. Voll brennender Ungeduld wartet er auf das nächste Zusammentreffen mit dem Bruder, um Verzeihung von ihm zu erlangen. Der Tag kommt, doch es stellt sich heraus, dass der Jüngere den Vorfall inzwischen vollständig vergessen hat. »Ist das wirklich passiert?«, fragt er, ungläubig lächelnd und ohne jeden Vorwurf. Doch ohne Anklage kein Freispruch. Die Schuld des älteren Bruders, des anmaßenden Zerstörers, bleibt bestehen. Der Drache, Symbol des Frühlings und des schutzlosen Lebens, wird nie wieder heil. Am Ende stehen bittere Zeilen winterlicher Hoffnungslosigkeit.

Als ich die wimmelnde Menge begeisterter Leute sah, die an einem schönen Sonntag im Volkspark in den von Drachen gepunkteten, von Staub und Smog verdreckten Himmel schauten, musste ich an diese Geschichte denken.

DUNKELHEIT

Warum haben die Fahrräder kein Licht?

Es kursieren etliche Theorien, die dieses merkwürdige Phänomen zu erklären versuchen. Fahrradlampen würden durch das ungünstige Klima hier zu schnell kaputtgehen, wird behauptet. Auch heißt es, wenn es Fahrradlampen gäbe, wären sie binnen kurzem von Dieben abmontiert. Einer weiteren Theorie zufolge existiert sogar ein Gesetz, das Lampen an Fahrrädern verbietet, um zu verhindern, dass Verkehrsteilnehmer geblendet werden. Ich möchte diesen Erklärungen meine eigene hinzufügen.

Aus europäischen Städten ist die Dunkelheit vertrieben, die Nacht wird immer mehr zum Tag gemacht. Der Grad der Beleuchtung ist ein Maßstab der Städtischkeit geworden. Was kommt heraus, wenn man diesen Maßstab hier anlegt?

Abseits der großen Durchgangsschneisen flackern nirgends Neonröhren auf, wenn die Sonne sinkt; auch die größeren Nebenstraßen der Innenstadt sind nur spärlich durch Lampen markiert; in den Wohnvierteln sind Verbindungsgänge, Höfe, Treppenhäuser nicht beleuchtet. Die Dämmerung ist kurz. Die schwere Luft scheint sich plötzlich zu materialisieren, Fledermäuse taumeln durch den grauen Stoff. Das Sirren der Zikaden in den sommerlichen Platanendächern verstärkt sich (wenn man nah herankommt, meint man, den gellenden Ton von Kreissägen zu hören). Die gespreizten Hände der Fingerpalmen strecken sich sehnsuchtsvoll der Nacht entgegen. Und sie kommt, ungehindert von Lampen und Lichtern, heißt die Zikaden schweigen, den Abendwind sich legen, den Menschenrhythmus sich verlangsamen, steigt von unten herauf wie eine stille sanfte schwarze Flut.

In schweren Tropfen fällt die Feuchtigkeit von den riesigen Blättern der Bananenstauden, und in den Pfützen, Residuen der letzten Regengüsse, brummen und quaken die Frösche. Der Abfall stinkt, die Ratten regen sich. Nach dem Abendessen kommen die Kinder zu ihrem Recht; endlich sind sie mit den Hausaufgaben fertig. Händler stapeln Gemüsekisten. In den Schneiderwerkstätten werden die fertigen Kleider gebügelt. In den Zigarettenläden ratschen die Alten, in den Videospielbuden sitzt gebannt die Jugend. Fernseher laufen. Männer hocken auf den Fersen und spielen mit Babys. Frauen waschen sich die Haare, sitzen auf Bambusstühlchen strickend mit Nachbarn zusammen. Allmählich geht die große Veränderung vor sich – die Stadt scheint nicht mehr aus festen Volumen zu bestehen, sie löst sich auf in Geräusche, in Gerüche, Wärmewellen, Dunkelheit.

Verwaiste Busse stehen in langen Reihen am Straßenrand. Hauseingänge, Geschäfte senden kein Zeichen einladenden Lebens mehr aus. Melonenverkäufer schlafen zwischen Melonenbergen. An manchen Ecken sieht man von rotem Kochfeuer erleuchtete Imbissstände, an denen Arbeiter nach der Spätschicht Suppe löffeln. Vereinzelte Gruppen junger Männer spielen bei Funzellicht auf dem Bürgersteig endlose träumerische Kartenspiele.

Die Nacht ist das große Aufatmen. Die Nacht befreit die Stadt von der Last, die auf ihrem Nacken liegt, die Last der

Kämpfe, die Last der Zwecke, die Last des ewigen emsigen Sichmühens. Und die Stadt sinkt in sich zusammen und lauscht dankbar der Stille, die sich nur in der Dunkelheit entfalten kann.

Gelbliche Scheinwerfer der letzten Autos streichen über schlafende Fassaden. Fahrräder ohne Licht huschen vorüber, Schatten, eine Schattenwelt bevölkernd, Sendboten und Wächter der Stille.

Warum haben die Fahrräder kein Licht? Es ist ein Tribut, den die Stadt der Nacht zollt, ihrer Wohltäterin.

EMPFANGSHALLEN

Über den Türen steht Plaza oder Mansion, Center oder Tower. Vor den Türen rauschen Brunnen. Hinter den Türen warten Pagen. Klimaanlagen arbeiten geräuschlos. Sessel laden zum Verweilen ein. Aufzüge schweben hinauf und hinab. Geschickt verteilte Lampen spenden freundliches Licht. Tiefe Teppiche tun den Sohlen wohl. Schmeichelnde Klänge tropfen von der Decke. Weiche Stimmen wünschen angenehmen Aufenthalt. Lächelnde Münder geben bereitwillig Auskunft. Gepflegte Hände weisen Wege, bringen Drinks. Goldene Uhren zeigen Weltzeit. Koreanische Limousinen präsentieren sich auf spiegelnden Podesten. Junge Mädchen wienern Marmor, gießen Palmen. Uniformierte Wächter sitzen vor Schalttafeln, beobachten Bildschirme. Ladentheken sind mit Büchern und Zeitungen, Spirituosen und Kosmetika, in- und ausländischen Spezialitäten gut bestückt. Wer Mangel leidet, könnte hier Fülle erfahren. Wer erschöpft ist, könnte sich erholen. Wem die Hitze zusetzt, könnte sich abkühlen. Wem der Smog in den Augen brennt, fände Erquickung. Wer friert, könnte sich wärmen. Wer den Lärm nicht mehr erträgt, fände Ruhe. Wen das Menschengewühl bedrückt, atmete freier. Es scheint nur Glas zu sein, was diese leeren Räume von der Straße trennt.

»Das arbeitende Volk, das auf den 9,6 Millionen Quadratkilometern der Volksrepublik China lebt, hat wahrhaft begonnen, dieses Land zu regieren!«, rief Mao Zedong. Das war 1958.

1997 führen Schüler der Fremdsprachen-Mittelschule einen Sketch auf. Der Sketch heißt: »Wir gründen eine Fabrik.«

Aus der großen Masse der begeistert schreienden, fingerschnipsenden Bewerber wird zunächst ein Manager ausgewählt, indem man den Kopfumfang von allen misst. Der Schüler mit dem dicksten Kopf bekommt den Posten. Sodann wird dem Manager eine Assistentin beigesellt. Aus der großen Masse der kichernden, fingerschnipsenden Bewerberinnen wird diejenige auserkoren, die einen unverständlich gebrabbelten Satz des Managers als Aufforderung, Kaffee zu bringen, zu interpretieren weiß. Es folgt der Buchhalter. Gewinner ist, wer die Zahlenreihe von fünfzig rückwärts am schnellsten fehlerlos herunterrattert. Dann der Telefonchef. Bestimmt wird, wer für den abwesenden Manager (der sich natürlich mit der Assistentin vergnügt) die lustigste Ausrede erfindet. Zuletzt der Auslandsrepräsentant, der vor allem als Doorman fungiert. Die Bewerber müssen ihre Weltläufigkeit unter Beweis stellen, indem sie in möglichst vielen Sprachen Begrüßungsfloskeln aufsagen. (Hier haben Provinzler als Angehörige entlegenerer Sprachfamilien natürlich die besten Chancen.) Nachdem auch dieser Posten besetzt ist, ist die Sache getan und die Spieler nehmen den verdienten Beifall entgegen.

FAHNEN

Rote Banner knattern im Wind. Ihre weißen Schriftzeichen verkünden an öffentlichen Gebäuden, über Plätzen, Straßen, Brücken die Weisungen des Parteitags. Die Fronten von Warenhäusern sind über und über mit bunten Bannern bedeckt. Die Beschriftung fordert zum Kaufen auf. Fabriktore, Auffahrten, Eingänge von Banken, Möbelgeschäften, Sportstätten, Universitäten, Parks werden zu bestimmten Anlässen mit Fahnen geschmückt, frisches Grün, Blau, Gelb, Rosa, Lila zwischen dem Braun und Grau schmutziger Fassaden. In Wohngebieten sieht man zwischen Bäumen und Laternenpfählen rote und weiße Spruchbänder, Mahnungen, die Straßen sauberzuhalten, Ankündigungen von Versammlungen, Willkommensgrüße für Gäste. Supermärkte machen mit langen Reihen bunter Wimpel auf Preisreduktionen oder besondere Angebote aufmerksam. An Festtagen sind ganze Straßenzüge mit solchen Wimpeln verziert. Auf Baustellen bezeichnen rote Fähnchen, paarweise in die Erde gesteckt, Gefahrenpunkte. Auch die großen Maschinen, die sich tief in den sumpfigen Boden bohren, und die mit Kies und Sand beladenen Kähne auf dem Huangpu sind rot beflaggt. An Straßenkreuzungen helfen Leute mit Trillerpfeifen und gelben Ordnerfähnchen, die Ströme der Fahrzeuge und Fußgänger zu regulieren. Im Klassenzimmer ist die Flagge der

Volksrepublik über der Tafel aufgespannt. Am Nationalfeiertag flattert sie als Standarte an Bussen, Lastwagen, Taxis, auf Schreibtischen, Fernsehern, Marktständen und hoch über den Dächern der Stadt. Dem Nationalfeiertag folgt der Waschtag auf den Fuß. An langen Bambusstangen hängen die Fahnen in allen Formen und Farben vor den Fenstern. Die Wäsche des Volkes schwingt im Wind.

FOTOS

Bei Familientreffen, Preisverleihungen, Empfangspartys, Abschiedsbanketten und Anlässen aller Art bricht regelmäßig wilde Fotografierwut aus, als traue keiner mehr der eigenen Erinnerung. Bei den immer beliebter werdenden Kurztrips der Neureichen zu den alten und neu-alten Stätten der Kultur bleibt nichts ungeknipst; die uralte Kiefer, der Tempel wie der Buddha hören auf, wirkliche, wirkende Gegenstände zu sein, und werden in Souvenirs verwandelt, die nur noch zum Füllen der Fotoalben taugen.

Das erinnert mich an eine Geschichte von Sun Wukong, dem rebellischen Affen, der sein will wie Gott. Das siebte Kapitel der *Reise in den Westen* handelt von seinem Kampf mit Buddha selbst und von seiner Bestrafung: Er wird in einem steinernen Kasten unter dem Gebirge der fünf Elemente eingeschlossen, von Berggöttern und himmlischen Generalen bewacht, und muss fünfhundert Jahre auf die Befreiung warten. Zuvor aber bietet ihm Buddha eine Wette an. Wenn es dem Affen gelingt, mit einem einzigen Purzelbaum seiner offenen rechten Hand zu entkommen, wird Buddha persönlich den Jadekaiser auffordern, zu ihm in den Westen zu ziehen und Sun Wukong den Palast des Himmels zu überlassen.

»Dieser Buddha ist ein kompletter Idiot«, sagt Sun Wukong, sich ins Fäustchen lachend. Denn er besitzt die Fähigkeit, mit einem einzigen Purzelbaum sechsunddreißigtausend Meilen weit zu springen.

Und Buddha streckt seine rechte Hand aus, die nicht größer scheint als ein Lotusblatt.

Sun Wukong springt auf und stürmt wie ein Wirbelwind vorwärts, bis er fünf rosafarbene Säulen erblickt, von den Nebeln des Himmels dunkel umflort. Er glaubt sich am Ziel, die Aufgabe gelöst. Nun verwandelt er eins seiner Haare in einen in Tusche getauchten Pinsel und schreibt, statt des Namens seinen anmaßenden Titel benutzend, DER GROSSE HIMMELSGLEICHE WEISE WAR HIER, groß und breit auf die mittlere Säule. Um ganz sicherzugehen, hinterlässt er am Fuß der Säule noch eine stinkende Pfütze. Dann kehrt er triumphierend dorthin zurück, wo ihn der Buddha erwartet.

»Jetzt hab ich dich, du Pissgeist eines Affen!«, hört er ihn donnern. »Du hast meine Handfläche nie verlassen!« Und Sun Wukong mit seinen Feueraugen, seinen goldenen Pupillen, sieht staunend hinab und erkennt seine Inschrift und seine Pfütze winzig klein in einer Falte am Mittelfinger von Buddhas Hand.

Heute würde sich Sun Wukong an der rosafarbenen Säule fotografieren lassen. Ein Foto ist unaufwendiger als eine Inschrift, es riecht kaum, und man kann es mit nach Hause nehmen. Das Foto liefert den schlagenden Beweis: Ein Ort ist zu *meinem* Ort geworden, eine Zeit zu *meiner* Zeit. Das Foto ist ein Instrument der Eroberung.

Doch Sun Wukongs Geschichte lehrt auch, dass die Sache einen Haken hat. Die Dinge, die schon unterworfen schienen, zeigen sich plötzlich in ihrer ganzen furchterregenden Unfassbarkeit. Das Merkzeichen der Eroberung ist von beschämender Lächerlichkeit. Die rosafarbene Säule ist keine rosafarbene Säule, der Aufenthalt an jenem Ort Illusion, die äffische Kunst nur Affentheater.

FRISEURSALONS

Dieser Friseursalon ist etwas Besonderes. Allein die Einrichtung! Halbdurchsichtige weiße Gittervorhänge mit Bambus-und-Panda-Muster, pistazieneisgrün lackierte Wandschränke mit karoförmigen schwarzen Plastikbeschlägen, Marmorkonsolen mit bröckelnden Fugen, große, an den Ecken blind werdende Spiegel, in offenen Fächern ein Sammelsurium von Dingen wie Spraydosen, Teegläser, Parfümflaschen, uralte, merkwürdig geformte Föhne, Porzellanköpfe mit angeklebten Wimpern und Hippieperücken; unter Glas stecken Fotos von lächelnden Kindern und Betriebsausflügen, auf der Konsole steht ein Minigrill, an eisernen Haken hängen die weder neuen noch sauberen Umhänge für die Kunden und die Krawatten der Angestellten. An der Decke drehen sich gemessen die großen, staubbedeckten Ventilatoren. Gewaschen und geföhnt wird in einem Extraraum, einem dämmrigen, leicht verlotterten Boudoir, das man durch ein in die Tapetenwand eingelassenes Mondtor betritt. Die Öffnung ist mit abgeschabtem, schwarzweiß gemustertem Papier beklebt. Die Uhr darüber gibt auf vergilbtem Zifferblatt eine ungefähre Zeit an.

Auf der ramponierten Bahnhofswartesaalbank mit Lederpolster, die den Salon in zwei Hälften teilt – links die Damen, rechts die Herren –, sitzen die Angestellten und warten auf Kundschaft. Sie sind sich bewusst, dass der Ruf des Etablissements von ihnen abhängt, und tragen ihre gepflegte dunkelblau-weiße Uniform mit Stolz und Grazie. Natürlich legen sie auch den größten Wert auf ihre Frisur. Die Frauen haben farbige Strähnen oder kunstvolle Hochfrisuren und Make-up. Am Sonntagvormittag zeigen sie sich mit Lockenwicklern auf dem Kopf, und ihre langen Nägel sind schön lackiert. Die mir zugeteilte Friseurin überprüft, während sie lässig meine Haare schneidet, immer wieder fachmännisch ihr Aussehen im Spiegel. Dann ist Mittagessenszeit, man holt vom Restaurant nebenan in Styroporschachteln verschiedene Gerichte, macht es sich bequem, plaudert mit Bekannten, die sich eingefunden haben, tauscht Leckerbissen aus. Ein Angestellter mit langen, nach vorn spitz zulaufenden Koteletten, ein Einzelgänger offenbar, steht mit melancholischem Blick an der offenen Tür und raucht. Jemand massiert einer Kundin liebevoll den Nacken. Jemand fegt in Zeitlupentempo den Boden und schiebt die mit verfilzten Bürsten, Scheren, Haarteilen und sonstigem Handwerkszeug beladenen antiken Wägelchen hin und her. Andere haben den Kopf auf die Lehne der Bank gebettet und machen ein Nickerchen. Weit, weit weg ist die Straße, das echte Leben mit all seinen unverschämten Anforderungen. Hier genießt man einen vorläufigen Aufschub. Während man sich selbst verwandelt, beobachtet man die anderen, die wie Schauspieler in der Garderobe systematisch und professionell, doch gleichzeitig ganz unbekümmert ihre Vorbereitungen treffen. Vertrauliches Scherzen und unermüdliches Schwatzen überspielt die Angst, es nicht zu schaffen, das Lampenfieber. Bald wird es mit alldem zu Ende sein, denke ich, denken vielleicht alle, während die Schere betont sorglos vor sich hin klappert und mir der weder neue noch saubere Plastikumhang die Kehle zuschnürt. Das hier ist der alte Schlendrian. Der Geist der Zeit aber verlangt Straffheit, Hygiene, fleckenlos weißes Furnier und klingelnde Computerkassen! Haben Sie noch nicht gehört, dass diese Trockenhauben nur noch in der Mongolei benutzt werden? Wissen Sie eigentlich, was eine Kosten-Nutzen-Rechnung ist? Und auch an Sonntagvormittagen darf nicht einfach so herumgestanden werden! … Gemach. Noch ist es nicht so weit. Noch sitzt die neue Maske nicht ganz fest, noch ist das Publikum ausgeschlossen, noch ist man unter sich, und die strenge Stimme ist noch nicht zu hören, die unweigerlich ertönen wird: Ihr Auftritt, bitte!

FRÜHLINGSFEST

Volle Geschäfte, hektisches Großreinemachen, auf dem Markt werden Hühner, Enten, Tauben, Wachteln am Fließband gemetzelt, Fische verenden in Plastiktüten auf dem Heimweg, Krabben warten mit traurigen schwarzen Augen auf den Tod im Feuertopf. Nachmittags beginnen Fernsehshows von gewaltiger Scheußlichkeit, der Bürgermeister schüttelt Hände, verteilt Blumen und Stofftiger, begrüßt Veteranen und Krankenschwestern und Containerschiffsbesatzungen. Die Nachrichten werden unter roten Lampions verlesen. Den ganzen Tag hört man es knallen.

Bei Einbruch der Dunkelheit, wenn die Familie auf das Essen wartet, verstärkt sich der Lärm. Riesige Mengen Kies rutschen von unsichtbaren Ladeflächen, wolkenbruchartiger Regen prasselt auf imaginäres Blech, Wasserfälle rauschen, Zeltdächer knattern, Urwaldtrommeln ertönen, Donnerschläge, Maschinengewehre. Um halb elf ist der Himmel rot von diesem allumfassenden elektrischen Beben, es zuckt und wetterleuchtet ununterbrochen. Von Minute zu Minute steigert sich das Knattern und Zischen, das Prasseln und Sausen, die wahnwitzige Knallerei. Doch kein Krieg, keine Naturkatastrophe kündigt sich hier an; nur das friedliche neue Menschenjahr.

Ein gigantisches Verdauungssystem entlässt monströse

Fürze gen Himmel, ein Panzer, der die Stadt eisern umklammert hielt, beginnt Stück für Stück zu platzen. Kometen mit langen irisierenden Schweifen verglühen haufenweise in den Gassen. Feurige Samen werden in die Luft geworfen und tragen sofort und überreichlich Frucht. Es regnet Blumen und Diamanten und blitzendes Konfetti. Funkensprühende Fische schwimmen in der rauchgeschwängerten Luft. Flammende Springbrunnen berieseln die Dächer. Weißäugige Schlangen suchen schillernd das Weite. Zwischen halb zwölf und Mitternacht ballt sich die Energie der Stadt zu einem einzigen ohrenbetäubenden Getöse, einer Orgie irrlichternd zuckender bunter Himmelslichter, einem alle Grenzen sprengenden Höllenlärm. Doch nicht im Himmel, nicht in der Hölle werden solche Feste gefeiert; nur die Erde gibt diese Freude.

FUSSGÄNGERBRÜCKEN

Diesem so nüchternen und praktischen Volk ist unübersehbar ein Hang zum Gemütvollen eigen, gerade dort, wo es ums Geschäft geht. Die Fußgängerbrücke Nanjing Lu Ecke Shimen Yi Lu ist dafür ein gutes Beispiel. Im Getümmel der nach Waren jagenden Menschheit ist sie eine wahre Oase! Der Aufgang ist nicht steil und kantig wie bei anderen Fußgängerbrücken, sondern verläuft in romantischen Kurven, und hier und da laden balkonartige Ausbuchtungen zum Genießen der Aussicht auf Reklametafeln und Taxikolonnen ein. Das Geländer ist hellblau und weiß gestrichen, was an Himmel und Wolken oder an Bettwäsche denken lässt. Der obere Teil ist in der Art eines Laubengangs gestaltet, mit grünen, wenn auch von einer schwarzen Dreckschicht bedeckten Zweigen und Blättern und roten Ackerwindenblüten aus Plastik, die sich um gewölbte Eisenstangen wickeln. Unwillkürlich verlangsamt der auf dieser Fußgängerbrücke entlanggehende Kunde seinen Schritt. Es ist ihm fast wie einem Flaneur zumute, der träumerisch in der Welt herumbummelt. Bereitwillig wirft er seinen Obolus in den Becher einer malerischen Bettlerin, die ihm die Schalen ihrer Sonnenblumenkerne vor die Füße spuckt, schon ist er geneigt, die ewig Purzelbaum schlagenden Pandabären und funkgesteuerten Polizeiautos der fliegenden Händler als durchaus originelle volkstümliche Hervorbringungen zu betrachten. Die Ladenmädchen, die ihm unter hängenden Ranken entgegenkommen, erscheinen ihm als interessante Müßiggängerinnen, mit denen er gern im Schatten lustwandelte, der junge Mann, der mit gerunzelten Brauen einen Kassenzettel studiert, sieht von weitem aus, als läse er in einem Band mit Gedichten.

Von all diesen Eindrücken fühlt sich der Kunde seelisch erhoben und gestärkt, so dass er, von der Fußgängerbrücke in sanftem Schwung zum Eingang des nächsten Kaufhauses geleitet, mit nüchternem Seufzen den Beutel aus der Tasche zieht, um den praktischen Zweck seines Daseins zu erfüllen.

GEDRÄNGE

(Aus den *Phönixflügen ins Paradiesland*)... Nun gelangten wir ohne Säumnis zum Tore jener Stadt, über dem in herrlicher Schrift geschrieben stand: »Weisheit und Güte, Kostbarkeiten ohne Zahl«. Wie erstaunten wir aber, als wir dort alles genauso gebildet fanden wie in jener irdischen Stadt über dem Meer, die wir vor langer Zeit verlassen hatten, Häuser und Straßen, Fahrzeuge in großer Zahl und Menschen, mehr als der Lange Fluss Sandkörner mit sich führt, wenn er trüb ist und geschwollen von Herbstregen. Tankstellen, Mittelschulen, Armeekrankenhäuser waren auf dieselbe Weise nummeriert, und auch in der Art der Kleider, der Haartracht und selbst der Weise zu sprechen fanden wir uns ganz daheim... Wir wandten uns also an einen Bürger, der den gutgebürsteten Rock, die weiße Haut, das schmale und wahrhaftige Auge des Edlen besaß, und fragten ihn, welchen Namen die Stadt trage, der wir uns anvertraut, und ob er eine Herberge wisse, wo wir nach den Anstrengungen des Fluges ein Weilchen der Ruhe pflegen könnten. Wie groß war jedoch unsere Enttäuschung, als er nach einem kurzen Blick auf unsere Füße verächtlich ausspuckte und davonging! Nun erst wurden wir gewahr, dass die Hiesigen nicht in unserer Manier die Füße zum Gehen und zum Treten von Pedalen benutzten, sondern, dem Straßenstaub enthoben, auf einzelnen pfirsichfarbenen Wolken vorwärtsschwebten, -glitten und -hüpften, wodurch der ganze Verkehr auf vorbildliche Weise abgewickelt werden konnte und auch der Himmel kein schlechtes Wetter mehr schickte, da er sich nicht mehr durch die zu ihm aufsteigenden giftigen Autoabgase beleidigt fühlte … Wir lernten, dass die Bürger dieser Stadt die Menschen nicht nach Haut und Auge beurteilen wie wir, sondern allein nach der Beschaffenheit der Wolke unter ihren Füßen, die klein oder groß, dünn oder dick, mehr rosig oder mehr grau sein konnte, im schlimmsten Fall aber gar nicht vorhanden war, wie bei uns Ausländern, und wie sonderbar und verdreht uns diese Beurteilungsweise auch anfangs vorkam, so konnten wir uns mit unseren gewohnten Begriffen doch schließlich einen Reim darauf machen, und sie schien uns allmählich sogar weniger unvernünftig und willkürlich als die unsrige, während das, was wir bald darauf erleben sollten, alle unsere Begriffe und Vorstellungen überstieg … So wenig die Marktbuden und Kramläden, die wir gesehen hatten, den Rumpelkammern glichen, als die wir sie kannten, so gering war auch die Ähnlichkeit zwischen unserer althergebrachten Art des menschlichen Umgangs und Verkehrs und der hier geübten … Freilich war die feine Sittlichkeit und gleichsam duftende innere Ordnung nicht auf den ersten Blick zu erkennen, und wir bemerkten oft erst im Nachhinein, in welch peinliche Diskrepanz zu den bürgerlichen Gepflogenheiten wir uns durch die rauen und scharfen Kanten unseres Verhaltens selbst brachten und wie viel Mühe es diejenigen, mit denen wir nach und nach bekannt wurden, zuweilen kostete, unsere unverständlich scheinende Grobheit ein wenig zu glätten, unsere plumpesten Schnitzer auszubügeln … Namentlich beim Besteigen von U-Bahnen und Bussen, aber auch beim Warten vor den Schaltern von Postämtern, bei der Essensausgabe in Kantinen und dort, wo es in Geschäften hinein- und herausgeht, wurden wir der Unangemessenheit unseres in entbehrungsreichen Erdenjahren gewachsenen und verfestigten Benehmens gewahr und schämten uns dessen bald wie eines barbarischen Lasters … Zwar gab es auch hier, in der luftigen Zwillingsstadt unseres staubbedeckten Herkunftsortes, die man nicht auf gewöhnlichen Wegen, sondern nur auf den Flügeln des Phönix zu erreichen vermag, zuweilen Wirrsal und Gedränge, doch dessen Ursache war nicht, wie bei uns, hässliche Anmaßung und schiere Gier und die unbeherrschte Sucht, andere hinwegzustoßen, um selbst den ersten und besten Platz zu gewinnen, sondern im Gegenteil äußerste Zuvorkommenheit, Höflichkeit und der tiefempfundene Wunsch, anderen unbedingt den Vortritt zu lassen und keinesfalls für sich selbst einen bequemen Sitz, eine gute Bedienung oder sonst irgendeinen noch so geringen Vorteil in Anspruch zu nehmen. An der Endhaltestelle einer U-Bahn-Linie zum Exempel – bei uns bekanntlich ein Ort grauenhaften Getümmels, zahlloser Püffe, blauer Flecken und zänkischer Worte – herrschte auch hier ein mächtiges Gedränge, und zunächst glaubten wir uns zu Hause in dem Pulk einander schiebender und stoßender, schwitzender und schreiender Menschen auf dem breiten Bahnsteig, dann jedoch erkannten wir, wie schlecht wir beobachtet hatten! Es verhielt sich hier nämlich so, dass jeder Einzelne unbedingt *nach* seinem Nachbarn in die wartenden Waggons einzutreten wünschte und nicht sich selbst mit aller Kraft nach vorn zwängte, sondern seinen edlen Nachbarn, dem er fortwährend auf das hitzigste zusprach, dass er sich doch *bitte* nicht weiter zieren und *unbedingt* zuerst eintreten solle, andernfalls er, der Drängende, sich in seiner Seele getroffen und beleidigt fühle, worauf der Gedrängte in wohlgesetzten Ausdrücken zur Antwort gab, dass ein um so viel höher stehender Bürger wie der edle Nachbar nicht das *Recht* habe, einem nichtswürdigen stinkfüßigen Wurm wie ihm, dem nun seinerseits Drängenden, den Vortritt zu lassen, er wolle die Strecke eher auf seiner dünnen Einzelwolke rutschend bewältigen, als eine solche unverdiente Ehre anzunehmen u. Ä. m. – so dass das Einsteigen all dieser sich zurückhaltenden und kleinmachenden Menschen in dem Übermaße an Bescheidenheit, die ihnen eingewurzelt schien wie uns die rücksichtlose und so oft plötzlich »wie der brüllende Tiger aus dem säuselnden Gehölz« zum Ausbruch kommende Eigensucht, zu dem nämlichen Phänomen eines fürchterlichen Geschiebes und Gedränges führte, das uns von Erdentagen her noch so gut im Gedächtnis haftete und in dem wir um ein Haar tatsächlich zerquetscht worden wären … Als wir in unserer Herberge ankamen, wo es so ruhig und reinlich zuging und das Abendessen nicht von Öl triefte und von scharfen Gewürzen brannte, sondern auch hier voller Bescheidenheit, mit wenig Fett und mäßig im Gebrauch der Gewürze zubereitet wurde, sprachen wir von all dem, was wir erlebt hatten, und erinnerten einander an die ersten Eindrücke von dieser Stadt, da uns alles falsch und verdreht vorgekommen war und wir uns doch allmählich in das Fremde hineingefunden und schließlich festgestellt hatten, dass vieles in Wahrheit besser sei als bei uns … Und wir konnten uns des Missmuts nicht enthalten und sagten traurig zueinander, dass es in unserer Erdenstadt in so vielem noch ungeübt und bäurisch zugehe, und fragten uns, wie lange es wohl noch dauern würde, bis wir den Stand jener auf Wolken schwebenden Edlen erreichen, deren Wohnort voller Wirrsal doch mit vollem Recht eine Perle genannt zu werden verdient, »von schimmernder Reinheit und sanftem Feuer«, weithin leuchtend am freudespendenden Ufer des Ostmeers und überquellend von Kostbarkeiten ohne Zahl…

GITTER

In der älteren Architektur finden sich überall Gitter, aus Holz und Stein und Metall, an Brücken und Pavillons, Wänden, Balkonen, Türen. Gitter, im Winter mit Papier beklebt, waren Fenster. Auch heute liebt man sie noch, zur Dämpfung grellen Lichts und gegen Diebe. Gitter trennen den Außenraum vom Inneren, ohne beide Bereiche voneinander abzuschließen, es sind Schwellen, akzentuierte Übergänge, offene Grenzen. In Gärten sind Gitter, oft als Blüten, Zweige oder Schriftzeichen gestaltet, kunstreich behandelte Themen. Sie halten den Blick auf, zerstückeln, entrücken, verrätseln, was man im Rahmen von Fenstern und Toren konzentriert betrachten soll. Die Wahrnehmung wird verunsichert, die Grenzen zwischen dem, was »Bild« ist, und dem, was als »Wirklichkeit« gilt, verwischt. Gitter wollen die Befreiung des Blicks. Gebrochen, erlangt er eine neue Sicht.

GRÄBER

Der erste Aufstand der chinesischen Bevölkerung Shanghais gegen die Ausländer, die das Recht, auf ihrem Boden zu siedeln und sich zu bereichern, mit Waffengewalt erzwungen hatten, fand 1874 statt, zweiunddreißig Jahre nach dem Ende des Opiumkriegs, der Unterzeichnung des Vertrags von Nanjing. Er forderte auf der Seite der Ausländer einige Verwundete, auf chinesischer Seite sieben Menschenleben, nachdem die Besatzung eines im Hafen vor Anker liegenden französischen Kriegsschiffs nachts mordend und brennend durch die Stadt gezogen war. Der Grund für den lodernden Zorn der Chinesen war der Plan der Franzosen, ihre Konzession nach Westen hin zu erweitern und den weitläufigen Friedhof einer angesehenen Handelsgilde durch eine Straße zu entweihen. (Die Mitglieder dieser Handelsgilde stammten aus Ningbo, einer Hafenstadt circa hundert Kilometer südlich von Shanghai, die jahrhundertelang das wichtigste Zentrum des Küstenhandels gewesen war und erst zu Beginn des 19. Jahrhunderts von Shanghai überflügelt wurde. Aus Ningbo kam wesentliches Know-how, vor allem auf dem Gebiet des Schiffbaus und des Bankwesens; Zugewanderte aus Ningbo hatten viel zum Aufstieg Shanghais beigetragen.) Am Ende einigte man sich gütlich. Den Chinesen wurde die Zahlung von 37 000 Taels zur Strafe für die Beschädigung ausländischen Eigentums auferlegt. Die Franzosen sollten den Familien der Opfer 7000 Taels zahlen. Der Friedhof sollte auf ewig unverletzt bleiben.

1898 wurden die Friedhofsmauern niedergerissen. Bald darauf wurde die Straße gebaut.

Inzwischen hatten die Ausländer mehr Erfahrungen mit Aufständen – ein Jahr zuvor hatten die Rikschakulis aus Protest gegen die Erhöhung ihrer Lizenzen mehrere Tage lang gestreikt – und verhinderten durch eine militärische Blitzaktion jegliche effektive Gegenwehr der Gilde. Es gab wilde Proteste, die sofort erstickt wurden. Die Aufständischen hatten zwölf Tote zu beklagen, unter den ausländischen Soldaten gab es keine Opfer. Es folgte ein monatelanger Boykott. In chinesischen Geschäften weigerte man sich, Ausländer zu bedienen. Viele chinesische Hausangestellte verließen ihren Arbeitsplatz in der französischen Konzession. Die Sache verkomplizierte sich durch Streitigkeiten zwischen Engländern und Franzosen, bis im folgenden Jahr die chinesische Regierung, nach dem verheerenden Krieg mit Japan geschwächt, der Erweiterung der Niederlassungsgrenze offiziell zustimmte, was zu einer Verfünffachung des ausländischen Territoriums auf Shanghaier Boden führte.

In neuerer Zeit wurden in Shanghai keine Friedhöfe mehr gebaut.

Shanghai gehört auch heute zu den acht Provinzen und Städten des Landes, die die Bestattungsreform vorbildlich durchgeführt haben. Diese Reformen, die der Förderung der »geistigen Zivilisation des Sozialismus« und der »Reinigung der gesellschaftlichen Umwelt« dienen, beinhalten vor allem die platzsparende Feuerbestattung, aber auch die Abschaffung vieler alter Totenbräuche: Aufbahrung der Leiche und kniefällige Verehrung der Verstorbenen, Grabopfer, lautes Trommeln und Abbrennen von Feuerwerk, Verbrennen von Geistergeld u. a. Stattdessen werden von den zuständigen Stellen neue, d. h. westliche Formen des Trauerns empfohlen.

Die Urnen werden in die Vororte gebracht. Zum Totengedenktag im April werden Bustouren zu den Friedhöfen organisiert. Wer es sich leisten kann, kauft ein Grab in der Umgebung von Hangzhou oder Suzhou. Die Toten sollen in einer schönen Umgebung ruhen, wird erklärt. Denn es gibt an jenen Orten Berge und Blumen und klares Wasser und gute Luft. Merkwürdige Verkehrung! Einst rebellierte man im Namen der Ahnen gegen Barbaren, die im Namen des Profits darangingen, die Wohnungen der Toten zu zerstören. Heute ist die Stadt von Gräbern befreit, der ganz den Lebenden geweihte Boden darf schrankenlos ausgenutzt werden, und wenn da einer nicht mitkommt und im Zuge dieses großen, reinigenden Zivilisationsprozesses die Wohnung verliert, kann er nicht einmal mehr auf die Hilfe der Geister rechnen. Denn womit sollen sie die Fahrkarte bezahlen?

GRILLENVERKÄUFER

Der Sommer ist da! Der Grillenverkäufer kommt! Gemächlich trottet er die Straßen des Viertels entlang, ab und zu stehen bleibend, um mit einem Kunden zu fachsimpeln oder den Preis der Ware auszuhandeln. Die Grillen sitzen in Käfigen aus gelblichem Bambusgeflecht, kleinen, mit Löchern durchsetzten Waben und Würfeln; vielleicht hundert davon sind jeweils mit einer Schnur verschlungen und hängen als dicke Pakete vorn und hinten an der Stange, die der Grillenverkäufer auf der Schulter trägt.

Die Stadt, die Welt – Haufen, Berge, Gebirge von Grillenkäfigen, und der alte Mann, von dessen Schultern wir baumeln, wie soll er wissen, dass es Protestgeheul ist, was ihm als Wolke süßen Gezirps lieblich in den Ohren klingt?

HEPING-PARK

Vor dem Eingang des ummauerten Parks, der mitten in der Stadt liegt, auf einer Fläche, die kaum einem der größeren Hochhauskomplexe entspricht, wird Kinderspielzeug verkauft, Roboter, Funkautos, blonde Puppen, martialisches Kriegsgerät. Es gibt Stände mit Drachen, Windrädern, Luftballons und Zuckerwatte. Ein Händler bietet Goldfische in Gläsern feil, ein anderer winzige grün-rot gemusterte Schildkröten, der nächste einen Korb voller flaumiger Küken. Am Tor stauen sich die Familien. Es ist Sonntagnachmittag. Im Innern des Parks sind die Bäume mit Papierschmetterlingen geschmückt. Auf einem künstlichen Berg aus zerklüftetem Kalkstein sitzen Stoffaffen, die nach ihnen haschen. Es gibt auch einen Käfig mit echten Affen und ein Raubtierhaus, wo ein Gepard, ein Tiger, ein Löwe und ein Bär zwischen Eisenstangen und Beton traurig und apathisch ihr Leben fristen. (Ohne Frage gibt man dem Gezähmten und Gemachten vor dem Rohen und Wilden den Vorrang.) In den Büschen singen unermüdlich Vögel. Sie sind krähengroß, haben rotbraunes Gefieder und einen weißen Augenstreif. Die hübschen Bambuskäfige mit Ess- und Trinknäpfen aus blau-weißem Porzellan sind so eng, dass die Vögel sich gerade einmal um sich selbst drehen können. Nachmittags werden sie von ihren Besitzern hierhergebracht. Genießerisch dem Gesang lauschend, sitzen die alten Männer auf Bänken am See. Über den See hallt das aufgeregte Geschrei der Bootsfahrer, die alle Mühe haben, nicht dauernd miteinander zusammenzustoßen. (Der See ist klein, aber so geschickt angelegt, dass man mehrmals Gelegenheit hat, ihn an schmalen Stellen auf gewölbten Brücken zu überqueren.) Nach der Bootsfahrt brauchen Väter, Mütter und Kinder eine Erfrischung. Imbissstände halten Eis, Limonade, Gebäck bereit. Am Ufer sind luftige Pavillons, wo man, wenn es nicht gerade Sonntagnachmittag ist, einen Platz findet, um auszuruhen und zu picknicken. Unter blühendem Oleander sieht man Frauenrunden mit Babys. Auf niedrigen Hockern sitzen Männer, die Karten spielen. Kinder fahren Karussell. Das Karussell für die Kleinsten besteht aus einigen aneinandergehängten Wägelchen, jedes davon mit aufgemalten Augen, einem spitzzähnigen Maul und einem Horn auf der Stirn. Die größeren Kinder fahren mit der Eisenbahn. Ab und zu hat die Eisenbahn Maschinenschaden, und die Reisenden müssen aussteigen, was ihnen den allergrößten Spaß macht. Ein Mann schiebt die Lokomotive die Gleise entlang, die Kinder schieben begeistert mit. Nicht weit davon lockt ein großes, mit bunten Giraffen und Fischen unbeholfen bemaltes Schild. Man bezahlt ein paar Pfennige Eintritt und betritt einen dunklen Vorraum. Vier oder fünf Papageien mit Fußketten krächzen einem ins Ohr, ein struppiges angekettetes Äffchen springt hysterisch hin und her. Überall liegen völlig unbegreifliche Dinge herum, Drahtrollen, Stöcke, Schläuche, Platten, Wannen, löchrige Körbe. An der Wand lehnt ein Fahrrad. Über der Tür hängen Kleiderbügel ohne Kleider. Unter dem Sofa schläft ein Kätzchen. Auf dem Tisch steht eine Schale mit roten Chilischoten. Daneben eine rostige Thermoskanne, ein Abakus. Der Fernseher läuft. Von irgendwoher taucht ein hochaufgeschossener Junge in Gummistiefeln auf, der in den eigentlichen Schauraum führt, ein kahles Gewölbe, wo in schmutzigen Glaskästen Echsen, Schlangen, Schildkröten und Fische vegetieren. Die Welt der lebenden geht unmerklich in die Welt der toten Tiere über. Man bemerkt ein ausgestopftes Krokodil, ein furchterregendes hummerartiges Ungetüm mit langem Stachel und einen keinen Hund mit blauen Augen, der in einer undefinierbaren Flüssigkeit schwimmt. Der Boden der Glaskästen liegt voller Münzen. Der schweigsame Junge öffnet den Deckel eines Käfigs, ergreift die dort zusammengeringelt liegende Schlange am Kopf und trägt sie fort. (Wird er sie zum Abendessen essen?) Man folgt ihm und gelangt aufatmend wieder ins Freie, wo einen Prinzen und Prinzessinnen aus Pappmaché erwarten. Sich an den Händen haltend, entsteigen sie vielblättrigen roten Lotusblüten aus Papier. Zwischen diesen märchenhaften Figuren toben reale Kinder aller Altersstufen. Väter sitzen mittendrin geduldig auf den Fersen, rauchen und werfen ab und zu Bälle zurück ins Gewimmel. Eine quäkende Lautsprecherstimme macht darauf aufmerksam, dass die Tore bald geschlossen werden. Es dämmert. Alles strömt zum Ausgang. Die eisernen Rollläden der Buden rasseln herunter. Die Boote schaukeln unter ihrem rostigen Dach am Ufer. Die Vogelkäfige werden zugedeckt. Ein paar alte Männer machen allein unter Bäumen ihre langsamen und konzentrierten gymnastischen Übungen. Der Pavillon mit den gezackten Kalkfelsen und der Trauerweide daneben ist leer. Fledermäuse flattern über dem stillen Spiegel des Sees. Die erschöpften Kinder schlafen friedlich auf den Schultern von Vätern, Müttern und Großmüttern. Vielleicht ist es das, was dem Park den Namen gibt. Heping heißt Frieden.

HITZE

An einem Juliabend führt mich mein Weg durch die Renmin Lu am Rand des alten Stadtkerns. Die Türen der unzähligen kleinen Stuben, Läden und ebenerdigen Küchen stehen offen, Verkaufsgespräche sind zu hören, Streitereien; ein Mann steht auf einer Leiter und zählt laut Handtaschen auf einem Regal; am Getränkestand werden Flaschen zur Kühlung in Wannen gestellt, deren Wasser gleich wieder lauwarm ist; vom öffentlichen Abort her weht bestialischer Gestank; am Straßenrand werden mit Hackmessern Wassermelonen zerteilt; alte Frauen fahren Kinder in Wägelchen herum; alte Männer mit Fächern sitzen im Unterhemd auf Bambusstühlchen an der Kreuzung; Beos in ihren Käfigen rufen: »*Wei ni hao*«; Leute arbeiten und essen, dösen, spielen – in jeder Quergasse dasselbe, alles ist draußen, alles wartet auf den Sonnenuntergang, das Nachlassen der Hitze.

Das Bild gleicht jener bekannten Karikatur, die einen Querschnitt durch ein Mietshaus ohne Außenmauer zeigt. Jedes kleine Viereck ist ein Lebensausschnitt, die Andeutung eines Schicksals, das Wand an Wand mit hundert anderen Leben und Schicksalen seine aristokratische Unverwechselbarkeit verliert und zum gleichgültigen Atom des Volksgewimmels wird. Durch die Hitze wird das Innere der Stadt nach außen gestülpt. Es gibt kein Geheimnis mehr an einem solchen Tag. Wer hat dem anderen noch etwas voraus? Ich bin Teil eines einfachen Stoffwechsels, gebe aus, was ich habe, um zu bekommen, was ich brauche, genauso, wie ich ständig schwitze und die verlorene Flüssigkeit durch Trinken ständig wieder aufnehme. Der Körper hat keine Gelegenheit, Polster zu bilden. Reserve, Distanz, Vorteil, Besitz sind Illusionen des Nordens.

Die Hitze ist die große Gleichmacherin. Es gibt keine Einzelkörper mehr, nur noch Stadt, keine Sonne mehr, nur noch unergründliche opake Helligkeit, keine Luft mehr, nur noch vibrierendes Erz, versteinerte Dämmerung, Stadt, brütende, blinde, alles bannende, alles erstickende Stadt, die mit gichtigen Fingern den Himmel umklammert und ihn zu sich herunterzieht.

Leicht gehe ich in der Renmin Lu an einem Juliabend, schwitzend wie alle, erschöpft wie alle, unsichtbar in einem großen Einerlei. Nie war mir klarer, was die Faszination der Stadt ausmacht, nie sah ich sie nackter, nie wusste ich besser, dass es außer ihr nichts mehr gibt.

HOCHHÄUSER

Die Hochhäuser sehen aus wie Bauklötze, aufgespießte Basketbälle, Garagentore, Dunstabzugshauben, Triumphbögen, Kühlschränke, Brückenpfeiler, Kathedralen, Fleischspieße, Siegertreppchen, Rutschbahnen, Ozeanriesen, Eiswürfel, Bratroste, Raketenabschussrampen, Minarette, Futtersilos, Autobatterien, kaputte Stühle, Einkaufstaschen mit Henkeln, Kugelschreiber, Burgruinen, Nagelbürsten, gebackener Tofu, Hanteln, Knochen, Ziegelsteine, Essstäbchenbehälter, Kamine, Regale, Spiegelschränke, Finger mit Ringen, Pickelhauben, Parkuhren, Spritzen, Dolche, mit Silberband umwickelte Pakete, Brillenetuis, Computertastaturen, Gipsbeine, Schnapsgläser, Finger mit Warzen, verwitterte Grenzsteine, Glockentürme, Krückstöcke, Bienenstöcke, Peilstöcke, Mondfahrzeuge, Fieberthermometer, Helme mit Visieren, geschliffene Diamanten, angeknabberte Maiskolben, Schuhsohlen, Haarspangen, Zahnpastatuben, Bleistiftspitzer, Uhrbänder, Mikrofone aus den fünfziger Jahren, Totempfähle, Terrassentempel, Backenzähne, Geigenhälse, Schneidezähne, verfaulte Zähne, angebissene Zuckerstücke, Rolltreppen, Tortenheber, Handys, Taschenrechner, Zementmischer, entrindete Stämme, zusammengelegte Fächer, Frisiertische, Feuerwehrleitern, Pagoden, Flaschen, Särge, Kelche, Lippenstifte, Zahnstocher, Flaschenöffner …

HOCHSTRASSE

Die Hochstraße ist eine Autobahn auf Stelzen, die die Stadt ringförmig umgibt und in Nord-Süd-Richtung durchschneidet. Auf der Hochstraße ist man dem gefahrenreichen Verkehrsgewühl am Boden enthoben und kann sich ganz dem Genuss zügigen Autofahrens hingeben. Diese Bequemlichkeit geht mit einem sonderbaren Phänomen der Wahrnehmung einher. Man stellt fest, dass die Stadt von hier oben gesehen eine andere ist.

Wo sich unten das Leben im unendlich abwechslungsreichen Nebeneinander verschiedenartigster Sinneseindrücke darstellt, wo auswegloses Elend an prunkenden Reichtum grenzt, rücksichtslose Expansion an verzweifeltes Zurückbleiben, brutale Zerstörung an unbeschwert experimentierenden Neubeginn, scheint oben alles von der gleichen gespenstischen Starre erfasst. Hier hält das graue Alter der stürmischen, gierigen Jugend seinen bösen Spiegel vor. Ein kalter, vom Leben abgenutzter und ausgelaugter Riesenkörper zeigt sich in seiner ganzen schmutzstarrenden Hässlichkeit. Sein Atem ist stinkender Smog, seine Haut ist von einem grauen, schleimigen Film überzogen, den kein Regen mehr abwäscht. Wie lange weigert sich dieser Körper schon zu sterben?

Nachts ist die Hochstraße von Scheinwerfern grell erleuchtet. Daneben erscheint das Lichtermeer der Innenstadt wie eine Handvoll armseliger Funzeln. Kaum durchdringt ihr matter Schein die schwüle Luft, die wie ein nasser Scheuerlappen vom Himmel hängt. Hier und da sieht man sterngleich blinkende Reklamewände, mondblau schimmernde Fernsehschirme und andere vertraute Anzeichen geschäftiger menschlicher Aufschneiderei. Und doch kommt man von der Vorstellung nicht los, auf einsamer Piste eine wüste Gegend zu durchmessen. Welche Flut ließ diesen Haufen durcheinandergeworfener steinerner Würfel einst zurück? Wer mag zwischen diesen müden Mauern hausen, in diesen stickigen Labyrinthen umherirren? Wohin brachen die Menschen auf, die vor Zeiten aus Schwäche hier niedersanken? Was haben sie verloren, dass sie glauben, an diesem unbewohnbaren Ort sei etwas zu gewinnen?

HUANGPU-FAHRT

Wir haben eine River Tour auf dem Huangpu gemacht. Zuerst schien die Sonne. Alle Chinesen hatten Pullover an und saßen innen drin, die anderen hatten T-Shirts an und saßen auf dem Deck im Freien. Die Japaner haben gleich fotografiert. Die Taiwanesen gingen mit einer Videokamera an der Seite entlang. Die Deutschen haben Sonnenbrillen aufgehabt. Die Taiwanesen auch, aber nicht alle. Rechts waren die Wolkenkratzer von Pudong – alles neu, links war der Bund – alles alt. Der Huangpu war so breit wie der Rhein. Ein Lautsprecher sagte: »Hi, friends!« Dann etwas auf Japanisch, weil die Kassette falsch eingelegt war. Dann Musik und dass der Karaokeraum da und da ist. Zwei Männer haben unten die Taue hereingezogen, mit denen das Schiff an einem anderen festgebunden gewesen war. Unten hat man auch den Maschinenraum gesehen, aber da durften wir nicht bleiben, weil wir davon nichts verstehen. Rechts waren Docks und Werften, links auch, in der Mitte Schiffe. Rostige alte Containerschiffe, rostige alte Flusskähne, rostige alte Passagierdampfer, rostige alte Fischerboote, dazwischen nichtrostige neue Containerschiffe, Flusskähne, Passagierdampfer und Fischerboote. Manche Schiffe waren an einem Ding festgebunden, das wie ein rostiger Deckel aussah. Der Lautsprecher sagte noch einmal: »Hi, friends!« Dann sagte er, rechts und links sind

Docks und Werften und dass Shanghai der größte Hafen Chinas ist, wie viele Tausende von Schiffen hierherkommen und wie viele Millionen Tonnen Fracht umgeschlagen werden. Dann etwas auf Japanisch. Die Sonne war sehr heiß. Wir bekamen Sprite in Büchsen und je eine Tüte getrocknetes Rindfleisch, süß-salzige Pflaumen und Kartoffelchips. Rechts und links waren Docks und Werften, in der Mitte Schiffe. Die Kähne waren mit Sand und Kohle beladen. Wir sahen einen riesigen Frachter aus Manila und einen noch riesigeren aus Korea (aber wir konnten nicht erkennen, ob Süd- oder Nordkorea, weil wir nicht wussten, wie die Fahne davon aussieht) und einen aus Panama namens *Sky Treasure*. Ein Schiff hieß *Schneedrache*, weil obendrauf alles ganz weiß angestrichen war. Wir sahen auch orangene Fährschiffe, die Menschen, Fahrräder und Laster übersetzten, und ein altes Fischerboot aus Holz mit abgeblätterter Farbe und aufgerollten Netzen und ein graues Kriegsschiff, wo die Matrosen Wäsche aufhängten, sie hatten blaue Uniformen mit weißen Streifen an. Auf einem Schiff standen zwei Kinder, die schrien. Auf einem anderen waren Männer, die das Deck schrubbten. Einer schweißte etwas an einer langen Röhre, er hatte einen Helm auf. Das war ein Tanker. Eine Frau schüttete einen Eimer mit ganz dreckigem Wasser in den noch viel dreckigeren Huangpu. Überall hingen zerfledderte rote Fahnen, besonders an den kleinen Schiffen mit starkem Motor. Dann sahen wir links ein Kraftwerk. Der Lautsprecher sagte, das wievieltgrößte des Landes es ist und wie viele Millionen Kilowatt Strom es produziert. Es waren lauter Schornsteine mit schwarzem und weißem Rauch und schwarze Berge von Kohle und fünf oder zehn Reihen von rostigen Flussschiffen am Ufer, die wahrscheinlich die Kohle gebracht hatten und jetzt Pause machten. Es gab rote Stahltürme, und daran hingen Container. So werden die Containerschiffe beladen und auch entladen, aber wir wussten manchmal nicht, was gerade dran war. Dann fuhren wir unter der Yangpu-Brücke durch, und der Lautsprecher sagte, wie viele Tonnen die Brücke tragen kann und wie viele Meter und Zentimeter sie lang ist und dass sie die längste Hängebrücke der Welt ist. Das haben wir nicht geglaubt. Es kam jetzt Wind, und man hörte dauernd, wie die Schiffe überall tuteten. Ein Japaner hat sich auf den Boden gekniet und den Kopf auf den Stuhl gelegt und geschlafen. Die Amerikaner haben geschnürte Stiefel angehabt. Nach und nach haben sie Jacken mit Kapuzen aus dem Rucksack gezogen, denn es kamen dunkle Wolken, und unten am Himmel wurde alles heller. Wir sind unter Deck gegangen. Nur die Amerikaner mit den Kapuzen sind oben geblieben, und der Japaner hat weitergeschlafen. Unten haben uns die Chinesen zuerst groß angeguckt, weil wir Ausländer sind, aber dann nicht mehr, weil sie sich an uns gewöhnt hatten. Es gab Sitze mit rosa Polstern, aber die Polster waren locker, und es wackelte immer, wenn man sich bewegte. Auf den Tischen waren aufgerissene Tüten, Pappbecher, Coladosen, Teegläser, zerknüllte Taschentücher und Sachen zum Essen. Eine Frau hatte lange angeklebte Fingernägel. Die anderen kamen vom Land. Ein Baby bekam die Brust, es hatte eine grüne Mütze mit Ohren und einen roten Anzug mit Blumen und Schlitz. Es war in ein Männerjackett gehüllt, weil es jetzt nicht mehr so warm war. Die Kinder saßen am Fenster, nur ein dickes Kind nicht, das immer bei seinem Vater bleiben musste. Es waren auch alte Männer in alten blauen Jacken mit durchgescheuertem Kragen dabei. Manche Männer gingen ins Freie, und wenn sie zurückkamen, haben die anderen sie ausgelacht, weil sie zerzauste Haare hatten und auch nasse Kleider, besonders die Frauen. Es war Nebel überall. Rechts und links waren noch Docks und Werften zu sehen, aber undeutlich. Es gab auch viele Schornsteine, Fabriken, Kräne und Schiffe, an denen ganz kleine Männer hingen, die die Aufgabe hatten, das Schiff anzumalen, damit es nicht so schnell rostet, und einen Turm mit etwas, was aussah wie eine Uhr, aber mit weniger Zahlen, das war ein Windmesser. Der Huangpu war jetzt doppelt so breit wie der Rhein. Im Wasser waren Markierungen für die Schiffe, die aussahen wie die Spitzen von untergegangenen Pagoden. Wir haben uns gefragt, ob das noch der Huangpu ist. Das Ufer war auf einmal weg. Viele Männer sind aufgesprungen und rausgegangen, dann standen sie mit den Händen in den Hosentaschen am Geländer und haben nur so geguckt. Wir haben uns gefragt, ob das die Mündung ist. Der Lautsprecher hat nichts mehr gesagt, um uns etwas zu erklären. Vielleicht gehörte das Ufer mit Häusern und Anlegestellen und anderen Dingen, das wir sahen, zu einer der Inseln, wir wussten es nicht. Wir wussten nicht, ob dieses grauweiße Wasser der Jangtsekiang ist, in den der Huangpu mündet, bevor sie beide zusammen ins Meer fließen, alles war groß und unsichtbar, man wusste gar nichts mehr. Wir standen da, wo auch die Männer standen und ein paar von den Frauen, alle waren ziemlich aufgeregt und zeigten dahin und dorthin, wo man gar nichts sah. Dann war es uns zu langweilig, und wir gingen wieder rein, und auch wir wurden natürlich ausgelacht, weil wir von einer Welle erwischt worden waren. Aber der nasse Fleck auf dem Jackett hinten am Rücken von diesem jungen Mann war kein Huangpu-Wasser und auch nicht Wasser vom Jangtsekiang, aber so oder so, es hat ihm gar nichts ausgemacht. Dann hat das Schiff gewendet, alle unterhielten sich oder haben das Klo gesucht, zu essen gab es nichts mehr, also fuhren wir wieder heim.

HÜHNERFÜSSE

Die Souveränität beim Essen zeigt sich beim Essen von Hühnerfüßen, die man, gekocht und eingelegt, hier gern als kaltes Entrée genießt. Chinesen halten sich den Fuß auf die zierlichste Weise mit Stäbchen vor den Mund – wie beim Singen scheint es beim Essen aus ästhetischen Gründen verpönt zu sein, den Mund weit zu öffnen –, und nach einigem eher beiläufigen Knabbern und Kauen liegen in null Komma nichts die feinen Knöchelchen samt den fünf Krallen glatt und sauber rund um den Teller auf dem Tischtuch. Währenddessen müht sich der Westmensch, falls er sich dem ungewohnten Gericht nicht rundweg verweigert, auf die hässlichste, berserkerhafteste Art mit gebleckten Zähnen nagend und schabend, mit dem sperrigen Ding ab, versucht minutenlang, die gewonnene essbare Substanz im Mund zu zermahlen und gleichzeitig die Konversation aufrechtzuerhalten, bevor er verzweifelt – was wird nach einem solchen Auftakt wohl noch folgen? – aufgibt und, um das Tischtuch nicht zu beschmutzen, den halbgegessenen Hühnerfuß auf das Tellerchen legt, das für den Reis gedacht ist …

INNEHALTEN

In einer Stadt, die vierzehn oder fünfzehn Millionen Menschen auf einer nicht sehr ausgedehnten Fläche zusammenpresst, einer Stadt, die so ehrgeizig, so tatendurstig, so mitleidlos ist wie diese, scheinen Gewaltsamkeit und Verbissenheit im täglichen Verkehr unvermeidlich. Dass davon so wenig zu spüren ist, hängt vielleicht auch mit der kleinen, weitverbreiteten Gewohnheit des Innehaltens zusammen.

Mit Entsetzen vernehmen Chinesen Berichte von deutschen Sonntagen – ausgestorbenen Straßen, verschlossenen Geschäften, Sonntagsfahrplänen, vierundzwanzigstündiger kollektiver Erschlaffung. Hier ist der Sonntag zwar für die meisten arbeitsfrei, doch wird er nirgends heiliggehalten. Die Zeit der Arbeit und die Zeit der Ruhe stehen sich nicht antagonistisch gegenüber. Urlaub kennen nur Privilegierte.

Der Alltag ist von Pausen durchsetzt. Kaum zeigt sich irgendwo die Notwendigkeit, Müdigkeit zu bemänteln. An Bushaltestellen und überall, wo es gerade nichts zu tun gibt, sieht man Leute, die sich bequem auf die Fersen niedergelassen haben und den durch Lärm oder Hitze ausgelaugten Körper zu seinem Recht kommen lassen. (Europäer neigen in der gleichen Situation zu nervösem Auf-und-ab-Gehen.) Besonders im Sommer ist nach dem Mittagessen die ganze Stadt wie vom Zauberstab berührt. Der Pförtner am Tor,

Kinn auf der Brust, im zerschlissenen Korbsessel über der Zeitung – die Marktleute an ihren Ständen – der Fahrradmann auf dem Bürgersteig, der sonst an einer Plastikwanne mit schmutzigem Wasser unaufhörlich Schläuche flickt – die Sekretärin am Computer – Studenten beim Vortrag – Angestellte in der Zahnarztpraxis, auf den Wartebänken liegend, wo sich sonst die Patienten drängeln – der Schreiner in der Werkstatt, hingestreckt auf dem Tisch, den er eben zusammengeleimt hat – die Verkäuferinnen im Geschäft, Köpfe auf dem Ladentisch – der ausgemergelte Fahrer des Lastfahrrads, Kopf auf dem Lenker, am Straßenrand – alles ist in tiefen Dornröschenschlaf gesunken.

In den frühen Morgenstunden trifft man überall auf Leute, die mit geschlossenen Augen minutenlang still und gesammelt dastehen. Andere bewegen sich – langsam, in langen, komplizierten Folgen und Figuren. Keiner der dicht an ihnen Vorübereilenden beachtet sie, ebenso wenig wie sich die Übenden von den Passanten stören lassen. Die Entwicklung dieser erstaunlichen Fähigkeit der Konzentration, der zeitweiligen Abschottung des Eigenen von allem, was ringsum vorgeht, hängt vielleicht mit der Tatsache zusammen, dass Öffentlichkeit und Privatheit anders definiert, auf andere Weise voneinander abgegrenzt sind als im Westen. Bei der Arbeit, beim Lernen, in der Freizeit ist man fast nie vor den Blicken der Mitmenschen geschützt. Jene Fähigkeit ersetzt Wände und Türschlösser (und wird manchmal mit Teilnahmslosigkeit verwechselt). Sie hat weniger mit Ausruhen als mit bewusstem kurzzeitigem Zurücktreten von den praktischen Lebenszwecken, dem Geldverdienen und Vorwärtskommen, zu tun. Im weitesten Sinn ist auch sie eine der kleinen, vielgeübten Tugenden des Innehaltens, die ins große Kulturfach des Abstandwahrens gehört.

JING'AN-TEMPEL

Während der Kulturrevolution wurde er vorübergehend als Plastikfabrik genutzt. Heute ist der Tempel der Stille mit seinen leuchtend safrangelb gestrichenen Mauern zwischen funkelnden Riesenhotels, der Rückfront eines renovierungsbedürftigen Wohnhauses aus den sechziger Jahren und einer Großbaustelle eingeklemmt. Es ist ein Gebäudekomplex mit schönen alten, grauen Dächern, Höfen, Hallen und überdachten Gängen. Man findet darin ein Nudelrestaurant, Devotionalienläden, Arbeitsräume, Fahrradabstellplätze, Schlafräume und Büros. Überall knallen Türen, hallen Schritte, es wird nach Kräften geschwatzt und gekeift. Von weitem hört man die unaufhörlich hupenden Autos auf der Straße.

Im Hof steht neben dem großen Räuchergefäß eine immergrüne Magnolie mit staubigen braunen Blättern. Unter dem Vordach sind Tische und Stühle gestapelt. Rote Laternen baumeln an Messingständern. Der Schaukasten zeigt Fotos eines lachenden Abtes beim Bankett mit irgendeinem Politiker. Unter den Besuchern herrscht Wandertagsstimmung. Man zündet Räucherstäbchen an, wirft Münzen, bringt mit einem hölzernen Klöppel eine große bronzene Glocke zum Klingen. Zwei Mönche in langen Gewändern raufen. Ein Mann im Anzug mit Krawatte brüllt in sein Handy. Einen

Augenblick später steht er mit geschlossenen Augen, brennendes Räucherwerk in Händen, reglos da.

Vor der Gebetshalle wirbelt ein altes Mütterchen mit einem Reisigbesen Staub auf. Im Innern hängen bestickte Streifen roter Seide von der Decke. Auf dem Boden liegen abgenutzte seidene Kissen. Ein Besucher berührt den Opfertisch und streicht sich eine unsichtbare heilkräftige Substanz über den Kopf. Andere tun es ihm nach, mit nervösen Seitenblicken, als wüssten sie nicht, ob sie es auch richtig machen. In einer Ecke falten Frauen Silberpapier. An der Wand ist mit Reißzwecken ein Stadtplan befestigt. An einer anderen Wand hängt ein gerahmtes Schwarzweißfoto von einem alten Mönch mit Brille. Auf einem Regal sieht man Gummistiefel, Wasserkessel, Thermoskannen und andere Dinge von unbestreitbarer Unheiligkeit. Aber was ist heilig? Ein großer, weißer, glatthäutiger Buddha sitzt im Schneidersitz zwischen Glühlampen mit rosafarbenen Lotusblütenblättern aus Blech. Vor ihm sind Vasen mit Plastikblumen und Schalen mit Äpfeln und Pomelos aufgereiht. Er gleicht einem Händler auf dem Markt, der nach einem langen Tag auf seine noch immer nicht verkauften Waren hinunterblickt, oder einer Hausfrau, die nach dem Einkaufen nach Hause kommt und sich darüber ärgert, dass sie wieder einmal sinnlos Geld ausgegeben hat.

Ein Mönch am Eingang liest mit leerem Gesicht in einem Buch. Er kratzt sich mit schmutzigen Nägeln den Kopf. Er gähnt.

Was ist heilig?

KÄHNE

Der Bus biegt von der Beijing Lu in die Xizang Lu ein, ich bin eine Haltestelle zu weit gefahren und muss zurücklaufen. Es ist spät, die Füße tun mir weh, die Straße steigt ein wenig an und senkt sich gleich wieder, dieser kaum spürbare Buckel ist eine der vielen Brücken über den Wusong (oder Suzhou Creek), der hier nur noch eine kurze Wegstrecke zurücklegen muss, bevor er am nördlichen Ende des Bund in den Huangpu mündet. An der Brücke stauen sich Dutzende von Lastkähnen. Am Bug stehen Frauen in Gummistiefeln, Taue in Händen, schimpfend, schreiend, winkend. Die Männer stehen zwanzig Meter hinter ihnen an den Steuerrädern. Das erhöhte Kabinendach ist überall heruntergeklappt, denn die Brücke ist sehr niedrig. Es bedarf geschickten Manövrierens, um sie zu passieren. Einer der größeren Kähne ist steckengeblieben, die nachfolgenden wollen Gleiches verhindern, suchen, sich unendlich langsam, schwankend, schwerfällig bewegend, die beste Ausgangslage in der Mitte des kleinen Flusses, um unter der flachen Wölbung reibungslos durchzukommen. Auf der anderen Seite der Brücke wartet eine lange Reihe kleinerer, aneinanderhängender Boote auf die Durchfahrt in entgegengesetzter Richtung. Die Leuchtreklame einer Bowlingbahn wirft helle Lichter auf das braune, stinkende Wasser. Direkt unter mir liegen die Schiffe, deren ärmliche und schäbige Aufbauten zu ihrer imponierenden Größe, dem Freien und Majestätischen, das ihnen eignet, in groteskem Missverhältnis stehen. Die Ladung – Sand, Ziegel, Bauholz – drückt sie tief ins Wasser. Immer, wenn wieder ein Verband kleinerer, wendigerer Boote an ihnen vorbeizieht, werden die seitlichen Stege überspült, die Frauen, die die Kähne mit langen Bambusstangen in Position halten, waten in der träge schwappenden Brühe, auf der Unrat und leuchtende weiße Styroporschachteln schaukeln wie giftige Wasserlilien.

Die Unruhe auf dem dunklen Fluss überträgt sich auf mich, ich kann meine Augen nicht mehr von den Schiffen wenden, die auf merkwürdige Weise miteinander verschworen sind, hier einander schleppend, dort einander verdrängend – ein sonderbarer Kampf, eine sonderbare Gesellschaft. Das Durcheinander von Arbeitsutensilien, Eimern, Autoreifen, zerschlissenen Tauen, Fahrrädern, zusammengerollten Planen im Bug, das Unreinliche und Nachlässige der ganzen durch und durch prosaischen Szene fasziniert mich immer mehr. Scheinwerfer flammen auf, die in das Innere des stockfinsteren Brückenraums hineinleuchten, und hohl klingende Stimmen dringen von dort heraus wie aus einer Gruft. Die jungen Bootsfrauen mit langem, auf dem Rücken zusammengebundenem Haar rufen den Männern am Steuerrad zu, nicht länger zu zögern, endlich die Durchfahrt zu wagen. Stoßweise arbeiten die Motoren, die Schornsteine entlassen schwarzen Rauch in die feuchtkalte, neblige Luft, langsam dreht sich ein schwerer Kahn der Flussmitte zu. Die kleinen, wachsamen, doch nie bellenden Hunde gehen währenddessen ihren eigenen Geschäften nach, beschnüffeln einander und springen so selbstverständlich von Bord zu Bord, als wären alle Schiffe Planken eines einzigen riesigen zerbrochenen Floßes, das, vom großen Ozean hereingespült, an den steinernen Ufern des Wusong gestrandet ist.

Ich weiß nicht, wie lange ich schon hier stehe, mitten auf der Brücke, im Strom der Passanten, und hinuntersehe auf das dunkle Gedränge der Kähne, dem außer mir niemand Beachtung schenkt. Zeit und Weg und Abendessen sind gleichgültig geworden. Das Wasser glänzt und funkelt wie nasser Teer. Langanhaltendes Tuten ertönt von der anderen Seite der Brücke, es wird vom Verkehrslärm auf der Straße verschluckt. Um mich streben die Leute nach Hause. Sie sehen nicht, was ich sehe, sie sprechen ihre Sprache, als gäbe es nichts anderes. Aber ich bin fremd hier und will fremd sein an jedem Ort.

KALLIGRAPHIE

Kürzlich bekam ich eine Kalligraphie geschenkt. Ich hängte sie auf und vertiefte mich in ihre Rätsel. Die Worte wurden mir übersetzt, ich habe alles entziffert. Es ist ein tiefgründiges und strenges Gedicht, es handelt von der Zeit. Aber das ist der Inhalt und damit die einfache Seite der Sache. Was ist mit der anderen, wesentlicheren Seite, der Form, dem *einen* Zug der Schrift, der, kraftvoll, flirrend, sich verknotend, sich lösend vor meinen Augen als Bild entsteht?

Der Schreibkünstler, ein Professor der Malerei im Ruhestand, übt seit seiner Kindheit, oft mehrere Stunden am Tag, indem er, eine mit Wasser randvoll gefüllte Schale in der Armbeuge, den Pinsel handhabt. Lächelnd erzählt der alte Herr, wie sein Vater ihn in die Kunst einführte: durch Ohrfeigen bei jeder fehlerhaften Strichfolge, jeder unzulässigen Abkürzung, jeder unschönen Proportionierung der Zeichen auf dem Blatt. Heute ist er stolz, einer viele Jahrhunderte währenden Tradition anzugehören.

Sie geht auf Wang Xizhi zurück, einen gelehrten Beamten der östlichen Jin-Dynastie. Seit jener Zeit, dem dritten und vierten nachchristlichen Jahrhundert, das auch den Beginn der Malerei als selbständiger Kunstgattung markiert, zerstört und erneuert die Hand des Kalligraphen immer wieder das verbindliche Zeichensystem der Schrift. Diese Schrift ist, in ihren Grundzügen unverändert, seit über dreitausend Jahren im Gebrauch, hochbedeutend in der Verwaltung des kaiserlichen Staats. Kalligraphie als Auseinandersetzung mit Schrift hieß daher stets auch Auseinandersetzung mit der herrschenden Kultur. Mit ihr verband sich ein den Zwängen des politischen Zeremoniells, der ehernen Hierarchie der Verwaltung, den offiziellen Leitsätzen entgegengesetzter Geist der Einkehr, des kontrollierten Nichtdenkens, der konzentrierten Spontaneität. Gewünscht wurde, was im öffentlichen Leben verpönt war, der freie Ausdruck der innersten Persönlichkeit, des Individuums.

(Was bedeutet es für die Kalligraphie, wenn die Schrift als allgemeines Bindeglied und verlässliches Wissensreservoir verlorengeht und in wesentlichen Bereichen der kulturellen Produktion durch künstliche, schnell veraltende Codes zur Speicherung von Information ersetzt wird? Auf dem verwandten Gebiet der Landschaftsmalerei stellt sich die Frage vielleicht noch krasser. Auch wenn ihr Zweck nie die einfache Darstellung eines Ortes gewesen ist, so muss eine in vorindustrieller Zeit gemalte Landschaft doch anders beurteilt werden als ein heutiges Bild, das jenem in Technik und Thematik gleicht. Wird die bis jetzt unverändert hochgeschätzte Schreibkunst zum harmlosen Anachronismus herunterkommen, kann sie mehr sein als Folklore, belächeltes Hobby alter Männer, die sich, wassergefüllte Schale in der Armbeuge, sinnlosen Exerzitien hingeben?)

Heute findet sich Kalligraphie an vielen Orten, wo der Anspruch auf Kultur erhoben wird. Der Namenszug von Zeitungen wird von der Hand bedeutender Staatsmänner gestaltet; Universitäten tragen ihren Namen, geschrieben von bekannten Wissenschaftlern oder anerkannten Persönlichkeiten des gesellschaftlichen Lebens, in Stein und Gips über dem Tor und als Logo auf ihren Urkunden; Ehrentafeln, Gedenksteine, Mahnmale kommen nicht ohne Kalligraphien berühmter Literaten oder Politiker aus, und in Amtsstuben, Wartesälen, Geschäften und Restaurants hängen Kalligraphien gerahmt an der Wand, um allgemeine moralische Grundsätze bekanntzugeben oder den Duft von Speisen zu loben.

Nachdem ich im Shanghai Museum zum ersten Mal eine Anzahl berühmter Kalligraphien konzentriert betrachtet hatte, fuhr ich mit dem Bus nach Hause. Ich dachte über Balance und Rhythmik, die wilde, exzentrische Schönheit einiger Schriften nach, die ich gesehen hatte; ich versank immer tiefer in Gedanken über diese einzigartige Kunst, die Schrift ist und Bild und in den imponierendsten Beispielen von Texten in Kursivschrift sich auf einem äußersten Grat als symbolische Mitteilung behauptet, während sie gleichzeitig nichts ist und sein will als reine, konkrete, unverwechselbare und unwiederholbare Spur des Augenblicks. Der Bus geriet in einen Stau. Plötzlich sah ich mich mit einem Pappschild konfrontiert, auf dem mit dem Pinsel etwas wie ein Gedicht gemalt war. Die Schriftzeichen erschienen mir von ebensolcher Souveränität des Ausdrucks und Vollkommenheit der Komposition wie die soeben im Museum gesehenen, und es dauerte mehrere Minuten, bis mein in Bewunderung erstarrter Blick zu den Zahlen (arabisch geschrieben) vordrang, die den wesentlichen Bestandteil des Textes ausmachten und verrieten, dass es sich um ein Verkaufsschild für die darunter aufgehäuften Billigschuhe aus Lederimitat handelte. Ähnliches ist mir seitdem immer wieder passiert. Kaum meine ich, etwas von Kalligraphie begriffen zu haben, werde ich mir meiner völligen Ahnungslosigkeit bewusst. Diese Kunst ist Hand-Werk, alles kommt darauf an, wie flüssig, wie subtil, wie nah oder fern dem Muster der alten Meister der Pinsel geführt wird, und gerade das ist für den an andere Schrift und Schreibwerkzeuge gewöhnten Fremden am schwersten zu erkennen.

In einem ihrer Bücher über chinesische Kunst bemerkt Jessica Rawson, dass der Westen, geblendet von handwerklicher und ästhetischer Perfektion der Waren, die auf den Handelsschiffen der Portugiesen, Spanier, Holländer und Engländer von China nach Europa kamen, die von Chinesen selbst am höchsten geschätzten Hervorbringungen ihrer Kultur nie kennenlernte. Seide, Tee, Porzellan waren von jeher begehrte Luxusgüter. Doch von den großen kaiserlichen Sammlungen mit Bronzegefäßen, Jadeobjekten und Kalligraphien wusste man im Ausland lange nichts. »Hinter der Raffinesse der Oberfläche seiner Luxusgüter«, schreibt Jessica Rawson, »blieb das Land ebenso wirkungsvoll verborgen wie einst hinter den physischen Barrieren – Bergen und Wüsten – seiner Geographie.«

Kürzlich bekam ich eine Kalligraphie geschenkt. Hier hängt sie nun und gibt mir ihre Rätsel auf.

KARAOKE

Aufruf der Ersten Internationalen Antikaraokeliga (EIAKL). An alle denkenden Menschen! Von vielen unerkannt oder bewusst verharmlost, greift die verheerende Seuche immer mehr um sich. Tausende und Abertausende unscheinbarer städtischer Lokale stellen Tausende und Abertausende von Infektionsherden dar. Tausende und Abertausende von Buchhaltern, Spinnereifacharbeiterinnen, Assistant-Managern, Architektinnen, Rohrlegern, Pfannkuchenbäckern, Kindergartendirektorinnen und viele andere brave Mitglieder eines glorreichen Volkes haben sich angesteckt. Abend für Abend dröhnt und blökt, zirpt und säuselt es aus Tausenden und Abertausenden von Mündern. Tausende und Abertausende von unerträglich einfallslosen, banalen und stupiden Melodien, durchsetzt von unerträglich stupiden, infantilen, gemeinen und verlogenen Texten, begleitet von unerträglich billigen, stupiden, kitschigen, einfallslosen und verlogenen Bildern vereinen sich zu einem wahrhaft infernalischen Geheul, das die Stratosphäre durchdringt und den Saum des himmlischen Bühnenvorhangs in Schwingung versetzt. Was aber lauert hinter dem Vorhang? Was würden all diese mitleiderregenden Kranken erblicken, wenn sie es wagten, dem Applaus zu misstrauen, den Vorhang herunterzureißen, den Gott zu entlarven, den sie vor dem Altar ihrer

Bildschirme anbeten? Den Satan der elektronischen Ersatzwelt, den gefräßigen Moloch der Unterhaltungsindustrie! Ehrliche Arbeit und echte Geselligkeit verachtend, weiß er seine Opfer unter den Arbeitenden und Geselligen zu finden und schlägt gerade dort auf das brutalste zu! Wer einmal den würdigen Vorstand einer ernsten Institution, die holdselige Mitarbeiterin einer ruhmreichen Bürogemeinschaft mit dem Mikrofon in der Hand schief und befangen vor dem Bildschirm stehen sah, wo sie mit blecherner Stimme die Begleitung zu einem Video herunterleiern, das sich an Peinlichkeit mit nichts auf der Welt vergleichen lässt, dem muss das Herz bluten wie dem Schreiber dieser Zeilen. Gibt es noch Hoffnung? Bürger! Genossen! Freunde! Lasst nicht zu, dass die Seuche weiter um sich greift! Setzt den profitgierigen Verbrechern, die aus geselligen Runden primitive Horden stammelnder Sklaven zu machen suchen, euer entschiedenes Nein entgegen! Erinnert euch! Denkt an die anregenden Erzählungen und aufmunternden Gespräche, den herzlichen Austausch, das schöne gemeinsame Liedersingen, das man einst in freudvoller Runde pflegte! Grabt aber auch die schlimmsten Szenen des letzten großen Angriffs auf die Kultur unseres Vaterlandes aus dem erschöpften Boden eures Gedächtnisses aus – kaum drei Jahrzehnte liegt sein Beginn zurück –, um euch gegen den ganz andersartigen Angriff eines ganz anderen Feindes zu wappnen! Unterschätzt nicht seine Vernichtungsgewalt! Nachbeten und Nachsingen ist eins! Wisst ihr nicht mehr, wohin das massenhafte Nachbeten verlogener Worte führte? Damals waren es Parolen, heute sind es billige Schlager! Karaoke zersetzt das Gehirn! Karaoke ist Vermarktung der Imagination, Vernebelung der Sehnsucht, Verhöhnung von Gefühl und Verstand! Karaoke ist Verdummung! Karaoke muss bekämpft werden! Diesem Aufruf werden weitere folgen. Verbreitet sie in Büros und Klassenräumen, Werkstätten und Kantinen! Knüpft Gespräche an! Macht Kollegen, Freunden, Verwandten klar, was auf dem Spiel steht! Bietet dem Übel die Stirn, wo es sich zeigt! Tretet der Ersten Internationalen Antikaraokeliga (EIAKL), der unbeugsamen Avantgarde der internationalen Karaokegegner bei! Seid wachsam! Widersteht!

KOMMUNISTEN

Man sieht sie im Fernsehen, bei Kongressen, Einweihungen, Urkundenüberreichungen aller Art. Man hört und liest von ihren unermüdlichen Bemühungen, die Staatsbetriebe umzugestalten und der Arbeitslosigkeit Herr zu werden, ihrem heldenhaften Kampf gegen Schlamperei und Korruption, ihren stets von Erfolg gekrönten Anstrengungen, das Land am Strudel der ostasiatischen Finanzkrise vorbeizusteuern. Aber im wirklichen Leben? Wo trifft man sie?

In meiner Klasse ist einer. An seiner Jeansjacke steckt die Flagge der Volksrepublik. Er ist vierundzwanzig. Er hat das Fach Marketing studiert, weil das seinem Vater aussichtsreich erschien, und nebenbei Bücher gelesen, ein paar Romane, vieles über Kultur und Gesellschaft, auch einige Werke von »Chairman Mao«. Sein Großvater, der in Yan'an lebte, habe »Chairman Mao« sogar einmal gesehen, sagt er lächelnd und etwas herablassend. Er lächelt dauernd, wegen seiner furchtbaren Schüchternheit. Er hat feine, weiche Hände und schlechte Haut, seine Stimme ist mädchenhaft leise. Er trägt eine große Brille mit dicken Gläsern. Er fragt mich, warum den Deutschen Honecker nicht gefallen habe. Honecker sei auch Kommunist gewesen. Kommunismus sei das Beste für die Welt und für China. Kommunismus bedeute, dass alle Leute Geld hätten und Arbeit und sich wohlfühlten. Einmal trank er bei einer Party ein paar Glas Bier, und weil er es nicht gewöhnt ist, Bier zu trinken, war er sofort betrunken. Er bekam kaum noch einen zusammenhängenden Satz zustande, kicherte ununterbrochen, stammelte unausgegorenes Zeug und schlenkerte auf eine merkwürdige Weise mit seinen langen Armen in der Luft herum. Nachdem er eine Weile in einem Sessel gedöst hatte, beugte er sich plötzlich vor und sagte, langsam und mit feuerrotem Kopf: »Alle Menschen sind Brüder.« Ich antwortete obenhin mit einem von den Umstehenden mit lautem Lachen aufgenommenen Scherz über die bei erhöhtem Alkoholkonsum proportional erhöhte Bereitschaft, Dinge dieser Art zu denken und zu glauben.

Das verzeihe ich mir nicht.

KOPFSTIMME

Die chinesische Oper – in Shanghai wird neben der Pekingoper in zahlreichen Theatern die ältere Kunoper dargeboten – ist eine aus vielen einzelnen, höchst komplexen und standardisierten Fertigkeiten zusammengesetzte Kunstform, in die nicht leicht einzudringen ist, wenn man mit westlichen Augen zu schauen und mit westlichen Ohren zu hören gewohnt ist. Die der Kunoper zugrunde liegenden Stücke stammen von Dichtern aus der Zeit der Yuan- und Ming-Dynastien. Sie sind zu lang, um an einem Abend zusammenhängend gespielt zu werden, man beschränkt sich daher auf einzelne Akte. Manchmal werden von Akt zu Akt die Sänger/Darsteller der Hauptrollen ausgewechselt, so dass das Publikum die Möglichkeit erhält, Vergleiche zu ziehen. Oft singen Frauen Männerpartien, es gibt auch Männer, die Frauenrollen spielen. Das Stimmtraining für die einzelnen Rollen beginnt im frühen Kindesalter, im Alter zwischen dreißig und vierzig erreichen die Sänger ihre höchsten Leistungen. Sie singen nicht nur lange Melodien in einer Sprache, die von Ungebildeten heute kaum noch zu verstehen ist, sondern müssen auch die jede Rolle charakterisierenden Gesten, die der Musik entsprechenden Schrittfolgen, Hand- und Fingerhaltungen, Kopfdrehungen, Augenbewegungen usw. beherrschen. Auch die Art, wie man Gewänder und Kopf-putz zu tragen hat, die langen Ärmel wie Flügel oder Fahnen einladend oder abweisend schüttelt, aufrollt, zurückschiebt, den Fächer als Ausdrucksmittel einsetzt, bedarf des jahrelangen Trainings. Dazu kommt das Wissen darum, wie man sich der Rolle entsprechend schminkt, Instrumentenkunde, Wissen um poetische Techniken und vieles mehr. Man kann nicht umhin, die Leistungen der Sänger, die somit gleichzeitig Schauspieler und Tänzer (und manchmal Akrobaten) sein müssen, zu bewundern. Wie kommt es, dass sich dennoch kaum ein Westmensch für die chinesische Oper begeistern lässt? Was macht uns Schwierigkeiten beim Verständnis dieser hohen Kunst?

Ich glaube, es sind vor allem die Töne der Kopfstimme, die uns abstoßen.

Das Spektrum der Töne, über die ein Sänger der chinesischen Oper verfügt, ist größer als in der westlichen Gesangskunst. Die für die weiblichen, aber auch manche männlichen Rollen kennzeichnenden hohen, grellen, gedehnten und kreisförmig ausgestalteten Töne werden in China gerade wegen ihrer extremen Künstlichkeit geschätzt, in Westeuropa aber, wo heute die dumpfen Klänge der Bässe höchste Popularität genießen, gehören sie kaum mehr in den Bereich dessen, was als Kunst ernst genommen wird. Sie werden als hysterisch und abnorm bewertet. Sie klingen nicht musikalisch.

Die Kopfstimmen der chinesischen Oper verlangen vom westlichen Hörer Kopfarbeit. Ohne Einsicht in die Beschränkungen der kulturellen Normen, die unsere Hörgewohnheiten formen, ist der Reichtum dieses Gesangs nicht zu vernehmen. Ohne Anstrengung des Denkens bleibt uns der Musikgenuss versagt. Ohne Wissen sind diese kunstvollen

Töne nur Katzenmusik. (Bedeutet das einen bloßen Wechsel der Normen? Wäre es möglich, unsere Hörgewohnheiten völlig zu überwinden? Könnte es gelingen – in einem Augenblick zwischen Wissen und Vergessen, Entdecken, Verwerfen und Neulernen –, zur Erfahrung dessen vorzustoßen, was Töne sind, bevor Musik aus ihnen wurde?)

LASTER

Staubig sind sie, himmelblau. Lehmbespritzt und grob von Gesicht, breitnasig, mit Gaben hoch bepackt. (Eisenträger Stahlstangen Honigmelonen Kabelrollen Eierkartons Zementsäcke Ziegelsteine schnatternde Gänse Ölkanister Reissäcke) Die Achsen durchhängend. Die Ladung mit Stricken verschnürt. Vom Dreck des Landes die Scheiben verschmiert. An den Kotflügeln fressend der Rost.

Von weit her kommen sie.

Der Phönix tanzt.

Sie haben die Straßen des Südens gesehen. (Betonweiler stinkende Kanäle Wäscherinnen pinkelnde Kinder Melonenverkäufer schnatternde Gänse Maulbeerbäume magere Rücken der Straßenarbeiter Strohhüte Wasserbüffel Schlaglöcher Fabrikschlote Schlaglöcher) Sie werden erwartet.

Nachts kommen sie.

Der Himmel glüht.

Braune Männer sitzen in der Kabine, zugeknöpfte Jacken, Zigaretten im Mund, aneinandergelehnt.

Drei Könige.

Mit müden Augen starren sie die Stadt an, den neuen Stern.

Der Duft des Südens klebt in ihrem blauen Haar. Der Rost des Südens frisst an ihren Flügeln.

Amulette am Spiegel. (Glöckchen Fische zarter Phönix mit hellem Schweif) Was vermögen Phönixe gegen die Macht der Stadt?

Der Phönix bebt und tanzt.

Nachts höre ich sie. (Nachts wenn ich wach liege in meinem Käfig) Sie tuten wie Schiffe.

Sternhell die Augen der Schlaflosen.

Rauch im Mund, verschwiegen der Blick.

Der Staub des Südens wirbelt in der Luft. Ratternde Räder. Lose Stricke, Kronen im Sturm. Der Duft der Erde erfrischt den Asphalt. (Gebeugte Rücken der Bauern Strohhüte grüner Reis leuchtende Felder Brücken Kanäle Boote Wäscherinnen Wasserbüffel pinkelnde Kinder dampfende Felder graue Wolken) O Licht!

Der Morgen graut, der falsche Stern verglüht.

Die Stadt ist ein enger Käfig. Doch der Himmel des Südens ist nah.

LAUTSPRECHER

Menschen aus dem Westen assoziieren Lautsprecher, aus denen frühmorgens Marschmusik, mittags Schlager, bei besonderen Anlässen Kommandos, Parolen oder über mehrere Stunden die Reden politischer Führer dröhnen, quäken, scheppern, gern mit dem totalen Staat orwellscher Prägung, besonders wenn sie gezwungen sind, eine Zeitlang (auf dem Gelände einer Schule oder Universität) direkt neben einem dieser Lautsprecher zu wohnen. Die Musik ist laut und roh, die Parolen sind einfältig, die Reden ohne Witz und Wahrheit. Lautsprecher stören. Lautsprecher dringen in die Privatsphäre ein. Lautsprechern ist man hilflos ausgeliefert. Man hat allerdings immer weniger Anlass, sich über den Lautsprecherterror zu beklagen, denn Lautsprecher sind heute seltener in Gebrauch. Heute gibt es Fernsehen. Fernsehen stört nicht. Im Fernsehen spricht man manierlich, die Informationen sind interessant, die Programme vielfältig, die Bilder schuldlos. Die größte und am liebsten geglaubte Lüge aber ist die von der Möglichkeit, sich der Macht des Fernsehens per Knopfdruck zu entziehen.

LONGHUA-MÄRTYRERFRIEDHOF

Ein parkähnliches Gelände am Stadtrand, wo man zwischen Bäumen und Rabatten, Gedenksteinen, Springbrunnen und einschüchternden Monumentalskulpturen spazieren gehen kann. Trotz des Dunstes ist in der Ferne die Pagode von Longhua mit ihren sieben geschwungenen Dächern sichtbar. In der Mitte befindet sich das Museum, eine von terrassenförmig ansteigenden Steinwürfeln eingefasste gläserne Pyramide, an die Louvre-Pyramide in Paris erinnernd. Breite Treppen führen zu ihr empor. Unter aufgespannten Sonnenschirmen kontrollieren uniformierte Wächter die Eintrittskarten. Im Innern wird der spiegelnde Marmor, das Glas der Schaukästen von blaugekleideten Putzfrauen mit Staubtüchern und Wischlappen ständig gewienert. Von der Decke hängen rote geraffte Behänge. Auf Ölgemälden führen breitschultrige Helden mit Pistolen und roten Fahnen ihre zum Opfertod bereiten Genossen zum ewigen Triumph. Im ersten Stock hat man jenes unscheinbare Zimmer nachgebaut, wo im Juli 1921 in Shanghai die Kommunistische Partei gegründet wurde. Die Helden der ersten Stunde saßen auf einfachen Hockern, tranken Tee und rauchten. Diese einfachen Hocker, diese Teetassen, diese Aschenbecher sind zweifellos heilige Dinge. Von den sonntäglichen Ausflüglern werden sie andächtig bestaunt. An den Wänden hängen, durch die Vergrößerung unscharf geworden, die glühend ernsten Gesichter junger Männer und Frauen, hinter Glas sieht man die Titelseiten der von ihnen gegründeten Zeitschriften, man sieht Briefe, die sie aus dem Gefängnis an ihre Mütter schrieben, Fotos, die sie im Kreis der Kommilitonen in Frankreich zeigen. In den Vitrinen darunter liegen Gegenstände, die ihnen gehörten: »Wollschal, von Zhang Xihuan getragen«, »Petroleumkocher, von Lin Yunan benutzt«, »Ledertasche, von Li Hanjun benutzt«, »Yang Xingfus Tagebuch«, »Zhang Yuans Adressbuch« usw. Es sind Reliquien, von höheren Wesen auf der Erde zurückgelassen, die von uns Sterblichen die gebührende Verehrung verlangen.

Am Ausgang liegt das Besucherbuch. »Das Klo zu finden ist wirklich schwer«, lesen wir. Auf einer anderen Seite: »Wir schlagen Ihnen vor, ein paar kleine Geschäfte einzurichten, zur besseren Versorgung der Reisenden.« Darunter: »Die Kämpfer sind immer in unserer Erinnerung.«

Nach dem Museumsrundgang gelangt man zum ewigen Feuer mit dem Grabmal des unbekannten Märtyrers. Pomp und Kitsch. Dann führt der Weg durch einen unterirdischen Gang an das nördliche Ende der Gedenkstätte zu einem einst berüchtigten Gefängnis der Guomindang, wo im April 1927 Hunderte von aufständischen Shanghaiern gefangen gehalten und hingerichtet wurden. Es war der Beginn des Bürgerkriegs, der im ganzen Land Hunderttausende von Opfern fordern sollte. Da die Ausflügler nach dem langen Weg schon etwas fußlahm sind, wird das Gefängnis im Schnelldurchgang absolviert. Frauenzellen, Männerzellen, manche leer, andere mit engen Stockbetten und schmutzverkrustetem Eimer in der Ecke, winzige Fenster hoch oben unter der Decke, Stacheldraht, Vernehmungsräume, Folterkammern mit dunklen, abgetretenen Dielenbrettern. Eine Inschrift weist darauf hin, dass man nach Öffnung des Gefängnisses von den Revolutionären verfasste und in die Wände geritzte Gedichte fand. Weiter geht es zum Exekutionsplatz. Goldene Schriftzeichen auf Marmortafeln, Zahlen der Erschossenen, Verstümmelten, Vermissten. Wehendes Haar grimmiger Helden im Halbrelief, gereckte Fäuste aus Stein. Am Rand des Springbrunnens endlich Gelegenheit zum Ausruhen. Die Sonne sticht. Unter dem Dach eines weißen Betonpavillons sucht man Schatten. Wasserflaschen und Erfrischungen kommen zum Vorschein. Schlafenden Babys wird Luft zugefächelt. Man knipst einander. Lärm, Gelächter, Geschnatter. Vor der kahlen Wand am Exekutionsplatz spielen drei dicke Kinder Blindekuh.

MÄRKTE (1)

Hier das Gemüse, grüne Tomaten, hellrote, dunkelrote, zu Pyramiden aufgetürmt, und Rettiche, kleine runde und große ovale, lila und weiße und lila-weiße ... ein großer Haufen dünner, grellrot leuchtender Auberginen ... Kartoffeln, Morcheln, Erbsenberge ... grün-rote Blätter, was ist das? ... und das, zartgrün und weiß, wie Sellerie ... und das, und das ... die schmutzigen, rotbäckigen Kinder der Gemüsefrauen jagen ein mageres Kätzchen mit Glöckchen um den Hals ... hier das Obst, daneben der Abfall ... eine alte Frau stochert darin herum, steckt dies und das in die Tasche ... klingelnde Fahrräder, der Kopf eines halbtoten Huhns baumelnd auf dem Gepäckträger ... und hier die Fische, zahllose Arten in Plastikwannen mit plätschernden Wasserschläuchen ... grün-schwarz gescheckt, mit Bart, wie Drachen ... lang und träge, mit spitzem Maul ... flach, braun, monströs ... klein, rund, regenbogenschillernd ... und das, und das ... die Fischhändler in hohen Gummistiefeln ... rote Hände ... sie schlagen die Fische ein paarmal nachlässig auf den Boden, dann schneiden sie die zuckenden Leiber mit der Schere auf ... silberne Schuppen schwimmen auf dem Blut, dem klebrigen Gedärm ... blutige Köpfe, die Mäuler schnappen nach Luft ... die Zähne, die Augen, tiefschwarz und glasig ... lange Reihen ausgeweideter, mit Hölzchen aufgespreizter Trocken-fische … rosa Adern im farblosen Fleisch der Tintenfische … und Krebse, Garnelen, Schildkröten, Schlangen … quakende Frösche, sie springen gegen das Netz, klettern übereinander, gleiten aus und springen und fallen zurück … gelbe Streifen auf moosgrüner Warzenhaut … und das … hupend bahnt sich ein Motorrad seinen Weg, *wei, wei!* … kleine Aale werden aus dem Wasser geholt, lebendig an einen Nagel auf ein Brett gespießt und enthäutet … Blut, Blut gurgelt im Gully … Uiguren mit bunten Käppis halten gelbe fette Rosinen feil … und hier der Tofu, ein Stand und noch einer … und Hühner, Enten, Tauben, Wachteln, piepsend, gurrend, schnatternd in schmutzigen Käfigen übereinandergestapelt … da hängt ein Vogel, der sich zwischen den Gitterstäben selbst stranguliert hat … alte Männer schneiden den Vögeln mit der Schere die Hälse durch, rupfen sie mit beiden Händen, die Federn stieben durch die Luft … und Eier, blaue Enteneier und Eier in erdigem Pelz … und Ingwer und Chili und Zimt … Geschrei … der Händler nimmt die Waage, Zigarette im Mund, die Frau keift auf ihn ein … und Algen und Quallen und Glibberfrüchte, in Fässern eingelegt … ist das Seegurke? … und das, und das … Frauen stricken … eine bricht große Muscheln auf und holt mit einem Schnitt das weiche Innere heraus … Kinder in Laufställen, alten Körben ohne Boden, an Orangen lutschend … Schweinsköpfe, Schweinsfüße, Kutteln … eine braune Rinderzunge in einer Schüssel mit Brühe … ein Berg von Herzen und Nieren, ein Schwarm Fliegen … ein schielender Mann wetzt sein Messer … eine alte Frau mit einem Bottich, auf einem Puppenwagen montiert, verkauft Tee-Eier … an der eisernen Standwaage werden Reissäcke gewogen … und hier die Säcke mit Trockenobst, und schwarzer Sesam … und Bohnen und Bambus und Lotus … und das … wo ist das gewachsen, wie schmeckt das? … und das … ein Korb voll duftendem Korianderkraut … Hühnerfüße mit langen Nägeln wie Leichenhände … und das, und das …

MÄRKTE (2)

Es ist noch nicht lange her, dass freie Märkte wieder erlaubt sind in China. Zu Beginn der fünfziger Jahre wurde der überregionale Handel im Zuge der Fünf-Anti-Kampagne als kriminelle Spekulation und damit besonders schlimme Form kapitalistischer Ausbeutung bezeichnet und vom Staat übernommen. Not und Mangel, das Warten in der Schlange im Morgengrauen, um ein paar frische Lebensmittel zu erstehen, haben die Städter längst noch nicht vergessen.

Märkte sind Bilder des Überflusses.

Die Freude an der Öffnung, an der Möglichkeit, auf eigene Faust Geschäfte zu machen, die Lust, frische und neue Sachen zu arrangieren, zu betrachten und auszuprobieren, ist heute überall spürbar. Märkte sind Augen- und Ohrenweiden. Kein Wohngebiet kommt ohne Markt aus. Außer Lebensmittelmärkten gibt es Kleidermärkte, Blumen- und Vogelmärkte, Teemärkte, Märkte für Schuhe, Stoffe, Werkzeug und Schnürsenkel. Wer tagsüber nicht das Rechte gefunden hat, versucht sein Glück auf einem der Nachtmärkte, wo es unaufhörlich dudelt und plärrt und klimpert und krakeelt, weil Musikinstrumente, Fernseher, Radios, Wecker den stets skeptischen und überkritischen Kunden zeigen müssen, was in ihnen steckt.

Märkte sind keine Supermärkte, keine bloßen Warenumschlagplätze. Das Handeln, das den Tausch begleitet, ist mehr als das Fixieren von Preisen. Man betrachte die Metamorphose braver Hausfrauen und Mütter beim täglichen Einkauf – wie sie mit wilder Gier nach allem greifen und grapschen, was vor ihnen ausgebreitet ist, alles betasten, beschnüffeln und in der Hand herumdrücken, um wegen eines winzigen braunen Flecks, einer kaum sichtbaren Delle den wackeren Landmann höhnisch und giftig zu beschimpfen – wie Letzterer kleinlaut sein Angebot nach noch saftigeren, noch makelloseren Produkten durchwühlt – wie sich jene Hausfrauen und Mütter nun ins Zeug legen mit Jammern und Schmeicheln, Zanken und Keifen und der Händler mithält und nach minutenlangem schrillem Gefeilsche hin und her missmutig nach der Waage greift und zähneknirschend das Wechselgeld herausgibt – diese Käufer sind keine bloßen Verbraucher, diese Verkäufer keine Businessmen; hinter den Masken der Warenhüter und Geldbesitzer kommen die Leute mit ihren Bedürfnissen zum Vorschein, hinter dem Austausch von Gegenständen hitzige Beziehungen, Herausforderungen, Demütigungen, Kämpfe und Arrangements.

Märkte sind Orte, wo man sich trifft und vergleicht. Wer auf den Markt geht, genießt auch das, was er als Einzelner sich nicht leisten kann. Begehrliche Blicke versichern sich des Überflusses, der neben der Knappheit des privaten Daseins anschaulich und greifbar vorhanden ist, eines Überflusses, der sich in der noch so großen Zahl käuflicher Dinge nicht erschöpfen kann und mehr ist als alles, was es zu kaufen gibt.

Wenn es Abend wird, die Käufer und Gaffer sich verlaufen und die Händler die übrig gebliebenen Waren verstaut, die Einnahmen gezählt haben, kehrt Ruhe ein auf dem Markt. Man setzt sich zum Essen. Man wäscht sich an demselben

Wasserhahn auf der Straße, wo man eben noch die Fische für die Kunden säuberte. Viele Marktleute schlafen hier, in winzigen Hinterstübchen, in denen auch die Waren lagern, auf dünnen Matratzen, hinter Plastikplanen und Bretterwänden. Einsam und elend zeigt sich der Markt, wenn der Glanz des Begehrens ihn nicht mehr erleuchtet, und die Illusion des Überflusses ist ebenso schnell verflogen, wie der Duft der frischen Früchte in den fauligen Modergeruch übergegangen ist, der über diesen Bruchbuden hängt.

MENSCHENFRESSER

Es gibt keinen objektiven, übernationalen Standpunkt, wenn es um die Barbarei geht, zu der eine Gesellschaft sich fähig gezeigt hat. Die Negation der eigenen Kultur, das Innewerden der eigenen Destruktivität ist schlimmer als das Wissen um die Grausamkeit anderer. Das Entsetzen über die Gräuel der eigenen Geschichte, die eigenen Landsleute, sich selbst, ist tiefer als der heilige Zorn über die Verbrechen der anderen. Doch vielleicht beginnt mit diesem Entsetzen das notwendige Sichauseinandersetzen, in dessen Verlauf man zu dem, was naturhaft über einen gekommen ist, Distanz gewinnt und Freiheit, die Zukunft in die Hand zu nehmen.

Lu Xuns *Tagebuch eines Verrückten* beschreibt dieses Entsetzen. Ein Mensch wird sich allmählich der Barbarei bewusst, die für seine Landsleute alltägliche Wirklichkeit ist. Seine Nachbarn und Freunde, die Mitglieder seiner Familie sind Menschenfresser, und sie haben es auf ihn abgesehen. Ist Schlimmeres denkbar? Der Verzweifelte hält den Barbaren eine flammende Rede: »Ändert euch sofort, ändert euch von Grund auf! Ihr müsst wissen, die Zukunft wird für Menschenfresser keinen Platz mehr haben …« Noch glaubt er an seine eigene Unschuld, noch kennt er nicht die ganze Geschichte. Erst am Ende wird er des Schlimmsten gewahr: dass auch er vom Fleisch seiner Schwester gegessen hat, dass er selbst zu den Menschenfressern gehört.

Lu Xun schrieb diese Erzählung 1918. Sie erschien in der berühmten Zeitschrift *Neue Jugend* und war der erste erzählende Text der chinesischen Literatur, der in der Volkssprache abgefasst war. Die Zeitgenossen verstanden sie als Anklage gegen den seit Jahrhunderten das Land auszehrenden erstarrten Konfuzianismus. Aber sie ist mehr als das. Denn jede Generation hat mit ihren eigenen Menschenfressern zu tun, und immer ist die Menschenfresserei ein Phänomen, das nicht nur die anderen betrifft. Vielleicht steht die Kraft dieses Textes, sein aus tiefster Bitternis, aus wahrem Entsetzen entspringender Humor mit der Kraft der damaligen Bewegung zur Erneuerung und Verbesserung der Gesellschaft in Zusammenhang. Und umgekehrt könnte man mutmaßen, dass die verharmlosenden Interpretationen, die der Erzählung in neueren Ausgaben beigepackt sind, mit der Schwäche der heutigen Bewegung zur Erneuerung und Verbesserung der Gesellschaft in Zusammenhang stehen.

Heute spricht niemand von Menschenfressern. Viel ist von Fehlern die Rede, von Verirrung und Verblendung. Aber niemand äußert Entsetzen. Daraus kann geschlossen werden, dass die Auseinandersetzung mit der Barbarei, zu der diese Gesellschaft sich fähig gezeigt hat, noch nicht begonnen hat.

MONDFEST

Im Herbst verschenkt man den Mond in Form von kleinen, kreisrunden Kuchen mit üppiger Füllung verschiedener Art. Wochen vor dem Fest gibt es sie schon überall zu kaufen. Es gibt Mondkuchenreklameplakate in den Schaufenstern, Mondkuchenreklamespots im Fernsehen, Mondkuchenreklameparaden mit trommelnden Mädchen in Phantasieuniformen auf den großen Geschäftsstraßen. Vor dem Laden des berühmtesten Mondkuchenherstellers der Stadt bilden sich endlose, von Ordnern in Schach gehaltene Schlangen. Am Eingang ein lärmendes, schwitzendes Gewoge, ab und zu Handgreiflichkeiten. Autos hupen, Kinder spielen zwischen den Beinen der Wartenden, Fahrräder und Lastkarren schieben sich durch den Menschenauflauf, Zeitungsverkäufer rufen, auf und ab defilierend, ihre Zeitungen aus. Jeden Tag wiederholt sich das, von früh bis spät, bis zum Mondfest.

Am Mondfest soll sich die Familie versammeln und den Mond anschauen, heißt es. In Wahrheit ist es der Mond, der, erschreckend dünn und kalt und blass vor Neid, herabblickt auf die lärmende und schwitzende, mondkuchenbäuchige Erde.

NACHTWÄCHTER

Wenn es dunkel geworden ist, machen ältere Männer und Frauen des Nachbarschaftskomitees, eine Glocke schlagend, ihre tägliche Runde durch die schlechtbeleuchteten Gassen der Wohnsiedlung. Es ist Zeit, sich für die Nacht zu rüsten, die Türen zu schließen, das Gas abzudrehen … Mit dem Ton der Glocke taucht wie auf einem versenkbaren Podest die Gestalt des Nachtwächters vor mir auf, und mit ihm all die anderen – der Reifenflicker, der Altmetallsammler, der Grillenverkäufer, der Scherenschleifer, der Nachttopfleerer, der Schlüsselmacher, der Entenröster, der Schwammschneider, der Uhrenreparierer, der Abfallsortierer, die Duftblütenverkäuferin, der Baumwolldeckenweber, der Scherenschnittmeister, der Nudelmacher … Und plötzlich scheinen zwei Zeiten nebeneinander zu existieren, eine, die den globalen Maschinen gehorcht, und eine andere, die von einer anderen, kleineren und näheren Ordnung abstammt und andere Lebensweisheiten, Tätigkeiten, Verhältnisse hervorbringt. Doch schon springt, elektronisch gesteuert, der Zeiger meiner Uhr auf den nächsten Strich; die andere Zeit weicht klaglos der einen, einzigen, die selbstsicher die Weltherrschaft beansprucht; der Nachwächter verschwindet mit seinem ganzen Gefolge in den stockfinsteren Gassen, und der Ton seiner Glocke macht dem Lärm der Fernseher Platz.

NESCAFÉ

Wer modern ist, trinkt Nescafé. Jeder kennt die Leuchtreklame über dem Bund: eine rote Tasse mit schwarzem Inhalt, davon aufsteigend eine ständig sich neu formierende Wolke weiß wabernden Dampfs. Der Werbespot im Fernsehen ist eine Angestelltenromanze im vollcomputerisierten Büro. In Supermärkten bietet man das teure Pulver im Glas auch im Geschenkkarton an, auf glänzendem rosa Stoff, zusammen mit Kaffeeweißer, Kaffeebecher und Kaffeelöffel oder mit beliebten Schlagerkassetten. Ob der jungfräuliche Markt, nach westlicher Berührung lechzend, das neue Konsumgut angenommen hat? Das ist die Frage. Mit allen Wassern gewaschen, findet sich das braun gedeckelte Schraubglas auf Werkbänken und Schultischen, neben Fahrersitzen, hinter Postschaltern und überall an den Stätten profanen östlichen Lebens wieder – mit Tee gefüllt.

ORDNUNG

Bei der Eröffnung der Achten Nationalen Sportmeisterschaften werden von Tausenden von Gymnastikern in der Arena des gerade fertiggestellten Shanghai Stadium lebende Bilder vorgeführt. Diese (vom Fernsehen übertragenen und fürs Fernsehen eingerichteten) Bilder sind zum Staunen gemacht, und man kann nicht umhin, sie zu bestaunen: Zahllose Körper bilden in schnellem und exaktem Wechsel Spiralen und geometrische Figuren, Schriftzeichen, wehende Schleier, Blüten, die sich öffnen und schließen, taumelnde Schmetterlinge mit schlagenden Flügeln, rollende Meereswellen mit Segeln, Fahnen im Wind und vieles mehr; am Ende der stundenlangen Darbietung formiert sich ein riesiger goldener Drache, der sich, während die Zuschauer in frenetischen Jubel ausbrechen und ein Feuerwerk gezündet wird, zu den Klängen der Nationalhymne phantastisch hin und her bewegt. Was aber ist hier eigentlich staunenswert? Die Choreographie, Massentraining und Massenorganisation? Die Disziplin, mit der all diese Menschen an ihrem Platz die vorgeschriebenen Bewegungen zur vorgeschriebenen Zeit vollführen? Die gigantische Harmlosigkeit ihrer Hervorbringungen? Das Spektakel selbst als Bild einer Ordnung, die darauf beruht, dass jeder an seinem Platz bleibt und an seinem Platz das Rechte tut? Diese Ordnung, vom Sohn des Himmels eingesetzt und legitimiert, konnte so lange aufrechterhalten werden, wie gewährleistet schien, dass jeder einen Platz und an seinem Platz das ihm Zukommende erhielt. Sie war also eine Mystifikation, und man glaubt sich zu erinnern, dass sie als solche vor nicht allzu langer Zeit außer Kraft gesetzt wurde. Sie hier wiederzufinden, unter dem dünnlippigen Lächeln Jiang Zemins auf der Ehrentribüne, das ist es, worüber man eigentlich staunen sollte.

PFUSCH (1)

Ein Samstag im November. Ein Mensch, aus dem Westen kommend und als ausländischer Experte in Shanghai tätig, wird durch das laute Rotzhochziehen und Ausspucken seines linken Nachbarn, der sich anschickt, unter der Platane seine Morgengymnastik zu machen, wieder einmal viel zu früh aus seinem wohlverdienten Morgenschlaf gerissen. Dann hängen sie im zweiten Stock Wäsche auf. Jedes Mal, wenn sie die Balkontür öffnen, fällt das eiserne Fliegengitter mit lautem Scheppern hinter ihnen ins Schloss. Sind diese Chinesen denn alle taub? Ist er der Einzige, dem das ständige Rotzhochziehen und Ausspucken und das Scheppern des Fliegengitters auf die Nerven geht? Überhaupt, diese Fliegengitter!, denkt der ausländische Experte mit innerlichem Hohnlachen. Warum ist noch keiner von diesen Chinesen auf die Idee gekommen, diese völlig nutzlosen durchlöcherten Fliegengitter abzumontieren? Warum sind diese Chinesen nicht in der Lage, überhaupt irgendetwas zu machen, was Hand und Fuß hat? Warum bringen diese Chinesen immer nur Pfusch hervor?

Mit dieser unheilvollen Gedankenkette beginnt ein düsterer Tag. Der ausländische Experte steht auf und begibt sich ins Bad. Mit einem Faustschlag auf den Lichtschalter bringt er die Lampe zeitweilig zum Brennen. Nun will er sich rasieren. Die Steckdose ist seit Tagen wacklig. Sie bricht aus der Wand, sobald er den Stecker seines Rasierapparates einstecken will. Die Schrauben, die schon zu oft ohne Dübel in die Wand gedreht wurden, haben zwei riesige Löcher und jede Menge bröckelnden Mörtel hinterlassen. Der ausländische Experte gibt das Rasieren auf und steigt in die Badewanne. Er dreht den linken Wasserhahn auf. Ein Strahl kochend heißen Wassers schießt aus dem Brausekopf. Dem rechten Hahn hingegen ist trotz endlosen Kurbelns in beide Richtungen kein Tropfen kalten Wassers zu entlocken. Der ausländische Experte ist gezwungen, über dem Waschbecken Katzenwäsche zu machen. Der Kitt in der Fuge zwischen Waschbecken und Wand ist schwarz und stinkt. Danach will sich der ausländische Experte mit Wattestäbchen die Ohren putzen. Die Watte bleibt in seinem Ohr stecken. Er muss sie mit Hilfe eines Bleistifts und eines Korkenziehers wieder herauspulen. Während dieser Prozedur vermeidet der ausländische Experte den Blick auf den Fußboden. Jeden Tag kommen zwei Frauen, die die Aufgabe haben, hier sauberzumachen. Ihr Besen besteht aus einem Stecken, an dem ein paar schmutzige Stoffstreifen befestigt sind. Mit diesem Gerät verschmieren sie den Schmutz auf dem Boden und fügen ihm einige ihrer Haare hinzu, die er nachher mit einem Stück Klopapier aufklaubt.

Heute ist es kalt. Die Fenster sind schlecht eingesetzt, es zieht durch alle Ritzen. Der ausländische Experte flieht ins Wohnzimmer. Dort gibt es Air-Condition. Er stellt den Schalter auf Off, woraufhin es in den Röhren hinter der Deckenverkleidung im Flur zu ächzen und zu quietschen beginnt. Er solle froh sein, dass es nur die Röhren seien, die dort rumorten, bekam er schon oft von erfahreneren Kollegen zu hören, früher seien es die Ratten gewesen. Der ausländische Experte ist seinem Schicksal ehrlich dankbar, dass es ihn damals nicht hierher verschlagen hat. Damals gab es auch noch keinen Kaffee. Der ausländische Experte aber kann ohne Kaffee nicht leben. Er geht in die Küche, um Kaffee zu kochen. Der Wasserkanister leckt. Der Wasserkessel ist rostig. Über die Wand mit dem granatapfelförmigen feuchten Fleck zieht eine Abordnung Ameisen in langer Prozession zum Schrank und wieder zurück. Mit großem Behagen zerdrückt der ausländische Experte jede einzelne Ameise, bis das Waschbecken schwarz gefleckt ist von Ameisenleichen. Dann legt er eine Kassette in den Recorder und drückt die Start-Taste, weil er sich bei ein wenig Musik erholen will. Die Kassette bewegt sich nicht. Wie immer hilft ein Faustschlag. Die Kassette bewegt sich, aber zu hören ist nichts, und aus dem geöffneten Kassettenfach quillt Bandsalat. Unnötig hinzuzufügen, dass der Recorder chinesischer Herkunft ist. Nun gut, denkt der ausländische Experte, dann eben Fernsehen. Er schaltet den Fernseher ein. Über den Bildschirm zucken rote Blitze. Er dreht an den Knöpfen, rüttelt an der Steckdose, umsonst. Der ausländische Experte nimmt nun zähneknirschend ein Buch zur Hand. Beim Aufschlagen des Buches reißt mit hörbarem Knacken die Bindung. Nun hat der ausländische Experte keine Lust mehr, sich zu erholen. Er will etwas Nützliches tun. Wäsche waschen. Nachdem er die Wäsche in die Trommel der Waschmaschine gelegt und den Deckel geschlossen hat, dreht er den Wasserhahn auf, und das Wasser strömt durch den Schlauch. Plötzlich löst sich der Schlauch vom Hahn und spritzt einen breiten Wasserstrahl an die Decke. Der ausländische Experte springt herzu und dreht, durch Wasser watend, den Hahn wieder zu. Er bemerkt, dass der Schlauch viel zu breit ist für das enge Gewinde des Hahns. Er ruft beim Service an, sie schicken einen Mechaniker.

Der Mechaniker ist klein und mager und trägt blaue Ärmelschoner. Er hat einen geheimnisvollen Stoffbeutel dabei. Nachdem er eine Weile an dem Schlauch herumprobiert hat, leert er den Stoffbeutel aus. Einige Zangen, viele rostige Nägel und zwei Essstäbchen aus Bambus kommen zum Vorschein. Der Mechaniker entnimmt dem Beutel einen Wollfaden, mit dem er das Gewinde des Wasserhahns umwickelt. Dann schiebt er den Schlauch darauf und dreht mit triumphierendem Blick zum stumm dastehenden ausländischen Experten den Hahn auf. Als es nach einer Minute wieder zu tröpfeln beginnt, nimmt der Mechaniker das Badelaken des ausländischen Experten von der Stange und legt es unter den nassen Hahn auf den nassen Boden. Dann sammelt er seine Sachen ein und verabschiedet sich mit höflichem Gruß. Der ausländische Experte ist am Ende seiner Kraft. Er denkt an gestern, an vorgestern, an die letzten Wochen und die letzten Monate. Er denkt an den nicht funktionierenden Computer, die nicht funktionierende Sekretärin. Er denkt an Elfi, die immer um seine seelische Gesundheit besorgt ist. Er beschließt, einen Spaziergang zu machen. Frische Luft entspannt den Geist.

Draußen regnet es. Er macht den Schirm auf und hat den Knauf in der einen, den Stock in der anderen Hand. Der Bürgersteig ist auf solche Weise gepflastert, dass überall tiefe Pfützen stehen. So ist der ausländische Experte binnen kurzem von Kopf bis Fuß durchnässt. Die Oberteile seiner Schuhe lösen sich von den Sohlen. (Die Schuhe sind chinesischen Fabrikats.) Die Jacke gibt ihre schwarze Farbe zuerst an das Futter, dann an die darunterliegenden Kleidungsstücke ab. (Die Jacke ist ebenfalls chinesischen Fabrikats.) Der ausländische Experte geht in den nächsten Supermarkt und kauft Bier.

Zu Hause zieht er die Vorhänge zu und trinkt eine Flasche nach der anderen. Nach drei Flaschen kann sein Magen nichts mehr aufnehmen, aber er ist immer noch stocknüchtern. Nicht einmal richtiges Bier können sie herstellen. Unten beginnt das Fliegengitter wieder zu scheppern. Jetzt wird gekeift, geschimpft – jetzt knallt die Wohnungstür – jetzt steigt der Duft von Sojasauce und Ingwer und Fisch in seine ausgehungerte Nase – und dann beschließt er, sich das alles nicht länger gefallen zu lassen. Nein, so lässt sich ein ausländischer Experte nicht behandeln! Schließlich waren *sie* es, die ihn gerufen haben! Und er hatte *wirklich* vor, hier nach dem Rechten zu sehen, ihnen beizubringen, wie man richtig arbeitet und wirtschaftet und alles besser macht!

Im Sturmschritt eilt er hinunter und hämmert gegen die Tür. Ein Mädchen in knapp sitzendem pastellfarbenem Kostüm öffnet lächelnd. »I am an expert!«, schreit er. »I want to rest!« Das Mädchen schüttelt lächelnd den Kopf. Im Zimmer sitzen ungefähr zehn Leute wie aus dem Ei gepellt um einen runden Tisch und schaufeln mit rundem Rücken Essen in sich hinein. Eine ältere Frau steht auf und bietet ihm den Plastikbadehocker an, auf dem sie saß. »I am an expert«, beginnt er von neuem. »I want – rest – work – no eat –« Zehn schwarze Augenpaare starren ihn an. Dann scheinen sie zu verstehen. Gelächter ertönt. Alles redet und schreit durcheinander. Man schiebt ihm Schalen mit Essen hin, man legt ihm Leckerbissen auf den Teller. Etwas wie Scham steigt in dem ausländischen Experten auf. Und plump und unrasiert, nach Bier stinkend und verbiestert, wie er ist, fragt er sich: Wozu bin ich hergekommen? Was mache ich eigentlich hier?

Für den Schluss der Geschichte gibt es zwei Alternativen: Entweder der ausländische Experte begibt sich, voll von Hass und Ekel und Weltüberdruss, schnurstracks wieder nach oben in seine Wohnung, wo ihn beim Versuch, eine Steckdose zu reparieren, der Schlag trifft. Oder er nimmt die Einladung an, unterhält die Gesellschaft mit ein paar Brocken seines überaus miserablen Chinesisch, verliebt sich in das Mädchen mit dem aprikosenfarbenen Kostüm, schlägt sich den Bauch voll und sinkt nach dem unvermeidlichen Wettbewerb im Schnapsglasleeren unter den Tisch, wo er zum weiteren Vergnügen aller Anwesenden sofort zu schnarchen beginnt, dass die Wände wackeln.

PFUSCH (2)

Ein Samstag im Februar. Der ausländische Experte wird durch lautes Rotzhochziehen, Schnauben und Spucken des Nachbarn wieder einmal viel zu früh aus seinem wohlverdienten Morgenschlaf gerissen. Er hat einen Traum gehabt. Mein Haus, denkt der ausländische Experte hinter geschlossenen Lidern und geschlossenen Vorhängen, innen mit Plastik beschichtet, damit kein Licht durchkommt, mein Haus ist kein Pfusch, mit meinem Haus passiert nichts. Unter ihm hängen sie Wäsche auf, wenn sie die Balkontür aufmachen, fällt das eiserne Fliegengitter mit lautem Scheppern hinter ihnen ins Schloss. Von der Fassade seines Hauses, des Hauses in der neugebauten Wohnanlage Am Erlenbach am Rand einer Stadt in Deutschland, in einem der südlichen Vororte, wo man die Autobahn nicht hört, weder die Autobahn noch sonst was, wie ihm versichert wurde, es ist totenstill totenstill, von der Fassade seines Hauses platzen plötzlich Brocken von Putz und halbe Ziegel ab, nicht von meinem Haus, denkt der ausländische Experte, nein, das ist hier gewesen, als es nach einer Woche Dauerregen auf einmal heiß und trocken wurde, die Kacheln platzten von den Fassaden der neugebauten Häuser ab wie die Kokosraspeln von dem Pudding, den Elfi gemacht hat, der ganze Tisch voller Kokosraspeln und Elfi auf meinem Schoß, weil die Kacheln stümperhaft verlegt worden sind, denkt der ausländische Experte, noch halb im Morgenschlaf, wie hier überhaupt alles völlig stümperhaft und dilettantisch gebaut wird, in Deutschland passiert so was nicht, und wenn doch, dann nimmt man sich einen Anwalt und kriegt sein Geld zurück, hör auf mit dem Gejammer, Elfi, weil es in Deutschland unabhängige Gerichte gibt, weil in Deutschland klare und geordnete Verhältnisse herrschen, man weiß, woran man ist –

Er macht sich einen Kaffee, er nimmt sich den Karton mit den Papieren vor, er hat Lust, heute seine Papiere zu ordnen, Kontoauszüge, Zinsbescheide, Kostenvoranschläge, Auftragserteilungen, die Mitteilungen der Immobilienfirma, der er die Überwachung der Mieteingänge und die Ausstattung seiner eigenen Wohnung im dritten, obersten Stock des Hauses Am Erlenbach übertragen hat, das Ordnen seiner Papiere beschwingt ihn und heitert ihn auf, er holt Klebestreifen und Schere, er klebt Zeichnungen und Musterblätter und einzelne Seiten der Möbelprospekte, die sie ihm zur Auswahl der Möbel geschickt haben, an die Flurtür, so dass ihm sein Eigentum immer vor Augen ist, das Bett Eiche massiv, die Polstergarnitur schwarzes Vollrindleder, die Küchenzeile Arbeitsfläche Carraramarmor, die gusseiserne Garderobe, keine Massenware aus der Fabrik, sondern etwas Besonderes, etwas Ausgefallenes, wie ihm versichert wurde, die Arbeit eines Kunstschmieds aus Portugal, so was hält ewig, das ist kein Pfusch, eigentlich ist das unbezahlbar, Ihre Familie wird es Ihnen danken, aber ich habe keine, denkt der ausländische Experte, höchstens Elfi, so was hält ewig, Elfi mit ihrem Gejammer, was jammert sie, sie hat doch alles, mit Haken, die nicht wie Haken aussehen, sondern wie Efeuranken und Tulpen mit gebogenen Stängeln, und hier und da sind Augen aufgemalt, die wie Mädchenaugen aus einem Dornröschengebüsch lugen, diese Augen haben ihm von Anfang an gefallen, Märchenaugen, Rehaugen –

Während er in seinen Kontoauszügen schwelgt, seinen aufgehäuften Schätzen, unserer sauer erarbeiteten Kohle, sagt Manne, in der Bar des Portman mittwochs nach dem Fitness, Manne mit seinem Golfurlaub, Ulf mit seinen Goldkettchen, denkt der ausländische Experte, sie denken nicht an später, kaufen sich Golfschläger Golfhotels Urlaub in Thailand Uhren für eine halbe Million, statt was Solides aufzubauen, kein Pfusch, was Solides, Ihre Familie wird es Ihnen danken, während er an sein Haus Am Erlenbach denkt, wo es garantiert ruhig ist, wo garantiert keine Ausländer wohnen, und der Wald in der Nähe, saubere Luft, sauberer Wald, hygienischer deutscher Wald, kein Pfusch, denkt der ausländische Experte, in seinen Kontoauszügen schwelgend, und Rehe, die Sie sonntags von der Dachterrasse aus beobachten können, Sie haben doch einen Feldstecher, während er daran denkt, meldet sich sein Darm, er geht ins Bad, es ist kalt im Bad –

Der Heizlüfter hat letzte Woche den Geist aufgegeben, der Heizlüfter steht kalt im Bad, und auf dem Heizlüfter steht die Klopapierrolle, die die Putzfrau gebracht hat, rote, geschwollene Hände, man kann sie nicht anfassen, denkt der ausländische Experte, auf dem kalten Klo sitzend, sie tragen ja nicht mal Handschuhe, sie wischen die Zahnputzgläser mit demselben Tuch aus, mit dem sie das Klo putzen, wenn ich daheim bin, gehe ich zuerst in den Drogeriemarkt, denkt der ausländische Experte beim Scheißen, und kaufe anständiges Klopapier, hygienisches Klopapier, sie wissen es nicht zu schätzen in Deutschland, dass sie unter zwanzig Sorten

Klopapier wählen können, dass sie die Freiheit haben, unter zwanzig Sorten Klopapier zu wählen, diese Sachen gehen einem erst hier auf, wo man sich mit diesem ewig gleichen kommunistischen Klopapier begnügen muss. Er macht das Papier ab, das die Klopapierrolle umschließt, dünnes, grün und rot bedrucktes Papier, er liest, was unter den chinesischen Schriftzeichen in lateinischen Buchstaben steht.

SHANGHAI
XUEHUAZHIPINGCHANG,

daneben eine Lilie, eine Lilie, das ist grotesk, denkt der ausländische Experte, während er das Klopapier in Dienst nimmt, eine Lilie, das beweist, dass sie lügen, die lügen wie sie beten, sagt Ulf in der Bar des Portman mittwochs nach dem Fitness, denen ist nichts heilig, denkt der ausländische Experte, während er die Spülung in Gang setzt, das Badfenster öffnet, bemerkt, dass es ein schöner Tag ist, schöne Tage sind für zu Hause, nicht für hier –

Weil es sonst nichts zu tun gibt, liest er die Briefe, die er in den letzten zwei Wochen bekommen hat, die verspätete Geburtstagskarte mit dem auf einer schief stehenden Schornsteinfegerleiter balancierenden rosa Schwein mit einer Art Kellnerinnenschürze um den Bauch und der Aufschrift: »Immer oben bleiben!«, und auf der Rückseite alle Unterschriften, der HAL rechts unten in der Ecke und Elfi daneben, ein Herz auf dem i, hör auf damit, denkt der ausländische Experte, ihre Kinderunterschrift betrachtend, hör auf mit dem Gejammer, es gibt nichts zu jammern, du hast doch alles, und dann Elfis Brief, ich heiße nicht Elfi, ich heiße Elfriede, acht Seiten ein Herzenserguss, hör auf mit dem Gejammer, denkt der ausländische Experte, während er den Brief in der Hand hält, ohne ihn zu lesen, was habe ich mit deiner Mutter zu tun, heute geht man nicht mehr ins Wasser, heute kann man schwimmen, selbst im allerdreckigsten Kanal kann man noch schwimmen und sich irgendwie ans Ufer retten, wahrscheinlich war sie blau, hör auf –

Er wählt die Nummer von Ulf, von Manne, aber keiner meldet sich. Er macht sich Spiegeleier und isst alten Toast dazu, der nach Schimmel schmeckt. Im Fernsehen gibt es einen Boxkampf, er zieht die Vorhänge zu, die innen mit Plastik beschichtet sind, damit kein Licht durchkommt, und macht sich an den Schnaps, den sie ihm geschenkt haben, chinesischen Schnaps, diese Geizhälse, oder wollen sie mich auf die Probe stellen, denkt der ausländische Experte, während er das erste Glas leert, das ihm die Kehle verbrennt, aber vom Four Roses ist nichts mehr übrig, Angeber, sie bilden sich ein, sie wissen alles, kaufen sich Uhren für zweihunderttausend, fünfhunderttausend, hängen diese Weiber mit Schmuck voll statt an später zu denken, wir machen diesen Job nicht ewig, irgendwann fängt das richtige Leben an dieser ewige Kampf Schnaps, der einem die Kehle verbrennt, und irgendwie geht der Vormittag herum und dann der Nachmittag –

Die Platane ist kahl, sie haben sie beschnitten, sie sieht aus wie ein Galgen, denkt der ausländische Experte, als er, den Aufzug vermeidend, die Treppe geschafft hat, wie kann so ein Galgen je wieder Blätter kriegen, aber an der Hausmauer riecht es nach Seife, nach guter Seife, nach wirklich guter Luxusseife, denkt der ausländische Experte, so was kann's hier nicht geben. An der Hausmauer blüht ein Strauch, er blüht, obwohl er keine Blätter hat und erfroren schien, mit kleinen, weißlichen, traurig herabhängenden Blütentrauben, er hat immer geglaubt, der Strauch sei erfroren, aber jetzt blüht er, blüht mit plötzlich aufgerichteten flaumigen Blütenbüscheln ohne Blätter, zwischen kahlen schwarzen Zweigen im Licht, das aus dem Erdgeschossfenster fällt wie eine gelbe Schabracke –

Vor dem Malone weckt ihn die Stimme des Fahrers, er schreit irgendwas, schreien, das können sie, denkt der ausländische Experte, nach Münzen kramend, diese Sprache ist nichts als Geschrei Gekeif Gezisch, die Frauen mit den Zigaretten, den Wollschals um den Kopf umrunden ihn, er will diese Zigaretten nicht, auch wenn es Marlboro sind, er will sie nicht, die sind bestimmt geschmuggelt oder sonst was, geschmuggelt gefälscht vergiftet, warum bin ich so erschöpft, denkt der ausländische Experte vor dem Malone, die Frauen mit den Wollschals um den Kopf abwehrend, das Geschrei abwehrend, den Krach aus dem Malone, das ist der Schnaps, gepanschter Schnaps geschmuggelt gefälscht die lügen alle, sagt Ulf, denen ist nichts heilig, aber vom Four Roses war nichts mehr übrig –

Ein Mädchen steht vor dem Eingang, verschränkte Arme, Handschuhe ohne Finger, er mag diese Handschuhe nicht, diese klammen Arme, diese dünnen Dinger, besonders wenn sie nach Mitternacht ins Malone kommen, aber es ist noch nicht nach Mitternacht, das Mädchen lacht mit weißen Zähnen roten Backen rot wie das Herz auf Elfis i, er lässt sich nicht mehr von denen täuschen, die lügen wie sie beten, sagt er, wenn er mit Ulf und Manne in der Bar des Portman sitzt, mittwochs nach dem Fitness, mir können die nichts vormachen, denkt er vor dem Eingang des Malone, Schneeweißchen und Rosenrot, ich glaube nicht an Märchen, die anderen haben ihre Maßstäbe verloren, wir sind zu lange hier wir fangen an, diese klammen dünnen Dinger schön zu finden schwarzes Haar wie Bast wie Seide wie Ebenholz geben das Geld aus, statt es zu Hause in Eigentumswohnungen zu stecken Miete zu kassieren Monat für Monat die Fensterbriefe der Dresdner Bank, kaufen irgendwelche Lis und Lans und wissen nicht, ob sie gesund sind, aber es gibt auch andere –

Im Malone trinkt er Four Roses und sieht einen Boxkampf, den er schon einmal irgendwo gesehen hat, aber er weiß nicht mehr wo, zwei Schwarze prügeln aufeinander ein, auf den Oberarm des einen sind zwei blaue Blitze tätowiert, Schweiß trieft von ihren Gesichtern, Schweiß trieft von ihren glänzenden Körpern, und unter der Haut schwellen die Muskeln und bäumen sich auf wie Schlangen –

Die dunkle Straße nimmt ihn gleichgültig auf, warum bin ich so erschöpft, denkt der ausländische Experte, nachdem er das Malone verlassen hat, Malone wie alone, ich bin ein Schwächling, ich vertrage dieses Zeug nicht sie wollen mich auf die Probe stellen, er will das Mädchen finden, das eben vor der Tür gestanden hat wann war das mit den weißen Zähnen es gibt auch andere weiß rot schwarz Schneewittchen Hänsel und Gretel die Hexe mit dem Wollschal um den zahnlosen Kopf vergiftete Zigaretten vergifteter Schnaps Rehe im Wald Sie haben doch einen Feldstecher –

Die dunkle Straße führt ihn irgendwohin, Musikgehämmer, Geschrei, das Rattern der Laster, er hängt in den Seilen, der Trainer flüstert ihm etwas ins Ohr, der Arzt tupft ihm mit Wattestäbchen das Blut von der Braue, ein riesiger schwarzer Schatten wie ferngesteuert, ein Roboter, ich brauche sie, denkt der ausländische Experte, die dunkle Straße entlangtaumelnd, die ist anders kein Witz, denkt er, er wird es ihnen sagen, nächsten Mittwoch nach dem Fitness, das

Grinsen aushalten, Angeber, sie denken, sie wissen alles, fressen sich mit Lebkuchen voll und sehen die Hexe nicht die an den Kochtopf schlägt dass es scheppert –

Über der Tür des Restaurants ist eine Leuchtreklame mit roten und blauen Neonschlangen, die blaue streckt immer wieder den Kopf vor und lässt eine lange rote Zunge herausschnellen, du musst sie in der Suppe essen, schmeckt wie Karnickel, sagt Manne, man wundert sich immer, was die aushalten die trinken das Blut kein Witz mir hat's den Magen umgedreht, sagt Ulf in der Bar des Portman, denkt der ausländische Experte bei der Betrachtung der Leuchtreklame des Restaurants, die wollen uns auf die Probe stellen die lügen wie sie beten ich sage euch die ist anders, sie hat mir ihre Hände gezeigt vor dem Kino ich heiße nicht Elfi ich heiße Elfriede weiße Fingerspitzen erfrorene Fingerspitzen ohne Blut wärme mich hol die Karten ich warte –

Beim Betreten dieser schmuddeligen und mit schmatzenden Menschen vollgestopften Lokale hat er immer mit einer unbestimmten Furcht, einem unbestimmten Ekel zu kämpfen gehabt, jetzt ist alles anders, es ist niemand mehr da, auf den Tischen stehen Zahnputzgläser mit Servietten drin, an der Wand ein fettbespritzter Kalender mit Goldfischen, eine Nische mit elektrischen Lichtern vor dem Gott des Reichtums, die Schlangen in Glasbehältern an der Wand, wie schön sie sind, denkt der ausländische Experte, sich über die Schlangenbehälter beugend, wie stark, kalt, eiskalt wie Elfis Fingerspitzen, du musst sie in der Suppe essen ich kann nicht mehr, wir denken wir helfen ihnen, sagt Ulf in der Bar des Portman, wir denken wir sind hier die Kings, wir bauen ihnen die Hochhäuser die U-Bahn die Autos wir legen ihnen die Telefonleitungen, und wenn sie alles aus uns rausgeholt haben, was sie brauchen, dann schmeißen sie die Atombombe und uns ins Arbeitslager die sind nicht wie wir, wir vergessen immer, dass es Kommunisten sind, sagt Ulf, Shanghai ist nicht China, sagt Manne, wer aufmuckt, wird erschossen, sagt Ulf, man darf nicht vergessen, was die hinter sich haben, bei jedem Regierungswechsel Millionen Tote, die haben sich gegenseitig abgeschlachtet Millionen Tote dagegen ist Hitler ein Waisenknabe, als wir geackert haben, Deutschland aufgebaut haben, Deutschland zu dem gemacht haben, was es heute ist, da haben die Studenten hier ihre Lehrer gefressen kein Witz aufgehängt aufgeschlitzt gebraten gefressen irgendwo im Süden nicht weit von hier –

In der Küche sitzen vier Männer in schmutzigen weißen Kochkitteln und Kochmützen um einen Tisch und spielen Karten. Das Mädchen gießt ihnen aus einer roten Thermoskanne mit durchgerostetem Boden Wasser in die Zahnputzgläser mit dunklem Teeblättermatsch. Die Männer grinsen, einer tritt seine Zigarette aus und wirft die Karten hin, er geht zu den Glasbehältern und holt die Schlange heraus, die mit der schwarzweißen Zeichnung dem schwarzen Kopf dem weißen Fleck an der Seite, er nimmt sie mit zwei Fingern hinterm Kopf, sie baumelt träge in der Luft, kalt und träge, der Mann legt sie auf den Boden wie ein Stück Telefonkabel, tritt mit dem Fuß auf sie, die langen Unterhosen ein Wulst in den Socken, schwarze Handschuhe kein Leder, denkt der ausländische Experte, ich bin ein Schwächling, er nimmt eine Schere und schneidet ihr den Kopf ab. Das Blut sprudelt wie eine Quelle, die Schlange windet sich unter dem Fuß des Mannes dem Plastikschuh des Mannes auf dem mit Melonenkernen Kippen Staubflusen übersäten Beton, das Mädchen hält das Zahnputzglas in der ausgestreckten Hand, das Mädchen hält ihm das rote Blut hin das heiße schäumende Schlangenblut die Quelle der Kraft das Grinsen der Köche, ich bin ein Schwächling, denkt der ausländische Experte, sich an der Schwingtür der Küche festhaltend, verpfuschtes Leben, ich bin ein Waisenknabe, das Blut strömt über ihren glänzenden Körper wie Schweiß, kalter Schweiß, Roboterschweiß, ich bin k. o., aber er hat keine Ahnung, wie er von hier wegkommt, nach Hause, denkt der ausländische Experte, sich mit klammen Fingern an der Schwingtür festklammernd, Wohnzimmer Schlafzimmer Kinderzimmer Dachterrasse ein Paradies für Kinder, wie ihm versichert wurde, aber die lügen ja alle keine Autos totenstill ich warte auf dich weg hier was habe ich mit deiner Mutter zu tun schau dir die Mutter an dann weißt du wie die Tochter mal wird, sagt Manne in der Bar des Portman mittwochs nach dem Fitness, kann sie nicht schwimmen was jammert sie in Deutschland gibt es unabhängige Gerichte sichere Renditen Fensterbriefe der Wald mit Rehen saubere Rehe hygienische Rehe wenn Sie einen Feldstecher haben weg hier –

Das Klo ist im Hof, er pisst in das stinkende Loch, er kotzt in das stinkende Loch, die Fenster sind kühl, irgendwas fällt um, es scheppert es ist dunkel es ist kalt, weiter, die kennen keine Straßenbeleuchtung ganze Stadtteile total dunkel das ist doch keine Stadt das ist ein Witz ein Witz, denkt der ausländische Experte, während er sich an der Mauer entlangtastet wie ein Schwerkranker, wo ist die Brieftasche, wahrscheinlich haben sie ihm auch noch die Brieftasche geklaut, den Pass nehme ich nie mit ich werde mich hüten den Pass mitzunehmen auch wenn sie im Malone englisch reden das haben die gepaukt you want special service no problem nur die Autobahn ist beleuchtet garantiert keine Autobahn außer bei Ostwind aber Ostwind ist selten das wissen Sie ja ich weiß gar nichts –

Unter der Hochstraße steht ein Laster. Der Laster ist mit Ananas beladen. Am Fuß des Ananasberges liegen irgendwelche Gestalten und rühren sich nicht, sie sehen aus wie Leichen Kanalleichen, er schreit ich schreie ich schreie um Hilfe, denkt der ausländische Experte, während er auf den Laster gezogen wird, weil es auf der Straße zu kalt ist zum Schlafen, aber das ist ja alles völlig egal, das Rattern der Laster über seinem Kopf die Schatten die Ratten wie halten die das aus die sind nicht wie wir Kinder Familie richtiges Leben kein Pfusch –

Das Mädchen bettet seinen Kopf auf irgendetwas Weiches, Ananasduft steigt ihm in die Nase, sie hält ihm etwas an den Mund, er schluckt, seine Kehle brennt, der Schweiß bricht ihm aus und rinnt über sein Gesicht wie Wasser wie Tränen Schneewittchentränen Dornröschentränen, denkt der ausländische Experte, in tiefen Schlaf sinkend auf dem Ananaslaster, gusseiserne Haken aber sie sehen nicht wie Haken aus eigentlich unbezahlbar warum dieser ganze Kampf diese ewige Prügelei Blut strömt von der Braue ins Auge und vom Auge übers Gesicht, das Mädchen tupft es mit Wattestäbchen vorsichtig ab schwarzes Haar wie Ebenholz weiße Haut weiß wie Elfis Fingerspitzen weiß wie Elfis Mutter im Kanal lilienweiß das stinkende Klopapier, wann war das heute Morgen oder letzte Woche als die Nachricht kam von Elfis Mutter als wir geackert haben wir bauen ihnen die U-Bahn wir legen ihnen die Telefonleitungen wir machen Deutschland zu dem was es ist –

PUDONG

Das World Center ist leer. Es ist ein Grundstück an der Pudong Dadao, von einem verwitterten Bretterzaun umschlossen, mit einem pompösen Eingangstor an der Seite, wo ein Pförtner Zeitung liest. Mehrere Gruppen von Hochhäusern, strahlend weiß, mit Balkonen und Klimaanlagen, griechischen Säulen und barocken Giebeln auf dem Dach – an einem der Giebel ist zusätzlich eine große Uhr –, stehen herum, und zu ihren Füßen stehen ein paar zweigeschossige Häuser vom Typ »Villa« in Reih und Glied, die irgendwie entfernt an Neuengland erinnern, aber eigentlich an gar nichts, und aus langsam grau werdendem Beton und langsam braun werdenden Dächern mit undefinierbarem Belag und spitzen sechs- oder achteckigen Türmchen und Erkern und schmiedeeisernen Geländern und gigantischen Satellitenschüsseln auf dem flachen Teil des Dachs bestehen, und all das ist unbewohnt. Nur die grauen Waben der Bauarbeiterhütten, die aus irgendeinem Grund noch da sind, obwohl alles längst fertiggebaut ist, sehen belebt aus, dort sieht man Leute ein und aus gehen, vor einer Tür steht ein Fernseher, vor den Fenstern hängt Wäsche. Auf der Straße, die um das Areal herumführt, sieht man riesige Rohre aus Beton, Berge von Ziegeln und Bauschutt, Berge von Abfall. Der Abfall wird von einem jungen Mann mit Mundschutz und einer älteren Frau ohne

Mundschutz mit einer rostigen Drahtzange sortiert und auf verschiedene Kübel verteilt. Es gibt auf dieser Straße keine Autos. Die Jungen aus der Siedlung nebenan haben Platz zum Fußballspielen. Der Pförtner lässt sie gewähren. Nur dürfen sie dem viereckigen, in einem Beet mit Unkraut schräg aufragenden rötlich glänzenden Marmorblock nicht zu nahe kommen, dessen Aufschrift verrät, dass es sich hier um das Weltzentrum handelt.

Die Siedlung nebenan besteht aus niedrigen, aneinanderklebenden, regellos und wie provisorisch aus Zement und Blech zusammengeschusterten Behausungen mit ein paar Gassen dazwischen, wo man sich und die Wäsche wäscht, Gemüse putzt, Zigaretten kauft und zum Friseur geht, wo die Alten im Winter in der Sonne sitzen und die Jungen mit den Händen in den Hosentaschen um ein Motorrad herumstehen, mit der öffentlichen Toilette, wo man den Nachttopf ausleert, und ein paar armseligen Imbissbuden und Läden, und all das ist übervoll mit Menschen.

Vielerorts trifft man auf diesen Widerspruch, aber er zeigt sich in Pudong besonders krass. Es ist der Widerspruch zwischen Arm und Reich, und es ist der Widerspruch zwischen einer Stadt, die ihr Gesicht von den dort wohnenden Menschen und ihren unterschiedlichen Interessen erhält, und einem Potemkinschen Dorf. Die Erneuerung Pudongs, das vernachlässigtes Randgelände war, Felder, Werften, Fabriken auf der östlichen Seite des Huangpu, ist eines der Lieblingsprojekte des neuen China. Doch das aufgesetzte Neue entbehrt der Wirklichkeit. Das Niedagewesene ist Phantom. Die höchsten Gebäude der Welt gleichen bloßen Tagesresten in einem anhaltenden Traum, in dem die negierte Wildnis als Wust von authentischer Hoffnung und realer Verzweiflung, als chaotische Ansammlung von Elendsbuden und Baracken allgegenwärtig ist.

Das Gesichts- und Geschichtslose dieses seltsamen Ortes wird in einem 1990 erschienenen Roman von Wang Anyi spürbar (dt. *Zwischen Ufern*). Er spielt in Shanghai. Ein noch unverputzter und doch schon traurig und verkommen wirkender Neubau in Pudong ist die Kulisse für eine Szene, in der die Heldin Mi Ni, betrogen und erniedrigt, verstört und gleichzeitig berauscht von Lust, ihre Initiation als Prostituierte erfährt.

Inzwischen gibt es nicht mehr so viele Schutthaufen, verwilderte Straßen und dröhnende Maschinen, wie im Roman erwähnt. Die Zahl der prunkvollen Fassaden hat sich vervielfacht. Es gibt Auffahrten und Empfangshallen, eine furchterregende Skulptur von springenden Stieren mit herausquellenden Augen auf einer »Plaza« mit hallend leerer »Shopping Mall«, eine giftgrüne Grünfläche mit einem Teich in Form des Stadtteils Pudong und mehrere gigantische Opferschalen vor dem World Finance Tower. Daneben die Baustelle des World Finance Center, das vierhundertsechzig Meter hoch werden soll. Berauscht wie Mi Ni feiert Pudong die Macht des Kapitals, wie ein ausgehaltenes Mädchen hält es trotzig an seinen Illusionen fest. Aber die schwarzen Schlieren sind unübersehbar, die blinden Fenster, der beißende Smog, die trüben Massen eines unheimlichen Nebels, in dem sich die stolze Höhe der Wolkenkratzer bei hellem Tageslicht entmaterialisiert.

PUTZFRAUEN

Wir sind es gewöhnt, dass Putzfrauen ihre Arbeit tun, wenn niemand anders zugegen ist, öffentliche Gebäude werden nachts oder in den frühen Morgenstunden saubergemacht. Hier scheint es diese Regelung nirgends zu geben. In Behörden, Bahnhöfen, Banken verrichten Putzfrauen bei hellem Tageslicht und vollem Publikumsverkehr ihren Sisyphosdienst. Im Museum bewundert man die ausgestellten Gegenstände, während das Glas der Vitrinen von Putzfrauen gewienert wird. In der Universität wandert man durch Gänge voller Unrat, weil Putzfrauen gerade die Abfalleimer ausgeleert haben, um den Müll zu sortieren. In der Lobby des Hilton-Hotels erquickt man sich am Anblick eleganter Pagen und gutgekleideter Businesspeople und dem üppigen Angebot an westlichen Backwaren und Zeitungen, während Putzfrauen, breite, mit schmutzigen Lappen umwickelte Besen im Zeitlupentempo vor sich herschiebend, für fleckenlosen Glanz des spiegelnden Marmors sorgen. In ihren Kitteln und Ärmelschonern, mit ihren Mopps und Feudeln, ihren verbeulten Kehrblechen und zerfledderten Bambuskörben sind sie unübersehbar und dringen doch nur wie am Rand des Gesichtsfelds ins Bewusstsein. Man gewöhnt sich an ihren stummen Dienst wie an die Dienste von Vasen und Sesseln. Man könnte sie für bloße Erscheinungen halten, Gespenster, die an den herausgehobenen Orten gesellschaftlicher Repräsentation gemachte Männer an die Machtlosen erinnert, Gerettete an die Untergehenden, Räuber an die Beraubten, die kein Weg je hierherführt.

QIUXIA-GARTEN

Der Garten war am Anfang. Später hat man das Kino erfunden. Noch später kamen die kalten, körperlosen Sensationen der elektronischen Apparate, und die große Empfindungskunst des Gartenbaus geriet ins Hintertreffen.

Der älteste Garten Shanghais liegt im Vorort Jiading und wurde 1502 erbaut, zur Zeit der Ming-Dynastie. Besucht man ihn in der kalten Jahreszeit, bei gelegentlichem Nieselregen, so entgeht man dem üblichen Freizeitrummel, der die zum Verständnis des Gartens notwendige empfängliche und konzentrierte Stimmung unmöglich macht, und kann seine Wunder ungestört erfahren wie jene Privilegierten, für die er einst angelegt wurde.

Auf einer nicht sehr ausgedehnten ummauerten Fläche öffnet sich eine Welt. Jeder Schritt auf den gewundenen Pfaden führt zu einer neuen Aussicht, jede Aussicht enthüllt neue Tiefen, jede Wegbiegung neue Raffinessen, andere Perspektiven. Dichter Bambus verbirgt einen Pavillon, dessen Giebel geschnitzte Fledermäuse zieren; Gruppen uralter Kiefern, mehrstämmige Ginkgos säumen einen Höhenweg; Felsen türmen sich auf und bilden einen Miniaturberg; der Hang ist vom berauschenden Duft des gelben Schneeflockbaums umwölkt, am Gegenhang ist der Fels bizarr durchlöchert, der Weg führt durch eine stumme, schwarze Höhle, in der für Augenblicke das Zeitgefühl verlorengeht; doch schon ist man wieder im Hellen; der weiche Klang einer Bronzeglocke weht über das graue Wasser eines Sees; immergrüne Gewächse, deren gefleckte Blätter an sommerliche Schattenmuster denken lassen, trotzen der Kühle; jäh ragt eine Klippe auf, ein Bach rieselt herab, der sich alsbald mit dem See vereint; kleine Boote liegen unter Trauerweiden zur Spazierfahrt bereit; Fenster, Tore, Wandgitter der um den See gruppierten Pavillons erinnern an Blüten und Monde; man blickt hindurch wie durch Rahmen, die einzelne malerische Gruppen und Effekte bühnenhaft hervortreten lassen; Brücken und Arkaden verbinden verschiedene Pflanzenfamilien, Farbgruppen, Bereiche von Hell und Dunkel und reizen stets aufs Neue die Aufmerksamkeit.

Das wellige Auf und Ab von Hügeln und Tälern, das kalkulierte Nebeneinander von Wäldchen und Gewässern, Fels und Haus und Ton und Duft machen aus der engbegrenzten Fläche eine abwechslungsreiche und geräumige Miniaturlandschaft. Bis ins Kleinste ist die Natur durchdacht und geformt. Überall finden sich Überraschungen und Korrespondenzen, überall zeigt sich, in welchem Maß man hier der Natur anhing und sich ihr als Gestalter und Betrachter entgegensetzte.

Die Wege des Gartens führen nirgendwohin. Der Garten ist ein Labyrinth. Endlos das Spiel des Himmels, des Lichts mit den eingewurzelten Erdwesen, endlos die Sinnesreize, endlos der Wechsel der Empfindungen von Abschweifung und Zielsicherheit, Verwirrung und Klarheit, Taumel und Halt. Der Garten ist eine Metapher. Endlos das Spiel der durch Muster und Formen, Farben und Namen hervorgerufenen Bedeutungen, endlos die Bilder, die der wache Geist zu einem einzigen großen, gedankenreichen Gemälde zusammenfügt.

Die sanfte Stimme des Regens übertönt den Verkehrslärm jenseits der Mauer. Menschen, die nah sind, entfernen sich. Unter dem geschwungenen Dach des Pavillons am Wasser ruht der Betrachter aus. Er gleicht dem Einsiedler, wie er auf den Bildern der alten Landschaftsmaler dargestellt ist, in tiefer Versenkung angesichts der Leere, die sich im Wechselspiel der Naturerscheinungen offenbart. Regentropfen lassen den fleckenlosen Spiegel splittern. Der Geist ist getrübt, der See ist ein graues Fenster mit Icecrackle-Muster. Doch schon hält der Regen wieder inne. Der leere Himmel bringt Fülle hervor, das stille Wasser spiegelt endlos ziehende Wolken. Dieselben Wolken – von der Sonne rötlich gefärbte Herbstwolken *(qiu xia)* –, von einem entzückten Besucher sinnend betrachtet, mögen dem Garten einst seinen Namen gegeben haben.

REGEN

Der Himmel hängt tief, ein schmutziggraues Laken, zwischen Wolkenkratzern aufgespießt, von gigantischen Gießkannen gewässert. Die trüben Scheinwerfer haben einen Hof aus schwebenden Tropfen. Die Magnolienblüten sehen traurig aus. Ebenso die Pflaumen und Päonien und die anderen, die ich nicht benennen kann. Die Luft ist frühlingshaft weich, die Schlaglöcher sind voll Wasser. Vor mir, hinter mir, neben mir fahren sonderbare stumme Wesen, Kapuzenmännchen, auf ihren zwei- bis dreirädrigen Untersätzen, in unabsehbaren, langsam dahintreibenden Pulks. Im wogenden Wolkengrau leuchten ihre Einheitsplastikregenumhänge in allen Farben des Regenbogens. Aber nach einer Weile sehe ich keine Kapuzenmännchen, keine Räder und keine Regenbögen mehr, nur noch rotblaugelbgrünlila Kleckse. Es wird dunkel. Meine Füße sind nass. Meine Hose ist nass. Mein Hals ist nass. An den Brillengläsern rinnt das Wasser herab. Ich setze die Brille ab und versuche, mich mit kurzsichtigen Augen irgendwie zu orientieren. Überall blinken wie feindselige Tigeraugen im tropfenden Dschungel unentzifferbare Neonschriftzeichen auf, die das Gefühl des heimatlosen Umherirrens auf einem von seelenlosen Regenwesen bevölkerten Planeten, das mich befallen hat, zur tiefen Trostlosigkeit steigern. Doch schon naht Rettung! Wie gut, dass es seit neuestem hier Mode ist, die Regenumhänge mit englischen Aufschriften zu bedrucken! Ein MANHATTAN STYLE GUARANTEED QUALITY, der unversehens vor mir auftaucht, ruft sofort Urvertrauen in mir wach. Ich folge ihm blind, und er führt mich sicher an den prustenden Bussen, den spritzenden Lastern vorbei. Als er im Dunst verschwindet, finde ich einen SPORTSTIME, einen COLONIES OF SPARKLE, der mich hurtig über die nächste Kreuzung bringt. Jetzt habe ich das Gefühl, es ist Zeit, nach links abzubiegen – schon setzt sich ein RACE KNIGHT ERRANT vor mich, der prompt eine Lücke im Strom der hupenden Taxis findet. Auf der anderen Seite löst ihn ein erfahrener CHALLENGE, ein WE STAND OUT, ein JUST DO IT ab, Letzterer ein echter Haudegen, der vor nichts Angst hat. Der chaotische Kreisverkehr ordnet sich wie von selbst, als ich ohne Zögern einem unverdrossenen MY FIRST MILLION folge, und endlich bringt mich RICH FORTUNATE SHANGHAI zuverlässig vor das heimatliche Tor.

RESTAURANTS

Von den Restaurants liebe ich am meisten die vollen und großen, ungemütlichen, bahnhofshallenähnlichen. Manche befinden sich in alten Fabriken oder Lagerhäusern, auch Kirchen sind zu Restaurants umgebaut worden; die Neubauten – vorzugsweise Seafood-Lokale – sind großspurige Kästen mit mannshohen Neonschriftzeichen an der Stirn oder riesigen gemalten Werbeschildern. Heerscharen von Mädchen in kurzen Röcken mit roten, goldbeschrifteten Schärpen um den Leib heißen die Gäste willkommen. In Vorräumen werden in Kühltruhen und sprudelnden Wasserbecken oder in einfachen Plastikwannen die Rohstoffe zur Schau gestellt, lange Reihen von Fischen und Krebsen, Muscheln, Schildkröten, Ochsenfröschen, Schlangen. In kleineren Abteilen die geräucherten und gebratenen, an Haken aufgehängten Enten, Wachteln, Fasane. Beim Betreten des Gastraums wird man von einem solchen Getöse empfangen, dass man kaum noch sein eigenes Wort versteht. An vielen überquellenden runden Tischen sitzen Gruppen von Menschen. Da und dort wird noch mit der Serviererin die Auswahl der Speisen aus der stets unübersehbar dicken Speisekarte beratschlagt. An anderen Tischen sind die Gesichter schon rot vom Essenseifer. Es wird geraucht und getrunken, geschrien, gelacht. Die Wassereinschenker gehen herum und treffen mit ihren

Kupferkannen aus drei Metern Abstand ihr Ziel, die Teetasse (manchmal auch nicht). Dutzende von Bediensteten bringen immer neue Speisen herbei, zünden den Kocher an, auf dem zugedeckt die Suppe brodelt. Ganze Männerrunden stehen immer wieder auf, um anzustoßen. In den Séparées jagen sich Neureiche in dunklen Anzügen mit jungen Damen in hautengen geschlitzten Seidenkleidern um den Tisch herum und brüllen dabei wie am Spieß. Lächelnd weichen ihnen die Serviererinnen aus. (Sie lächeln, wie man über Kinder beim Kindergeburtstag lächeln würde.) Handys piepsen, Beeper beepen. Kleine Mädchen sitzen brav auf dem Schoß der Oma oder rennen vor den Fischbecken herum. Die Väter telefonieren und pulen dabei mit dem Zahnstocher in den Zähnen. Beim Bezahlen holen sie dicke Geldscheinbündel lässig aus der Hosentasche. Und dann, plötzlich, wie auf ein geheimes Kommando hin, erhebt sich alles und strebt dem Ausgang zu.

Es ist noch nicht neun Uhr. Die Halle ist leer. Die Tische sind verwüstet. Die weißen Tischdecken sind mit Schalen, Knochen, Gräten besudelt. In fettigen Gläsern schwappt schales Bier. (Man hat die Gewohnheit, die Gläser nicht ganz auszutrinken, auch in den Schalen und Schüsseln mit Essen lässt man gern etwas übrig.) Die Serviererinnen machen sich daran, das Chaos zu beseitigen. Die Köche kommen heraus, um noch ein Weilchen zu rauchen und zu plaudern. In der Küche werden Töpfe und Schneidebretter geschrubbt. An der Kasse wird Geld gezählt. Bald gehen überall die Lichter aus. Auch nach den größten Ausschweifungen begibt man sich pünktlich ins Bett.

ROST

Ob als Folge der hohen Luftfeuchtigkeit oder aufgrund des schlechten Stahls – was in dieser Stadt aus Metall ist, ist bald rostig. Aus dem Westen kommend, setzt man rostige Dinge mit defekten Dingen gleich, und defekte Dinge sind aus dem Verkehr zu ziehen. Von den Hiesigen wird diese Auffassung offenbar nicht geteilt. Der westliche Mensch lernt einen anderen, weniger dem Schein als dem Sein verhafteten, praxisbezogenen Umgang mit den Dingen kennen.

Nehmen wir Fahrräder: Rostige Fahrräder werden von dunkelhäutigen Provinzlern in blauer Arbeitsmontur und Stoffschuhen ebenso benutzt wie von milchweißen Großstädtern im eleganten Businessdress. Auf rostigen Fahrrädern werden Wasserkanister, Mehlsäcke, Polstermöbelgarnituren, Garküchen, Baugerüste, wird überhaupt alles transportiert, was überhaupt transportfähig ist. Auf rostigen Fahrradgepäckträgern sitzen rosige Kinder in Weiß und Türkis, die von Vätern und Müttern zum Kindergarten, zur Schule gefahren werden. Rostige Fahrräder werden von Parkwächtern ordentlich in Reihen aufgestellt, von Luftpumpenmännern aufgepumpt, von Reparateuren am Straßenrand in Windeseile repariert. Solange rostige Fahrräder im Gebrauch sind, klingeln rostige Fahrradklingeln, was das Zeug hält. Rostige Fahrräder sind so lange im Gebrauch, wie sie fahren. Manche gestatten sich in aller Bescheidenheit, die Welt auf den Namen ihrer einheimischen Herstellerfirma aufmerksam zu machen. In Gold und Silber prangt er auf dem rostigen Gestänge: *Forever.*

SCHAUKÄSTEN

Bedeutende Ereignisse im Leben einer Arbeitseinheit, einer Firma oder Fakultät werden gern in Schaukästen dokumentiert, die eine Art öffentliches Fotoalbum darstellen. Auf bunter Pappe, schön beschriftet und mit allerlei Ornamenten verziert, kleben Fotos von Preisverleihungen, Banketten und Politikerbesuchen, wellig von der Feuchtigkeit, ausgebleicht vom Sonnenlicht, langweilig wie alle Fotos dieser Art, und kein Mensch, der nicht selbst mit abgelichtet wurde, bleibt stehen, um sie sich anzusehen.

Anders die Schaukästen, in denen auf die gleiche Weise die Fotos eben festgenommener Straftäter ausgestellt sind. An einer Hausmauer vor einer Polizeistation in der Fuzhou Lu stehen immer Leute, die lebhaftes Interesse an diesen Schnappschüssen bekunden, und auch ich bleibe, von einem schwer fassbaren Gefühl getrieben, immer wieder davor stehen.

Im Fernsehen sind Berichte über Durchsuchungen und Razzien, Festnahmen, Verhandlungen fester Bestandteil von Nachrichtensendungen. Doch es scheint, dass das Fernsehen mehr an der Aktion interessiert ist – den sich anschleichenden schwerbewaffneten Polizisten, den überrumpelten, ins Scheinwerferlicht blinzelnden, in Unterhosen an der Wand zusammengetriebenen Verbrechern, der Vorführung bei Gericht, der Unterschrift unter das Protokoll (oder das Urteil) mit von Handschellen zusammengepressten Händen – und lieber die Beute ausstellt – beschlagnahmtes Rauschgift, Kisten voll gepanschtem Schnaps, Raub-VCDs, gefälschte Autoschilder, Banknoten, Uhren – als die Personen. Im Schaukasten an der Fuzhou Lu hingegen werden solche Personen einzeln präsentiert, in ganzer Figur oder als Brustbild, mit zerknitterten Kleidern, halb zugeknöpften Mänteln, kahlgeschorenen und mit Schorf bedeckten Köpfen. Um manche Hälse liegt ein Strick. Sind das die Todeskandidaten, die man zur Hinrichtung führt? Mild, menschlich scheint mir in diesem Augenblick die Todesstrafe gegen die Grausamkeit der Bestrafung nach dem uralten konfuzianischen Prinzip der öffentlichen Beschämung. Diese abgeknipsten Gesichter sind verloren im doppelten Sinn, preisgegeben und ohne Daseinsgrund, und das Böse, das man in ihnen sucht und findet, ist nur die Maske dieser ungeheuren Verlorenheit.

SHANGHAI LILY

Josef von Sternberg drehte *Shanghai Express* Anfang der dreißiger Jahre in Hollywood. Marlene Dietrich spielt die Hauptrolle. Sie ist Shanghai Lily, eine Frau mit zweifelhaftem Ruf, einem überschaubaren Repertoire an Körperhaltungen und Mimik, edler Seele und atemberaubender Garderobe. In ihrem Gefolge treten auf: britische und französische Militärs, ein englischer Pfarrer, eine englische Pensionsbesitzerin, ein englischer Diamantenschmuggler, ein englischer Opiumhändler, eine steinreiche Chinesin. Ihr Gegenspieler ist ein blutrünstiger, frauenschändender Kommunist. Auch wenn der Film nicht den Anspruch erhebt, sich mit geschichtlichen Tatsachen auf seriöse Weise auseinanderzusetzen, enthält er in seinem völligen Unverständnis dem Land gegenüber, in dem er spielt, doch eine tiefe historische Wahrheit. Die zwielichtige Enge des nachgebauten Zuges, die Sternberg so eindrucksvoll dazu benutzt, den von ihm erschaffenen Star in mondänen Roben und Pelzen in Szene zu setzen, ist die Welt der ausländischen Bedrücker. Die Revolutionäre stürmen den Zug. Im Kampf um den als Geisel genommenen englischen Major zeigt Shanghai Lily, was in ihr steckt. Die Fahne, unter der sie kämpft, ist der mit Kranichen bestickte Ärmel des seidenen Morgenrocks, der an ihrem lässigen Körper schmeichelnd herabfließt. Der Kampf geht zu ihren Gunsten aus, der Zug fährt weiter zu seinem Bestimmungsort. Das Zwielicht, das Shanghai Lily umgibt und das ihr Element ist, hat sich als den Revolutionären überlegen erwiesen.

SHANGHAI STAR

Auch wenn es die Freiheit der Presse als einklagbares Recht in unserem Sinn nicht gibt, hat man in Shanghai die Möglichkeit, sich über die großen nationalen und internationalen politischen Ereignisse umfassend zu informieren. Als nicht Chinesisch lesender Ausländer ist man keineswegs auf den *Shanghai Star,* die einzige englischsprachige Lokalzeitung, angewiesen. Und doch gewöhnt man sich an ihn, wie man sich an jede Lokalzeitung gewöhnen kann, weil sie über Dinge berichtet, die man selbst kennengelernt hat. Aber »berichten« ist vielleicht das falsche Wort, und selbst das Wort »Zeitung« weckt falsche Assoziationen.

Der *Shanghai Star* erscheint zweimal wöchentlich und wird von *China Daily* herausgegeben. Er hat 16 Seiten, mehrere davon in Farbe. Die Anzeigen lassen unschwer erkennen, wen man als Hauptleserschaft im Auge hat: Royal Apartment Towers wirbt monatelang ganzseitig mit Fotos von einem blonden Golfer auf grünem Rasen und einer muskulösen Männerhand, die eine Hantel umfasst, der Begleittext verspricht Sauna, Squashplatz usw. zusätzlich zum Ultimate Dream Home. Ikea wirbt, ebenfalls ganzseitig, mit Duschvorhängen, Deckenflutern und Hi-Fi-Gestellen. Mindestens eine Farbseite gehört jenen gastronomischen Unternehmungen, die mit mexikanischen Drinks, echter belgischer Schokolade, Poolside Barbecue, einer neuartigen Kombination von Hummeressen und Pottery Creation Workshop sowie Sonderangeboten zum Muttertag locken. Die Rubrik »Around Town« informiert über Dining, Fitness und Entertainment in den großen Hotels. Daneben das aktuelle Angebot der internationalen Fluglinien und die gehobenen Immobilien. In der Rubrik »Events« die Abfahrtszeiten der Sightseeingbusse, Hinweise auf gastierende Balletttruppen, Ausstellungen, Briefmarkenauktionen und Neuzugänge im Zoo.

All das wäre nicht weiter bemerkenswert, der *Shanghai Star* nichts als eine harmlose Touristenpostille, keines zweiten Blickes wert, gäbe es da nicht unübersehbar die Artikel, die Fotos auf den vorderen Seiten, die, unter den Rubrikbezeichnungen »City«, »Pudong«, »Business« firmierend, auf charakteristische Weise die Stimmung widerspiegeln.

Man hat es mit einem großen, grob und schlecht gemalten Bild in der Art des Sozialistischen Realismus zu tun, dessen Gegenstand der Kapitalismus ist. Der Titel des Bildes lautet: Shanghai im Jahre 2000.

Heller als die Sonne strahlt diese magische Zahl über der Stadt und lässt Erwartungen aus dem Boden schießen, deren wucherndes Wachstum nur noch in Millionen und Milliarden zu messen ist: Bis zum Jahr 2000 werden im Hafen 4 Millionen Großcontainer umgeschlagen! Die Stromerzeugung steigt auf 12 000 Megawatt! Die neugegründete Light Industry Holding Company erwartet, Produkte im Wert von 10 Milliarden Yuan zu verkaufen! Kurz: Shanghai wird größer und mächtiger sein als New York, Tokio und Hongkong zusammen. Das Jahr 2000 krönt eine Entwicklung, die sich wie ein unbesiegbarer Strom von den gefährlichen Höhen und Klippen der sozialistischen Vergangenheit fortwälzt hin zu den breiten Ebenen ungehemmter marktwirtschaftlicher Produktion und vor allem Konsumtion: In den ersten 6 Monaten des Jahres erschienen 7300 neue Konsumgüter auf dem Markt. Der Marketingdirektor von Dupont lässt verlauten, dass die neu eingeführten teflonbeschichteten Küchenutensilien in überaus befriedigender Weise gekauft werden. Der Präsident von Clairol lobt die Shanghaierinnen für ihren Mut zum Haarefärben. Herr Zhu wird als Besitzer des dreimillionsten Telefons in der Stadt beglückwünscht, die Telefoninstallationskapazität der Stadt hat die von Hongkong überrundet. Im April wurden 22 000 Santanas produziert, über 2000 mehr als im März. Der Jahresoutput der Computerindustrie beträgt 14 Milliarden Yuan. Das bedeutet einen Zuwachs von …

Alles wächst, alles steigert sich. Als Faustregel gilt: Je brisanter das Problem, desto phantastischer die Zahlen.

Selbstverständlich wird der mit giftigen Chemikalien hochgradig verseuchte Stadtfluss Wusong in ein bis zwei Jahren gereinigt sein und für die selbstverständlich ansteigenden Touristenmassen eine weitere Attraktion darstellen, die sie dazu bringen wird, unermessliche Mengen von Dollars auszugeben. Wieder einmal wird das Jahr 2000 seine Zauberkräfte entfalten. Wozu diesen Kräften mit eigenen ökologischen Entscheidungen ins Handwerk pfuschen? Hier und da bepflanzt man ein paar Meter Ufer mit bunten Blumen, begleitet diese Maßnahme mit Farbfotos und zitiert den Festredner, der gesagt hat, dass bald, bald jedem Einwohner 2,75 Quadratmeter Grünfläche zur Verfügung stehen werden. Zum Thema Abwasser gibt es Schlagzeilen über Zukunftsprojekte, Zahlen und wieder Zahlen, doch keine einzige, die über die wirkliche Situation erhellend Auskunft gibt. Wenn es um Abfallbeseitigung geht, weist man mahnend auf die Styroporschachteln hin, die täglich millionenfach benutzt und weggeworfen werden. Dann die triumphierende Meldung, dass Shanghaier Betriebe in der Lage sind, 900 Millionen Styroporersatzschachteln aus Reisstroh herzustellen. Doch vergeblich sucht man nach Antwort auf die Frage, warum sie nirgends benutzt werden; warum überhaupt von all diesen Projekten im täglichen Leben so wenig Wirkung zu verspüren ist. Dass es an allen Ecken und Enden an Geld fehlt, um die katastrophalen und immer katastrophaler werdenden Umweltprobleme in den Griff zu bekommen, gesteht man nicht gern ein. Erst reich werden, dann sehen wir weiter! Davon scheinen Zeitungsschreiber ebenso überzeugt wie die Mehrzahl der Shanghaier, mit denen man darüber spricht.

Was die Abrisse der alten Viertel, die Umsiedlung der Bewohner in oft weit außerhalb gelegene Vororte, die tiefgreifende Veränderung der ganzen Innenstadt betrifft, wo gewachsene Wohngebiete in reine Geschäfts- und Verkehrszentren umgewandelt werden, so findet man Fotos von lachenden Familien, die unter neidvoller Anteilnahme der Nachbarn vom Taxi in ihr neues Wohngebiet gebracht werden, lachende Menschen, die zwischen sauber gestutzten Vorstadthecken den Umzugslaster entladen und vor den blütenweißen Wänden ihres neuen Heims lachend die Blumen des Vizebürgermeisters in Empfang nehmen, der seinen Antrittsbesuch abstattet.

Auf gewohnt praktische altchinesische Weise geht man mit dem Problem der Arbeitslosigkeit um. Da es von den höchsten Politikern auf höchster Ebene öffentlich zur Sprache gebracht worden ist, kann auch der *Shanghai Star* nicht umhin, es gelegentlich zu erwähnen. Doch wenn anderswo von den zahllosen Verzweifelten die Rede ist, die vor dem Nichts stehen, spricht er in stolzen Schlagzeilen von der Zahl der Spindeln, die man im Zuge der Reform der staatlichen Textilfabriken vernichtet hat, und wartet mit Statistiken über die zunehmende Zahl der privaten Unternehmen auf, die den entlassenen Textilarbeitern eine strahlende Zukunft bieten. Sollte es dem einen oder anderen Arbeitslosen an Ideen mangeln, so hilft er durch großzügig über alle Ausgaben verstreute Fotos von lachenden Menschen in adretter Kleidung, die wie Millionen anderer verelendeter Erwerbsloser ihre Arbeitskraft als selbständige Dienstleistende verkaufen. Die Legenden lauten folgendermaßen:

»Jiang Sha (rechts), Direktorin der Firma Zili Reines Wasser, im Gespräch mit einer Verkäuferin. Der Betrieb wurde 1996 von Frau Jiang und 50 anderen Männern und Frauen gegründet, nachdem sie ihre Arbeit bei der Textilmaschinenfabrik Nr. 4 verloren hatten. Die Verkäufe des hier abgefüllten Wassers steigen ständig.«

»Zhang Wenlong (links), ein entlassener Arbeiter, gründete eine Reparaturfirma für Haushaltsgeräte. Heute besitzt er 11 Werkstätten und beschäftigt 42 ehemalige Arbeitslose.«

»Ding Tiansong (Mitte), ehemals Arbeiterin einer Fabrik, die Wollpullover herstellte, startet ihr eigenes Geschäft. In Heimarbeit verpackt sie Souvenirs für Touristen.«

»Jiang Lizheng, ehemals Arbeiterin bei der Baumwollspinnerei Nr. 10, putzt Waschbecken im Shanghai Landmark, einem Einkaufs- und Bürokomplex an der Nanjing Lu. Frau Jiang, 44, freut sich über ihren neuen Job.«

Was hier entworfen wird, weist in seiner öden Schönfärberei zwar noch gewisse Ähnlichkeiten mit dem verordneten

Optimismus jener Ära auf, deren Anfänge ihre Kraft aus den großen Gedanken des Sozialismus zog. Doch die – vielleicht utopischen – Ziele, die man damals vor Augen hatte, wirken heute lächerlich und abstrus wie Maojacken und Mandschuzöpfe. Wo gibt es eine gläubigere Gefolgschaft des Kapitalismus als hier, in diesen Texten, geschrieben und gedruckt in einer Stadt, deren Arbeiter vor siebzig Jahren als Erste aufstanden, um die westlichen Bedrücker aus dem Land zu werfen? Von Arbeitern – namentlich dem Millionenheer der Wanderarbeiter, die aus den armen Provinzen in die Stadt strömen, um zu niedrigsten Löhnen die Wolkenkratzer der Reichen zu bauen – ist nicht mehr die Rede. Umso mehr von A-Shares und B-Shares, Profitraten, Börsengängen. Wie schnell scheint man verstanden und akzeptiert zu haben, dass man durch Arbeit heute auf keinen grünen Zweig mehr kommt! Am liebsten meldet der *Shanghai Star* Ereignisse, die die Modernität und Weltstädtischkeit Shanghais beweisen, wie die Eröffnung der neuen Valentino-Boutique oder das von den Konsumenten endlich entdeckte Bedürfnis nach einer Antifaltencreme. Die Tatsache, dass die Zahl der Aidskranken in der Stadt ständig steigt, wird von der Nachricht verdrängt, dass eine Shanghaier Firma ein neues Aids-Wundermittel auf den Markt gebracht hat. Es heißt XQ-9302, und weil in Shanghai die Tradition dem Fortschritt dient, sind über 20 traditionelle Heilkräuter darin enthalten. Auf der Titelseite feiert man das moderne Leben bei der Einweihung einer neuen Coca-Cola-Abfüllanlage in Pudong. Der Vizebürgermeister prostet mit einer roten Coladose dem Präsidenten von Coca-Cola zu, und man erfährt, dass ein Shanghaier 86 Flaschen Coca-Cola pro Jahr trinkt, 81 Flaschen mehr als der Landesdurchschnittsbürger. Die Steigerungsrate bis zum Jahr 2000 beträgt …

SÖCKCHEN

Grausam war die Unterdrückung, die Frauen im alten China zu erdulden hatten. Als Mädchen verkaufte man sie an prügelnde Ehemänner, als Witwen trieb man sie zum Selbstmord, als mittellose Bäuerinnen machte man Konkubinen, Prostituierte, Arbeitssklavinnen aus ihnen. In Stadt und Land wurden Frauen misshandelt, gedemütigt, der fundamentalsten Rechte beraubt. Emblematisch für ihre Lage ist die jahrhundertelang geübte Praxis des Füßebindens geworden, wodurch man ihnen die Freiheit der Bewegung nahm und sie zwang, sich auf die wenigen häuslichen Tätigkeiten zu beschränken, die man ihnen zugestand.

Heute werden die winzigen, schön bestickten seidenen Schühchen, in denen noch vor zwei, drei Generationen die gebrochenen Füße der Frauen steckten, als Kuriositäten auf Flohmärkten verkauft. Aber das Füßebinden war keine Kuriosität, und die einst erlittenen Torturen sind dem kollektiven Gedächtnis der Frauen vielleicht tiefer eingeschrieben, als man es sich mit einem einzelnen heutigen Kopf vorzustellen vermag. Wie ist es zu erklären, dass man sehr kurze Röcke und sehr durchsichtige Stoffe, doch auch bei heißestem Wetter öffentlich kaum einen Frauenfuß zu sehen bekommt, der unbekleidet im Schuh steckt? Sollen die bei Busfahrerinnen, Professorinnen, Köchinnen, Managerinnen, Verkäuferinnen gleichermaßen beliebten, zu Hosen wie zu Röcken getragenen dünnen, hellfarbenen Söckchen die Füße hervorheben oder den Blicken entziehen? Steckt in diesem merkwürdig verschämt anmutenden Utensil außer einer letzten glimmenden Erinnerung an traditionelle Kleidungsvorschriften nicht auch der Hinweis auf eine schwer zu fassende, tiefsitzende Furcht vor Verletzung der gerade erst befreiten Füße?

STEMPEL

Stempel werden in China seit über dreitausend Jahren benutzt. Zuerst waren es hohe Beamte, die offizielle Dokumente mit roten Siegeln beglaubigten, später benutzten mehr und mehr gebildete Privatleute, Literaten, Maler und Kalligraphen Stempel als künstlerische Form der Gestaltung ihrer Namen, Gedanken und Maximen. Immer wieder wurden die für den Stempeldruck verwendeten Siegelschriften vereinheitlicht. Wer sich heute einen Stempel schneiden lässt, wählt häufig eine Schrift, die aus der Zeit der Qin- und Han-Dynastien stammt. Stempel waren anfangs flache Metallplättchen, die man auch als Anhänger um den Hals trug, später verwendete man wertvollen, oft durchscheinenden und farbigen Stein mit geschnitzten Tierfiguren als Schmuck. Das Stempelschneiden ist eine Schriftkunst wie die Kalligraphie. Auf kleinster, meist quadratischer Fläche werden die Zeichen so angeordnet, dass sich ein ästhetisches Ganzes ergibt. Im Shanghai Museum sieht man die Abdrücke sehr alter Stempel, bei denen man auf den ersten Blick nichts als ein gleichmäßiges Linienmuster zu erkennen vermag. Bei genauerem Hinsehen enthüllen sich dem Kenner die Linien als Schriftzeichen, die, von oben nach unten und von links nach rechts gelesen, einen Sinn ergeben – Beamtentitel, Gedichtanfänge, Sinnsprüche. Auf höchst kunstvolle Weise ähneln diese Stempelbilder dem Daumenabdruck, von dem das Stempeln und Drucken vielleicht einst seinen Ausgang nahm. Der Unterschied zwischen unserer Signatur und einem Stempel ist der zwischen einer zufälligen Kritzelei und einem Gemälde. Insofern bringt der Stempel die Individualität dessen, der ihn benutzt, genauer und mit mehr Autorität zum Ausdruck als seine Unterschrift. Maler versehen ihre Bilder mit Stempeln, aber ein altes Bild trägt oft auch noch die Kolophone und Stempel derer, die es besessen haben. Das Bild wird sprechend durch die sichtbaren Eindrücke all derer, die es betrachtet und Zwiesprache mit ihm gehalten haben.

STRASSENHÄNDLER

Vor den Toren unserer Wohnsiedlung herrscht ein buntes Treiben. Immer gibt es etwas zu schauen, zu kaufen und zu kosten, immer ist was los. Daran sind die Straßenhändler schuld. Sie sammeln sich auf dem Bürgersteig. Sie kommen pünktlich und gehen klaglos an die Arbeit. Jeden Tag werden es mehr.

Straßenhändler sind Leute, die auf der Straße sitzen.

Frauen in geflickten Jacken breiten Tücher über den Bordstein und legen Wäscheklammern, Kleiderbügel, Einlegsohlen, BHs und Pantoffeln billigster Machart darauf. Junge Männer hocken auf dem Mäuerchen und halten angesägte CDs, Glückwunschkarten, mit Maoköpfen bemalte Aschenbecher und alte Wecker feil. Männer mit Muslimkäppis sind mit Fellen behängt, die sie Passanten anbieten. Andere ziehen Tierschädel und Batikstoffe aus ihren Rucksäcken. Es gibt Sonnenblumenkerne, Nüsse und Obst. Es gibt auch »stinkenden« Tofu und duftenden Jasmin. Es gibt Zierschildkröten in Plastikwannen. Es gibt Krimskrams. Zum Frühstück die Fladenbäcker. Mittags die Garküchen auf Fahrrädern, die Schachtelreisverkäufer. Wenn es kalt wird, die Süßkartoffelröster mit ihren großen Tonnen. Abends die Lammfleischspießbrater, die Pfannkuchenbäcker …

Mitten im malerischen Gedränge rief plötzlich jemand:

»Polizei!« Und alle Straßenhändler packten in höchster Panik ihre Sachen zusammen und zogen ihre Wägelchen und Karren und Räder in die nächste Toreinfahrt. Zwei, drei Polizisten mit Schlagstöcken erschienen und zerschlugen alles, was sie noch vorfanden. Außer zerbrochenen Eiern, zerschmetterten Hockern und Öllachen zwischen den Pflastersteinen blieb nichts übrig. Wer beim Straßenverkauf ohne Erlaubnisschein erwischt wird, bekommt eine saftige Strafe. Es gibt regelmäßige Kontrollen und Verwarnungen, doch es gelingt den Behörden nicht, dem Straßenhandel Herr zu werden.

»Die Reform der Staatsunternehmen wird vor allem einen wirtschaftlichen Mechanismus etablieren, durch den starke Einheiten überleben und schwache untergehen.« So steht es treffend in der Zeitung.

Der Kampf zwischen den starken Einheiten und den schwachen wird vor aller Augen ausgetragen. Das traditionelle Kleingewerbe, das einst die Straße bevölkerte, stirbt aus. Heute kommen viele Straßenhändler aus industriellen Berufen. Nach der Entlassung aus der Fabrik ist die zermürbende und unsichere Arbeit auf der Straße die einzige Erwerbsquelle, die ihnen noch offensteht, und sie sind verzweifelt genug, um wegen ein paar Yuan – oft nicht einmal das – Razzien, Strafen, die allzeit mögliche demütigende Begegnung mit der Staatsgewalt in Kauf zu nehmen.

Straßenhändler sind Leute, die auf der Straße sitzen.

Nur uns gutbezahlten Blinden erscheint das täglich farbiger werdende Treiben vor den Toren unserer Wohnsiedlung bunt.

Unglaublich, aber wahr! Nach langen Monaten geduldigen Einhörens ist es der Berichterstatterin gelungen, das auf den Straßen Shanghais herrschende verwirrend vielstimmige Hupkonzert in Einzelstimmen zu zerlegen und das uns so fremd anmutende Idiom des morgendlichen Quäkens und Jaulens, Klingelns und Zirpens, Trötens und Orgelns ins Deutsche zu übertragen.

Im Folgenden ein Auszug:

(...)

Ein mit Kohlköpfen beladener schwerer blauer Lastwagen der Marke Ostwind (gutmütig, vom Land):

»He! Genossen! Macht frei die Bahn!
Uns braucht die Gesellschaft, wir müssen fahrn!«

Ein Bus der öffentlichen Verkehrsbetriebe, in dem die Leute stehen wie Sardinen in der Büchse (missgelaunt, brummig):

»Gesellschaft, Gesellschaft, das kennen wir!
Wer macht den Reibach, wer schuftet hier?«

Eine nagelneue Mopedrikscha (munter):

»Ihr wisst wohl noch nichts von der neuen Reform?
Privat muss man sein! Privat setzt die Norm!«

Der Laster:

»Ach, lass uns in Ruh. Wir rackern uns ab.
Ihr kläfft und meckert und fresst nicht zu knapp.«

Ein weiterer öffentlicher Bus, mit aus dem Fenster hängender lärmender Schaffnerin:

»Und wisst ihr, was wir am liebsten fressen?
Die Kameraden in ihren Ackerchaisen!«

Noch ein Bus (alt, schwarze Rauchwolken aus dem Auspuff schleudernd):

»Wir dienen dem Volk! Wir brauchen Platz!
Für pünktliche Leute gibt's keinen Ersatz!«

Ein Motorroller einheimischen Fabrikats (hustend):

»Ersatz gibt's heute für alle und jeden!«

Der alte Bus:

»Sei still! Lass die Erwachsenen reden!«

Ein halbleerer klimatisierter privater Nissan-Kleinbus mit wehenden Gardinen (nervös):

»Wer euch noch nimmt, ist selber schuld,
Die neue Zeit hat keine Geduld!«

Ein privater Iveco (gellend):

»Früh aufstehn, heißt's, und los mit Gebraus,
Mit den alten Gäulen ist's endgültig aus!«

Der alte Bus (empört, zitternd):

»Ich wette, ihr werdet vor uns verkalken,
Der Gaul ist alt, doch er kennt kein Halten!«

Ein Santana-Taxi (von hinten heranpreschend, mit quietschenden Bremsen):

»Wir fordern Freiheit und Vorfahrt für alle,
Und Fleisch jeden Tag und Geld auf die Kralle!«

Ein riesiger, strahlendweißer Daewoo (ruhig vorbeiziehend):

»Mein Gott, wie schmutzig hier alles ist!«

Der Ostwind (frech):

»Auch du kamst mal von 'nem Haufen Mist!«

Eine staubige schwarze Firmenlimousine mit schwarzen

Scheiben, Marke Rote Fahne, die schon bessere Tage gesehen hat (neidisch):

»Schaut her, der Affe auf Angebertour!
Ihr habt den Crash! Wir die Kultur!«

Ein Audi-Taxi (rechts überholend, kämpferisch):

»Ihr glaubt, wir wissen nicht, wie's geht,
Wie man ohne Arbeit Milliarden verbrät –«

Ein Passat-Taxi, dessen Insassen auf ihren Laptops Börsenkurse studieren (stehend, wissend):

»Und Schulden macht und vergisst, sie zu blechen –«

Ein Laster mit eingedrücktem Kotflügel und sich drehender Zementmischtrommel (zwischen den Zähnen):

»Lakaien! Euch sollen die Achsen brechen!«

Eine wacklige Fahrradrikscha mit Hilfsmotor und zerschlissenem Plastiksitz:

»Wir ehrlichen Leute, für uns ist es schlimmer,
Uns lassen sie bluten, einst und immer!«

Der Santana (unwirsch):

»Gejammer, Gejammer, sonst hört man hier wenig.«

Der Passat (höhnisch):

»So bleibt man ewig arm und sehnig.«

Ein Fahrrad, Marke Forever (hoheitsvoll):

»Wir Armen von der dritten Welt
Könn' tun und lassen, was uns gefällt!«

Ein privater Mitsubishi (unbeeindruckt):

»Ihr könnt ja nicht mal Autos baun!«

Der Rote Fahne (wütend):

»Weil uns die Amis die Ingenieure klaun!«

Ein Fahrrad mit selbstgebasteltem Beiwagen, in dem ein Kind sitzt und eifrig einen Comic liest:

»Du Ausländer da, mit der großen Lippe,

Wie kriegst du nur so viel Fett auf die Rippe?«

Ein rumpelnder alter Kleinlaster ohne Markennamen, auf dessen Ladefläche ein paar frierende Arbeiter zwischen Mandarinenbergen ins Leere starren:

»Uns fehlt's nicht an Fleiß, uns fehlt's nicht an Schwung,
Uns fehlt's an 'nem neuen Mao Zedong!«

Ein Fahrrad (beiseite):

»Der Mao wie der Jiang Zemin,
Die führn das Volk in den Ruin!«

Ein Moped, Marke Piaggio (arrogant):

»Hört mal! Wie schön mein Auspuff kracht!«

Ein Fahrrad (klapprig, müde):

»Das hab ich die ganze Nacht gemacht!«

Noch ein Fahrrad (solidarisch):

»Ach, wie gut konnt man einst pofen!«

Der Santana (energisch durchstartend):

»Nur kein Mitleid mit den Doofen!«

Das Fahrrad (träumerisch fortfahrend):

»Als man statt auf Motorkarkassen
Sich noch auf die eigne Kraft verlassen …«

Ein riesiges altmodisches Motorrad, Marke Glück, von zwei Lastfahrrädern eingekeilt:

»Nur Gier, nichts andres ist die Jugend!«

Ein Fahrrad (ironisch):

»Wo bleibt die Bildung und die Tugend?«

Ein Mountainbike, Marke Phoenix (in Schlangenlinien auf dem Bürgersteig überholend):

»Die alte Zeit geht brav am Zügel,
Der schlauen Jugend wachsen Flügel!«

Ein von zwei Menschenarmen gezogener hölzerner Abfallkarren mit Glöckchen (weinerlich):

»Seht, Brüder, mich und meinen Karrn,
Ich muss doch auch den Weg hier fahrn …«
Das Mountainbike (beiseite):
»So'n Schmarrn!«

SUN-YAT-SEN-HAUS

An einem eisigen Samstag kurz vor dem Frühlingsfest besichtigte ich das Haus in der Xiangshan Lu in der ehemaligen französischen Konzession, wo Sun Yat-sen nach dem fehlgeschlagenen Feldzug gegen die Warlords in Guangxi 1918 einzog und bis 1924 lebte, ein Jahr vor seinem Tod und der geplanten Nördlichen Expedition zur Wiedervereinigung des zerfallenen und zerstrittenen, ausgepowerten Landes, die er anführen sollte. Es ähnelt auf den ersten Blick einem Landhaus im europäischen Stil; erst bei Betrachtung der zum Garten sich öffnenden Front versteht man, dass es mit den großzügigen, vielteilig gegliederten Fenstern des überdachten Balkons und den schattigen Arkaden der Veranda ein durch und durch chinesisches Haus ist. Der vorgebaute, Licht und Luft einlassende Raum puffert das Innere gegen die oft so unbekömmliche Shanghaier Witterung ab. Die Farben – die Oberflächen sind nicht verputzt, sondern mit dunkelgrauen glatten Kieselsteinen beworfen, Fensterrahmen und Türen braunrot lackiert – gleichen denen der typischen chinesischen Fassaden überall in der Stadt. An diesem Tag bin ich die einzige Besucherin.

Die Tour beginnt in der Küche, wo mich ein freundlicher älterer Herr in Empfang nimmt, mir bedeutet, meine Schuhe mit den bereitliegenden Plastiküberzügen zu versehen, und mich in einem Kauderwelsch aus Englisch und Chinesisch auf den damals hochmodernen Heißwasserboiler und den Gasherd mit Ofen hinweist. Durch einen dunklen Gang mit verglasten Bücherschränken erreichen wir den Empfangsraum mit angeschlossenem Speisezimmer. Der Führer betätigt eine Kurbel, es erschallt eine Stimme, die auf Englisch die Einzelheiten der Einrichtung erklärt, der Führer deutet stumm auf das jeweils Erwähnte. Der Dielenboden ist mit einem schönen Teppich bedeckt, die Wände sind dunkel getäfelt, die klassischen Möbel aus wertvollem dunklem Holz. Auf schmalen Gestellen stehen alte Vasen und Statuen, ein silberner Pokal. An der Wand Kalligraphien in schwarzen Rahmen. Ein Wandschirm mit eingelegten farbigen Steinen, blühende Zweige und Vögel vorstellend. Ein Kaminschirm mit hellem Marmor, dessen Maserung einen breiten Fluss mit dunklen Bergen bildet. Auf dem Kaminsims ein Schwert aus Familienbesitz. Über dem Kamin das schwarz gerahmte Foto des Hausherrn. Es gibt viele Fotos von Sun Yat-sen. Die meisten zeigen ihn in der untadeligen Haltung und Kleidung (westlich und chinesisch im Wechsel) des Weltmanns, mit einem von Entschlossenheit, eiserner Selbstdisziplin und dünnlippiger Distanz geprägten Gesicht. Auf späteren Fotos zeigt sich die Andeutung eines unfrohen Lächelns, Einsamkeit, Verbitterung.

Etwas Düsteres und Bedrückendes liegt über den Räumen, die vom persönlichen Schicksal dieses umhergeworfenen und in seinen politischen Zielen so oft schwankenden schmächtigen Mannes nichts erkennen lassen. Doch mein Führer lässt mir keine Zeit, länger darüber nachzusinnen. Wir steigen eine enge, dunkle Treppe hinauf. Am Fuß der Treppe ein Schrank für die Geschichte der vierundzwanzig Dynastien.

Im Flur des ersten Stocks ein verglaster Bücherschrank neben dem anderen. Anders als andere Reformer seiner Zeit besaß Sun nicht den Hintergrund eines klassisch gebildeten konfuzianischen Gelehrten. Die Titel auf den abfotografierten Bücherrücken lassen auf eher westlich orientierte Bildung und breites Wissen über die politische Weltkonstellation schließen, die zu der für China so entscheidenden Situation in den zwanziger Jahren des 20. Jahrhunderts führte. Sie erinnern auch daran, dass Sun in diesem Haus zwei Bücher schrieb, in denen er seine Ansichten über die weitere Entwicklung Chinas darlegte. (Von der heutigen offiziellen Geschichtsschreibung werden sie bestenfalls gönnerhaft belächelt.)

Als Nächstes geleitet mich der kleine grauhaarige Führer ins Schlafzimmer, und hier erst wird mir durch die Anwesenheit einer Frisierkommode, einer weiß überzogenen Chaiselongue mit bestickten Kissen und einem Foto an der Wand klar, dass der Hausherr mit seiner Ehefrau hier lebte. Es gibt noch ein weiteres Foto Song Qinglings im Haus, es hängt über dem Kamin des angrenzenden Arbeitszimmers *(seines* Arbeitszimmers). Beide Fotos zeigen sie lesend, mit gesenktem Blick. Ich versuche mir vorzustellen, wie das Leben für diese schöne, sanfte junge Frau gewesen sein muss, die eben erst ihr Studium in Amerika beendet hatte und sich – als Einzige in ihrer berühmt-berüchtigten Shanghaier Familie – glühend für die Republik begeisterte, an der Seite eines fünfzigjährigen Schwerkranken (wann wurde es ihm bewusst, dass er nur noch kurze Zeit zu leben hatte?), der ihr Vater hätte sein können, in diesem Haus, das so streng und männlich und tadellos war wie er selbst.

Wie bei einer Geisterbeschwörung scheinen sich meine Gedanken auf den Führer zu übertragen. Er lenkt meine Aufmerksamkeit auf einen gepolsterten Stuhl neben der Balkontür. Er stellt sich vor ihn, geht in die Knie, beugt sich vor und legt beide Hände auf den Sitz. Dann richtet er sich auf und bedeutet mir, es ihm nachzutun. Ich weiß nicht, warum, aber ich tue, ohne zu zögern, wie er mir geheißen. Er bleibt neben mir stehen und lehnt sich mit seinem ganzen Gewicht auf meinen Rücken. »Heavy?«, fragt er. Ich bejahe verwirrt. Und bevor ich Zeit habe, mich wieder aufzurichten, spüre ich, wie sich das Gewicht auf meinem Rücken verstärkt – der Mann sitzt auf mir, und mit einer sonderbaren, hämisch gellenden Stimme ruft er: »Heavy! Heavy!«, bis mein stotternder Protest ihn endlich dazu bewegt, mit dem bizarren Spiel aufzuhören und wieder abzuspringen. Triumphierend lächelnd (so interpretiere ich es jedenfalls) führt er mich weiter in den kleinen Salon und das Arbeitszimmer, wo er wie üblich an den passenden Stellen des englischen Lautsprecherschwalls auf Landkarten, Schreibutensilien, gerahmte Urkunden und Antiquitäten deutet. Sodann entlässt er mich formlos am Fuß der Treppe.

Im Garten betrachte ich lange die Rasenfläche, auf der am 5. Mai 1924 Kommunisten und Nationalisten gemeinsam den dritten Jahrestag von Dr. Suns Einsetzung als außerordentlicher Präsident der Republik feierten – dieselben Männer, die sich wenig später im Bürgerkrieg auf das blutigste befehden sollten –, und noch einmal sehe ich zu dem Balkon mit seinen großen blinden Fensterbögen hoch, hinter denen die junge Schöne mit den revolutionären Ideen an einsamen Nachmittagen auf ihrer Chaiselongue saß und Tanzmusik aus dem Radio hörte, und dann löst sich die Spannung, ich kann das Lachen nicht mehr unterdrücken.

TÄNZER

In den Parks sind Leute zu beobachten, die an Seeufern, unter Bäumen, unter Pergolen aus Beton ein merkwürdiges Hobby pflegen. Ein Kassettenrecorder mit zwei Lautsprechern bläst dünne Musik in die kalte Vorfrühlingsluft, Tango und Foxtrott, Rumba und Cha-Cha-Cha. Die Leute wackeln mit den Hüften, wedeln mit den Armen, halten sich an den Händen wie Kinder, drehen sich umeinander wie Ponys. Sie sind steif und unbeholfen, arglos und ohne Prätention. Sie tragen schlecht geschnittene Hosen und schlecht sitzende Röcke, abgewetzte Pullover und unansehnliche Polyesterhemden, und ihre Schuhe sind unelegant und plump. Nüchtern, mechanisch halten sie den Takt. Ihre Füße kennen die Schrittfolge, aber ihre Körper lassen sich vom Rhythmus nicht mitreißen. Dass diese Sache etwas mit Gleiten und Schweben und erotischer Seligkeit zu tun haben kann, das ahnen sie nicht und wollen es nicht. Sie heben nicht ab. Sie bleiben auf dem Boden. Doch seltsam, auch darin ist Liebreiz.

TAXIFAHRER

Aus Stolz, nicht zu den körperlich Arbeitenden zu gehören, haben sich manche den Daumen- oder Kleinfingernagel lang wachsen lassen; manche berichten von bitterer Arbeitslosigkeit nach der Entlassung aus der Fabrik; viele nutzen den geschützten Raum des Taxis zu offenen Gesprächen über Politik; hin und wieder wird vom Fahrgast verlangt, den Weg zum Fahrziel anzugeben (der Gebrauch eines Stadtplans ist unüblich); zuweilen wird einfach irgendwo angehalten und behauptet, das da vorne sei das gewünschte Fahrziel (Ausländern kann man alles erzählen); manche haben ein Glöckchen um den Finger gebunden, um sich wach zu halten; der Gebrauch von Aufputschmitteln soll verbreitet sein; manche erhoffen sich von einem Maobild Schutz vor Unfällen; an fast jedem Rückspiegel baumeln Amulette. Gibt es etwas, was allen Taxifahrern gemeinsam ist?

Ich weiß es nicht. Sobald ich eingestiegen bin, bemühe ich mich, Auto, Chauffeur und die Fährnisse des Weges zu vergessen. Ich sehe nur seitlich aus dem Fenster und habe mir zum Grundsatz gemacht, niemals irgendein Wende-, Ausweich- oder Überholmanöver im Einzelnen zu verfolgen. Am bemerkenswertesten finde ich weniger die Taxifahrer als jene Fahrgäste, die imstande sind, neben ihnen mit zurückgelehntem Kopf und offenem Mund Mittagsschlaf zu halten.

TORSO

Ich gehe oft ins Shanghai Museum. Ich habe mehrmals die Abteilung für Skulptur besucht. Ich habe Skulpturen von Fabelwesen und Buddhas und Wächtergottheiten und Tänzerinnen gesehen. Ich habe mehrmals die Abteilung für Malerei besucht. Ich habe Bilder von Blumen und Vögeln, von Mönchen und Arhats und Damen, die Schmetterlinge fangen, und Landschaften betrachtet. Ich habe versucht, die Unterschiede in der Malweise der Maler verschiedener Dynastien herauszufinden. Ich habe mir Namen eingeprägt. Ich habe mir Techniken erklären lassen. Ich habe Bücher gekauft. Oft stand ich überwältigt von der unendlichen Weite und feierlichen Tiefe einer Berglandschaft mit Wasserfällen und Kiefern und Nebeln und Einsiedlern, die in Pavillons die Natur anbeten, vor einem Bild, und dann kam das nächste Bild, und ich hatte keine Kraft mehr, mich überwältigen zu lassen, weil es mir an Kriterien mangelte, ich sah nichts Genaues mehr, alles verschwamm zu einem nebulösen Berg-und-Wasser-Einerlei.

Im Shanghai Museum fand eine Ausstellung von Kunstwerken aus dem Besitz der Medici statt. Eines der Glanzlichter der Ausstellung war ein dreiundzwanzig Zentimeter hoher Terrakotta-Männertorso von Michelangelo auf einem hölzernen Sockel, in einem Glaskasten.

Der Torso war mir sofort vertraut. Mit meinem Blick folgte ich den von Muskeln, Sehnen, Fett und Haut gebildeten Erhebungen und Kuhlen, dem vorspringenden Bauch, den zwittrigen Hügeln der Brust, dem kühn geschwungenen Tal des Rückgrats, ich nahm das Harte wahr und das Weiche, das Herausgedrückte und das Eingezogene, das Kämpferische und das Nachgebende, das Befreite und das Gebückte. Ich setzte den Torso in Beziehung zu seinem Bildergefolge von florentinischen Renaissancemachthabern, den herausquellenden blauen Augen und Wüstlingslippen der Cosimos, den auftrumpfenden roten Waden Lorenzos, den spitzenumkränzten Jungfernwangen der Maddalena Strozzi, dem verhärmten und hochmütigen Gesicht der Cristina di Lorena. Ich sah die dem Torso beigesellten Allegorien und Schlachten und biblischen Szenen, Körper und wieder Körper, bloßes weißes wildes unbeherrschbares Fleisch.

Vor den Bildern und Glaskästen standen laut diskutierende Männer mit dicken Brillen und zwei Lagen abgetragener Pullover, Frauen in Stoffschuhen, mit rostigen Klammern im Haar, picklige junge Männer und Studentinnen in Miniröcken mit Rucksacktäschchen aus Kunstleder. Ich versuchte, den Torso mit ihren Augen zu sehen. Ich versuchte, ihn von den eleganten Buddhas und erhabenen Landschaften her zu sehen, die ich kennengelernt hatte. Ich versuchte, die Gewohnheit abzuschütteln, die Schulung abzuschütteln, mir diesen Torso fremd zu machen. Ich sah, dass dieser Torso, umringt von den Emblemen der Macht, der Dauer, der Unbesiegbarkeit, ein monströser Körper war, besessen von Tod und Verwesung und Untergang. Ich sah diesen kleinen tönernen Torso im Shanghai Museum *genau*. Und ich erkannte, dass das, was Kunstgenuss genannt wird, nur an dieser Grenze zu haben ist, wo Vertrautheit an Widerwillen grenzt, wo man für einen Moment die Freiheit gewinnt, mit anderen eigenen Augen zu sehen.

TRADER'S BAR

Man durchquert die Empfangshalle eines etwa dreißigstöckigen Hotels und gelangt mit dem Aufzug in den dritten Stock. Wenn man den Aufzug verlässt, glaubt man sich im Keller, denn es sind nirgends Fenster zu sehen. Ein goldener, metallisch glänzender Buddha mit Blumengestecken links und rechts sitzt neben dem Aufzug im Gang. Ein Empfangsfräulein im Qipao steht neben dem Eingang zur Bar an einem Pult, auf dem ein aufgeschlagenes Heft liegt. Das Empfangsfräulein lächelt und zeigt sein langes Bein im Schlitz des Qipaos, während es etwas in das Heft einträgt. Dann weist es mit einladender Geste auf die offene Tür. Im Innern herrscht schummriges Licht, und große braune Sessel stehen um kleine Tischchen herum. Die Tischchen sehen aus wie die Tischchen in Pariser Bistros. Hier sind sie allerdings – Platte, Bein und geschwungener Fuß – vollständig aus Marmor. In der Mitte des Raums zieht sich ein viereckiger Tresen mit Barhockern um den Ausschank. Über dem Tresen hängen zahllose Weingläser wie Glasglocken von der Decke. Hinter gläsernen Wänden sind Flaschen aller Getränkemarken der Welt ausgestellt. Auf den Barhockern sitzt niemand. Zwischen den Barhockern stehen Mädchen in Tennisröckchen, Hände sittsam hinterm Rücken verschränkt. Sobald man sich gesetzt hat, eilt eines von ihnen auf leisen

Tennissohlen herbei, um die Karte zu bringen. Man mag diese Mädchen auf Chinesisch ansprechen – sie antworten in jedem Fall auf Englisch. Ein Glas Bier kostet so viel wie ein ganzes Abendessen anderswo. Man bestellt, und sofort stehen die Getränke vor einem. Auf dem Tischchen ist ein blau-weißes Gefäß, in Form und Dekor einer Ming-Schale nachempfunden, mit gesalzenen amerikanischen Erdnüssen gefüllt. An der Wand hängt ein Ölgemälde, das eine Ansicht Venedigs im Stil Canalettos zeigt. Über den ganzen Raum verteilt hängen Fernsehapparate von der Decke, auf denen man abwechselnd ein Golfturnier in Pakistan und ein Autorennen auf dem Hockenheimring verfolgen kann. Auf einer Bühne, deren Prospekt wie ein Plattencover der sechziger Jahre aussieht, spielt eine chinesische Band amerikanischen Jazz aus den vierziger Jahren. Das Publikum besteht aus hünenhaften blonden jungen Männern, die Jeans, karierte Hemden, Turnschuhe und Geldgürtel tragen und australisch oder norwegisch reden. Es gibt auch eine Gruppe asiatischer Gäste, die Männer in schwarzen Anzügen, die Frauen in tief ausgeschnittenen Kleidern. Ein Mann dieser Gruppe filmt die Band mit einer Videokamera. Sobald ein Glas zur Hälfte ausgetrunken ist, erscheint eines der Tennismädchen, leert, auch wenn gar nichts drin ist, den Aschenbecher, füllt die Erdnussschale auf und fragt, ob man noch etwas zu trinken wünscht. Zu den vier Instrumentalisten auf der Bühne gesellt sich zu fortgeschrittener Stunde ein Sänger von kindlicher Zierlichkeit, in hautengen Hosen, mit Punkfrisur und Hornbrille. Sich schlangengleich vor dem Mikrofon hin und her windend, singt er mit der rauchigen Stimme von Billie Holiday: *Lost in a Masquerade.*

TRAUM

Ich bin in Deutschland. Es ist Nacht. Zugedeckt bis zum Kinn liege ich im Bett. Ein Geräusch weckt mich. Meine Mutter kommt aus dem Bad. Ich frage, was los sei. Sie setzt sich zu mir ans Bett und sagt, ihr Bein habe ein bisschen wehgetan. Ich frage, was mit ihrem Bein los sei. Sie erklärt mir, es sei abgestorben. Ich bin entsetzt. Wie kann man mit einem abgestorbenen Bein leben? Sie erklärt mir, die meisten Leute hätten abgestorbene Beine oder Arme oder sonstige abgestorbene Körperteile. Ob ich es denn noch nicht bemerkt hätte? Ich solle nur einmal herumfragen. Im Lauf der Zeit passiere das eben. Es sei ganz natürlich. Ich brauchte keine Angst zu haben. Die medizinische Technik sei so weit fortgeschritten, dass mit Einschränkungen im täglichen Leben kaum zu rechnen sei. Es tue ab und zu ein bisschen weh, aber wirklich nur ein bisschen. Das sei alles. Sie streicht mir sanft mit der Hand über die Stirn. Sie lächelt.

UNTERHOSEN

»Die Welt gehört allen«, schrieb Sun Yat-sen. Das war vielleicht zu ungenau formuliert. Den europäischen Handelsherren, die in der Stadt lebten, verdarb es jedenfalls nicht den Spaß. »Nach Shanghai kommt man, um Geld zu verdienen«, schrieb Vicki Baum rund ein Jahrzehnt später in ihrem berühmten Shanghai-Roman. Ein weiteres Jahrzehnt später wurden die Opiumhändler entmachtet, die Prostituierten umerzogen, die ausländischen Konzessionen geräumt, die ausländischen Schiffe vertrieben. Die Shanghaier bekamen ihre Stadt zurück. Dörfliche Stille zog ein, und es kam die lange Zeit des Darbens und Sichplagens.

Seit kurzem kommt man wieder nach Shanghai, um Geld zu verdienen. Die ausländischen Schiffe sind wieder da und Flugzeuge und Handelsniederlassungen und Prostituierte und bestimmt auch Opiumhändler. Auch die Frage, wem die Welt gehören soll, wird wieder gestellt. Man versteht sie als Frage der Verteilung von Märkten und Kapital.

An einer großen Kreuzung am östlichen Rand des Volksplatzes, dort, wo sich einst die Engländer zum Pferderennen trafen, wo sich heute der motorisierte Verkehr auf mehreren Spuren lärmend entlangquält, wo internationale Konzerne ihre Produkte auf einer gigantischen, triumphbogenähnlichen Videowand anpreisen, wo sich ein Geschäft ans andere reiht, wo zu fast jeder Tages- und Nachtzeit Tausende von Menschen unterwegs sind, auf Busse warten, die Treppen zum unterirdischen Einkaufszentrum oder zur U-Bahn hinauf- und hinabeilen, sich aus Kinos und Restaurants ins Freie ergießen, in Handys schreien, Taxis winken, Brieftaschen stehlen, Wasserkanister ausliefern, Sesamkuchen und *jiaozi* feilbieten oder auf der Suche nach Arbeit herumstreunen – dort also, wo das Herz der Stadt am lautesten und aufgeregtesten schlägt, hängen, an Bambusstangen zwischen zwei Strommasten knapp über Kopfhöhe aufgespannt, ein paar Männerunterhosen zum Trocknen.

Menschen aus dem Westen, mit diesem Faktum konfrontiert, kommentieren es mit weltläufiger Häme und kaum verhohlenem Ekel. Gern sprechen wir von Urbanität, an der es dieser Stadt mangle, und wenden uns hoffnungsvoll den kühlen Fassaden der neuen Hochhäuser im Westen des Volksplatzes zu, die besser als die engen und dunklen alten Quartiere zu einer Stadt passen, wie wir uns eine Stadt vorstellen. An den Fassaden hängen die Riesentransparente der Maklerfirma. Noch immer steht ein großer Teil dieser Häuser leer, weil sich Normalverdiener die geforderten Mieten nicht leisten können.

Jene, die mitten im unerträglichen Lärm und Dreck des modernen Verkehrs auf die alte dörfliche Weise leben, müssen auf einem Auge blind sein; sie hängen ihre Wäsche dort auf, wo längst keine Wäsche mehr aufgehängt werden kann, sie leben an einem Ort, der zum Wohnen nicht mehr geeignet ist. Wir aber sind blind auf dem anderen; wir sehen die Fassaden von Häusern und glauben, es handle sich um Orte zum Wohnen, wo es längst nur noch um Objekte zum Spekulieren, Gelegenheiten zum Geldverdienen geht. Gelänge es, mit beiden Augen zu sehen, würde man vielleicht weniger über Unterhosen nachdenken als darüber, was Sun Yat-sen damals gemeint hat.

VERGÄNGLICHKEIT

Auf meinem täglichen Weg zog eines Tages ein ärmlich gekleideter Mann mit der sonnenverbrannten Haut der Landbewohner meine Aufmerksamkeit auf sich. In der Hand hielt er dünne Stöcke, auf denen etwa fingerlange, aus frischen Grashalmen gefertigte Grillen und Libellen, Heuschrecken, Gottesanbeterinnen und Schmetterlinge steckten. Ich hatte schon von dieser volkstümlichen Kunst gehört, deren Produkte nicht länger haltbar sind als ein, zwei Tage – bis der Saft in den Halmen trocknet und sie welk und braun und schrumpelig geworden sind –, doch war ich einen Moment atemlos vor Überraschung, als ich im Vorübergehen die ungeheuer lebendig wirkenden Tierchen erblickte. Ich sah flache, dreieckige Köpfe, Panzer, sirrende Flügel, abgewinkelte, zum Springen bereite Beine, lange Stacheln, spitze Zangen, verletzliche Fühler, ich sah gewickelte, geknotete, geschnittene, geknickte, gefaltete Halme in allen Schattierungen von Grün.

Es war Mittag. Die Straße war voller hupender Busse und klingelnder Fahrräder, der Bürgersteig voller Leute, die wie ich Hunger hatten und zum Essen strebten. Ich blieb nicht stehen. Ich beugte mich nicht zu dem Mann hinunter, der auf seinen Fersen oder auf einem kleinen Hocker saß und feilbot, was er selbst für völlig bedeutungslos halten mochte, eine Spielerei für Kinder, sonst nichts. Peinlich standen mir meine mangelnden Sprachkenntnisse vor Augen, die Mühe der Kaufverhandlung. Doch von der Minute des Heimkommens an wartete ich ungeduldig auf den nächsten Tag. Ich rief mir die zarte Anmut jener künstlichen Gebilde ins Gedächtnis, ihre Schönheit, die die Vergänglichkeit des Frühlingsgrases, das flüchtige und flirrende Dasein ihrer natürlichen Modelle erfahren lässt. Ich nahm mir vor, den Mann, der sie verkauft und gemacht hatte, genauer zu betrachten und mehr über ihn zu erfahren. Ich wollte alles kaufen, was er zu geben hatte. Doch vergeblich hielt ich am nächsten Tag mein Geld bereit. Der Mann war nicht mehr da und kam nie wieder.

VERKEHRSPOLIZISTEN

Dass es keine Ampeln gebe, gehört zu den Märchen, die über den Verkehr in Shanghai im Umlauf sind. Doch, es gibt Ampeln, und sie funktionieren ausgezeichnet! Nur haben sie wenig mit der Regelung des Verkehrs zu tun. Es scheint nämlich, dass die Menschen hier noch nicht so weit sind, den ferngesteuerten Automaten mehr zuzutrauen als sich selbst. Deshalb kommt die Polizei den Ampeln zu Hilfe.

In der Mitte der Kreuzung steht ein rot-weiß gestreiftes Podest, auf dem gerade ein Mann Platz hat. Im Sommer und bei Regen ist ein Schirm über ihm aufgespannt. Der Mann trägt die gewöhnliche olivgrüne Polizeiuniform, ein weißes Koppel, in dem das Funkgerät steckt, weiße Handschuhe. Er hat soldatisches Training absolviert, das ist leicht zu erkennen. Bei den Drehungen, die er vollführt, hört man den trockenen Ton zusammenschlagender Hacken. Keinen Augenblick erlaubt er sich, die Schultern hängen zu lassen oder in der Hüfte einzusinken. Die Hände werden genau in Brusthöhe zusammengeführt, der gestreckte Arm wird im exakten Winkel zur Seite geführt. Doch je länger der Polizist seine Arbeit tut, desto gelassener, desto ausdrucksvoller werden seine Bewegungen. Der militärische Drill ordnet sich immer mehr den Erfordernissen der Bühne unter, auf der er hier steht.

Warnend oder ermunternd, schulmeisterlich oder schmeichelnd heben und senken sich die Arme. Bittend, beschwörend wird der Strom der Fahrzeuge mit erhobener Hand in Schach gehalten. Die behandschuhten Finger kleben nicht stumpf aneinander, sondern bewegen sich leicht und graziös wie die Federn eines Vogelflügels in der Luft. Pirouetten werden ausgeführt, zum Trommelwirbel des Verkehrslärms. Die Trillerpfeife fordert nicht eintönig zum zügigen Vorbeifahren auf, sondern wendet sich gezielt an einzelne ungeschickte, verwirrte, renitente Verkehrsteilnehmer, um sie gellend ins theatralische Gesamtgeschehen zurückzuführen.

Ab und zu muss auch ein Star seine Darbietung unterbrechen. Jemand geht einfach zu ihm hin und fragt nach dem Weg oder wo der Bus Nummer soundso viel abfährt. Dann beugt er sich mit einem Ohr hinab und gibt pflichtschuldig Antwort, bis das ohrenbetäubende Sympathiegehupe ringsum ihn davon überzeugt, dass das Publikum nicht länger ohne ihn auskommt. Oder er winkt ein Auto, das er mit Adlerblick in der dröhnenden Masse der Dahinziehenden ausgemacht hat, an den Straßenrand, um die Papiere zu überprüfen. Man gönnt ihm die Pause! Doch glücklicherweise trennt er sich nach kurzem Wortwechsel auch schon wieder von dem vor Ehrfurcht kleinlaut gewordenen Fahrer, salutiert knapp und elegant und erklimmt mit federndem Sprung erneut die Bühne. Mir aber, seiner ungeduldigen Zuschauerin, kommt nichts absurder vor als die Ampeln, die im Hintergrund blinken wie die schläfrigen Augen einer alten Gouvernante.

VOGELGEZWITSCHER

Der Taxifahrer in Peking schimpft auf die Shanghaier. Schmutzig und geldgierig seien sie, hochnäsig und geizig, und ihre Sprache sei – er sucht nach einem möglichst beleidigenden Ausdruck – wie Vogelgezwitscher. Tatsächlich hört sich das *Shanghaihua* mit seinen vielen kurzen Vokalen und Zischlauten hart und unmelodiös an, es ist keine Sprache, die ins Ohr geht, und auch wenn man als Ausländer des Hochchinesischen mächtig ist (ich bin es nicht!), erfährt man bald, dass einem hier immer eine ganze Welt verschlossen bleiben wird.

Ich verstehe nicht, worüber sich die Arbeiter am Nebentisch unterhalten, was das Kind auf dem Fahrradsitz so begeistert seinem Vater erzählt, was der Mann hinter mir im Bus in sein Handy schreit, was die Frauen mit den großen Strohhüten, die das Unkraut jäten, sich mitzuteilen haben, worüber die Studenten tuscheln, die Marktfrau klagt. Ich bin frustriert. Ich ärgere mich jeden Tag über meine Sprachlosigkeit und das, was mir durch sie entgeht.

Ein Bild, das ich in einem Buch finde, spendet Trost und neue Erkenntnis. Gemalt hat es der große Zhu Da, der Anfang des 17. Jahrhunderts in Nanchang, südlich des Jangtse, geboren wurde.

Das Original ist ein Meter acht hoch und achtundvierzig Zentimeter breit, der Grund ist gelbliches, hier und da verflecktes Papier. Oben rechts befinden sich Signatur und zwei Stempel. Im oberen linken Drittel sieht man einige verwischte schwarze Flecken und dicke Striche und zwei, drei mit nassem Pinsel hingeworfene Umrisslinien. Ein fast kahler, überhängender Fels ist dargestellt, auf dem ein kleiner Vogel mit gesträubten Federn und geöffnetem Schnabel sitzt. Im rechten unteren Drittel des Bildes sieht man wieder Felsen, mit dem gleichen flüchtigen und sicheren Pinsel skizzenhaft gezeichnet, die diesmal ein ragendes Steilufer bilden, darüber ein Fisch mit gezacktem Schwanz und feinen, fedrigen Flossen am Bauch. Der Blick des Fisches ist nach oben gerichtet, so dass der Eindruck entsteht, er lausche ruhig und aufmerksam dem lärmenden Vogel hoch über ihm.

Durch winzige Einzelheiten – die angestrengt vorgebeugte Haltung des Vogels, der Schnabel, der an einen scheltenden und zeternden Menschenmund erinnert, das fast lächelnde geschlossene Maul des Fisches, sein großes, rundes, komisch-treuherziges Auge mit der nach oben gerollten Pupille – wird ein größtmöglicher Kontrast hergestellt; zwischen der oberen Welt und der unteren, der Welt der Luft und der Welt des Wassers, der Welt der Handelnden und der Welt der Leidenden, der Welt des Redens und der Welt des Schweigens, der Empfänglichkeit, der Geduld. Betrachtet man das Bild auf dieser Ebene, »inhaltlich«, so ist der Widerspruch zwischen beiden Polen, Fisch und Vogel, in ihrer grotesken (und doch vollkommen natürlichen) Gestalt unauflöslich. Achtet man jedoch auf die Vielzahl der angedeuteten Perspektiven, lässt man sich ein auf das entschieden Nichtillusionäre der Darstellung, die kühne Abstraktion, so erschließt sich wuchtig das sublime Gleichgewicht, das dieses Bild so tief und so lebendig macht.

Zhu Da galt als überspannt, exzentrisch, krank. Seine Bilder signierte er gern mit dem Namen *lü* (Esel). Nach der Übernahme des Kaiserthrons durch die Mandschus und dem Selbstmord des letzten Ming-Kaisers (dessen Sippe er angehörte) beschloss er, nicht mehr zu sprechen und fortan als wandernder Mönch das Land zu durchstreifen. So will es die Legende. Offenbar traute man nur einem Sprachlosen jene Einsichten in das Wesen der Sprache und der menschlichen Kommunikation zu, die in seinen Bildern zu finden sind.

WESTEN

Schon lange weiß man hierzulande, dass das Paradies im Westen liegt. Aber seit man die Klassiker nicht mehr liest, sondern lieber Marketinghandbücher, Kosmetikratgeber und das jeweilige Buch zum allerneuesten Hollywoodhit, weiß man nicht mehr, was im Westen (und auf dem Weg dorthin) wirklich los ist: dass es dort manchmal so kalt ist, dass die Flüsse gefrieren, dass es ausweglose Wälder und blind machende Winde gibt und dunkle Höhlen mit heruntergekommenen Berggeistern und Länder, in denen nur Frauen wohnen. Keinem kann man trauen, weil jeder noch so gewöhnlich aussehende Mensch sich in null Komma nichts in einen mordlüsternen Ochsenkopfdämon verwandeln kann, und überhaupt ist alles von Monstern bevölkert, die Menschenfleisch essen und Kinderblut trinken, und es gibt viele senile Götter und korrupte Könige, falsche Buddhas und dumme Daoisten, sinnverwirrende Teufelinnen mit Fingern, so zart wie Frühlingszwiebeln, Rhinozerosgeister, Skorpiongeister, beleidigte und rachsüchtige Schildkröten, Leute, die eigentlich Wanzen oder Feuerwolken sind und beim ehrlichen Zweikampf zu den gemeinsten Tricks greifen, und alle möglichen sonstigen Dämonen und Barbaren. Treulich berichten von alldem die hundert Kapitel der *Reise in den Westen,* verfasst bzw. aus früheren, meist mündlich überlieferten Fassungen kompiliert in der Mitte des 16. Jahrhunderts von Wu Cheng'en. Die Helden des Buches, ein heiliger, doch ziemlich weinerlicher und unfähiger Mönch und seine beiden glorreichen Gehilfen Sun Wukong und Zhu Bajie, ein Affe und ein Schwein, zeigen als beispielhafte Kämpfer und listige Ratgeber, wie man sich aus dem Westen Sachen holt, die man braucht, um in der Welt den Anschluss zu behalten, die westlichen Dämonen in die Pfanne haut und dabei unsterblich wird.

Dies bedenkend, fragt man sich, ob es eigentlich stimmt, dass die Klassiker nicht mehr gelesen werden.

WINDRÄDER

Ich mag die bunten Windräder für Kinder. Es sind kleine Kreise aus rundgebogenen Bambusspänen mit einer Nabe aus Draht in einem Papierröllchen. Die Speichen bestehen aus dünnen, vielfarbigen, wie gebatikten Papierstreifen. Sie drehen sich an einem Bambusstäbchen, an dessen Spitze oft noch ein kleineres Windrad befestigt ist oder ein rotes Fähnchen aus Papier. Erst als ich einmal einen fliegenden Händler vor dem Jadebuddhatempel sah, der diese Windräder zusammen mit anderen Devotionalien verkaufte, wurde mir klar, dass es sich um ein altes und ehrwürdiges buddhistisches Symbol handelt, das Rad der Wiedergeburt vorstellend, das ewige Auf und Ab von Ursache und Wirkung in der bedingten Existenz, den Leidenskreis der Zeitlichkeit. Daraus haben die Chinesen ein Spielzeug gemacht.

XUJIAHUI-KATHEDRALE

Der Stadtteil Xujiahui ist nach Xu Guangqi benannt, einem berühmten Gelehrten der späten Ming-Zeit. Sein bronzenes Abbild mit Buch und Astrolabium befindet sich an der Caoxi Lu gegenüber dem Jiangguo-Hotel, wo man in der toten Saison mit Hilfe von allerlei rot-weißem Tand und einem Schriftzug aus mannshohen silbernen Lettern zahlungskräftige Gäste anzulocken versucht: MERRY CHRISTMAS.

Xu Guangqi konvertierte zum christlichen Glauben. Er war Schüler und Freund des großen Jesuiten Matteo Ricci, der 1583 China erreicht hatte und aufgrund seiner umfangreichen Kenntnisse in den Wissenschaften – namentlich der Astronomie und des Kalendermachens, der Mathematik, Geographie und Hydraulik – bei den Gelehrten des Hofes bald Anerkennung und Aufnahme fand. Nach Xu Guangqis Tod erwarb die jesuitische Mission Land aus seinem Familienbesitz, später wurde die dem hl. Ignatius von Loyola geweihte Kathedrale darauf erbaut. 1848 entstand ein katholisches Zentrum mit Waisenhaus, Gewerbeschule (in der die Zöglinge u. a. lernten, Madonnen in italienischem Stil zu malen), Bibliothek, meteorologischem Observatorium und einer Druckerei. Was ist aus all diesen Gebäuden und Projekten geworden? Was ist übrig geblieben von der anspruchsvollen jesuitischen Verbindung des geistlichen Lebens mit dem geistigen?

Der Umkreis der bescheiden wirkenden neugotischen roten Backsteinkirche mit den zwei erneuerten spitzen Türmen – während der Kulturrevolution waren sie abgehackt worden – ist von Baulärm erfüllt, nebenan entsteht ein Hochhauskomplex, dessen vorspringende Seitenfront durch schmale, hohe, weiß abgesetzte Fenster gegliedert ist. Der Architekt zeigt, dass er mit den Stilelementen des Gotteshauses generös zu spielen versteht. Es ist, als würde sich der neue Bau mit falschem Lächeln noch einmal herunterbeugen zu seiner betagten Nachbarin, bevor er sich zu seiner ganzen erdrückenden Riesengröße aufschwingt.

Über den drei vorderen Portalen der Kirche wachen Statuen bärtiger Kirchenmänner aus Stein. Im Innern steht Maria mit blauem Mantel und schwarzhaarigem Kind steif und still auf dem Tabernakel des Hochaltars. An der Chorwand hängt eine kunstlos ausgeführte Kopie von Leonardos *Abendmahl* mit vielen blonden Aposteln, die sich um einen wenig ansprechenden Esstisch versammelt haben. An den schön gearbeiteten Steinsäulen sind elektrische Ventilatoren angebracht. Da man sie im Winter nicht braucht, hat man ihnen adrette blaue Plastikhäubchen übergezogen. Zwischen den Säulen stehen Spucknäpfe mit rosa Blumendekor. Die dunkel lackierten Bänke im Hauptschiff ähneln Schulbänken. In den Seitenkapellen stehen Betstühle, manche mit Schnitzereien verziert und mit Kissen für die Knie. Bunte Bilder stellen Maria und Joseph auf der Flucht, das leere Grab mit Joseph von Arimatäa und andere einschlägige Szenen dar. Auf einem dieser Gemälde sieht man in einem Meer voll wilder, schaumgekrönter Wellen den in ihnen versinkenden blonden ungläubigen Thomas, der sich verzweifelt an seinen Herrn klammert. Hinter ihm drei weitere Apostel in einem Boot. Das blassrote

Segel flattert über ihren Köpfen wie eine Fahne. Parallel zur Fahnenstange bzw. zum Mast hat einer der Männer den rechten Arm hochgestreckt und die sehnige Hand zur Faust geballt wie ein heroischer Kämpfer auf den linientreuen Jubelbildern der sechziger Jahre. Das Pathos dieser Geste wird durch die ängstlichen Mienen der Apostel und ihre erschrockenen Blicke Lügen gestraft, mit denen sie den mühelos menschlichen Kleinmut sowie die Gesetze der Physik überwindenden Christus in leuchtendrotem Gewand auf seinem Weg übers Wasser verfolgen. In der nächsten Kapelle verwahrt man allerlei Kisten und Utensilien, mitten im Durcheinander ein ausrangierter Heiliger mit blutendem Herzen und segnend ausgebreiteten Armen. Im Seitenschiff ist auf einem zerklüfteten Gebirge aus braunem Packpapier die Krippe aufgebaut. Über Palmen und Blumen, einem echten Orangenbäumchen und zwei Plastiktannen, der heiligen Familie mit Schafen und Hirten und der Offering Box schweben weißgekleidete, schön frisierte barfüßige Barbiepuppen, die chinesisch beschriftete Spruchbänder durch die Luft flattern lassen. Eine alte Frau kniet in der vorderen Bank, laut betend.

Hinter dem Hochaltar, in einer bis auf etliche versprengte Barbiepuppen völlig kahlen, vergitterten Kapelle entdecke ich einen mit weißem Plastik bedeckten sargähnlichen Kasten. Liegt hier Xu Guangqi begraben, wie ich es in einem alten Buch gelesen habe, oder befindet sich sein Grab, einer englischsprachigen Informationstafel zufolge, in einem kleinen, nach ihm benannten Park, nicht weit von der Kirche entfernt? Umgeben von stillem Wasser und Bambus spielen dort in einem zugigen Betonpavillon ein paar alte Männer *weiqi*. Als ich vorbeikomme, heben sie die Köpfe und betrachten mich gleichmütig und schweigend.

YANGPU-BRÜCKE

»Im Zeitalter der höchsten Tugend war man in seinen Bewegungen schwerfällig, in seinen Blicken stetig«, heißt es im Buch *Zhuangzi.* »In jener Zeit gab es keine Wege über die Berge, keine Boote und Brücken, die Ströme zu überqueren. Die Zehntausend Wesenheiten wuchsen in Massen heran, jedes in seiner Sphäre.«

Doch bald ist die Selbstgenügsamkeit des ursprünglichen Lebens dahin. Die Blicke werden begehrlich. Unruhe greift um sich. Entfernungen gelten nichts mehr, Grenzen sind überwindbar. Die Ufer der Flüsse werden miteinander verbunden, dann auch Länder, Meere, Kontinente. Die Zehntausend Wesenheiten aber finden keinen Ort mehr, wo sie sich in Ruhe entfalten können, und zerstreuen sich in alle Winde.

Auf der Yangpu-Brücke erfährt man die neue Zeit als Bewegung. Unten die tutenden Frachter, die von Meeren und Flüssen hereinkommen, Schlepper mit schäumendem Kielwasser, schaukelnde Lastkähne, zu langen Pulks zusammengebunden. Am Ufer die Kräne, klein wie Spielsteine, die über den Bäuchen der wartenden Schiffe ihre Arme schwenken, flatternde Wäsche auf einem Heck, ein gelber Hund, der sich gähnend streckt, Taue, die ins Wasser klatschen, winzig, wie Stecknadeln, Matrosen, die auf schmalen Planken balancieren … Darüber der donnernde Strom der Fahrzeuge, mit Säcken, Kisten, Kanistern, Containern bepackt, auf dem Weg zu Lagerhallen, Fabriken, Märkten. Die Stadt, die bis vor ein paar Jahren nicht über den Fluss hinausgriff, dehnt sich nun zu beiden Seiten der glitzernden Schlange lückenlos bis zum Horizont. Am Himmel wälzen sich Wolken, vom Sturm getrieben, in riesigen Batzen und Ballen dahin. Der Boden unter den Füßen bebt. Mit den Stahltrossen, an denen sie hängt, scheint die Brücke selbst zu schwanken.

Auf der Yangpu-Brücke erfasst mich die alles verbindende, alles zerstreuende Bewegung der Zeit als Schwindel. Unendlich dehnen sich alle Richtungen vor mir aus; Entfernungen verschwimmen; die Zehntausend Wesenheiten wirbeln um mich herum wie Sandkörner, und ich bin mitten unter ihnen, herausgerissen aus meiner Sphäre, ankerlos, sprachlos, taub.

Das führt mich zu Zhuangzi zurück, dem (je nach Übersetzer) »Betäubung«, »Erschöpfung«, »Verwirrung«, »Von-Sinnen-Geraten« oder »Torheit« als Voraussetzung galt, das Dao zu erlangen. Von selbst kehren dann die Zehntausend Wesenheiten zu ihrer Wurzel zurück und blühen absichtslos, nach ihrer Natur. Welcher Ort aber wäre geeigneter als die große Brücke, wo alles kommt und geht und niemand bleiben kann, weder hier noch dort, ein Reich des Dazwischen, um in der Raserei der Zeit den Stillstand zu entdecken, die »große Versunkenheit«, die mit jenem berühmten Gebot des Daoismus gemeint ist: »Werde leer! Werde nichts!«

ZEICHEN (1)

Sehr geehrter Verlag der Hochschule für Sprache und Kultur!

Nach Lektüre des von Ihnen vor wenigen Jahren in Peking publizierten Werkes über die *Entwicklung der chinesischen Schrift am Beispiel von 500 Schriftzeichen* wende ich mich heute an Sie mit der Bitte, mir in einem äußerst wichtigen Punkt Gehör zu schenken, obwohl ich mich mit dem hochverehrten Autor des Buches, was natürliche Geistesgaben und wissenschaftliche Durchdringungskraft sowie die Kenntnis der Geschichte unserer ehrwürdigen Schrift betrifft, selbstverständlich nicht im Entferntesten messen kann. In meiner unentschuldbaren Dummheit und Rückständigkeit drängt es mich dennoch, ihm in einem einzigen Punkt (Seite 242) zu widersprechen.

Der ausländische Gelehrte Marcel Granet schreibt, unsere Schrift sei keine Sammlung von Bilderrätseln – doch habe sie schon in frühester Zeit als eine solche gewirkt. Wie Priester aus den Sprüngen der Knochen und Tierpanzer beim Orakel zogen unsere ersten Denker aus den Bestandteilen einzelner Begriffszeichen, die sie gegenständlich auffassten, die Anregungen zu ihrer Deutung, ihrem Gebrauch. Die von Menschen geschaffenen Zeichen wirkten wie übermenschliche Weisungen herrisch auf sie zurück. Ich weiß nicht, ob ich die Gedanken dieses Autors richtig verstanden habe, aber ich bin nach langem Nachdenken zu dem Schluss gekommen, dass er recht hat. In dem von Ihrem ruhmreichen Haus veröffentlichten Werk finde ich nun unter dem Zeichen 女 *(nü)* das Bild eines auf einem geflochtenen Bettvorleger knienden Mädchens mit zwei brezelartigen Zöpfen auf dem Kopf, in einem hässlichen, altmodischen Kleid mit weiten Ärmeln, in denen die Hände des Mädchens züchtig versteckt sind. Ihr überaus weiser und tiefschürfender Autor, mit dem ich mich, dessen bin und bleibe ich mir bewusst, in keinster Weise messen kann, behauptet in dem kurzen Begleittext am Fuß der Seite, dass sich das Zeichen 女 *(nü)* aus besagtem Bild entwickelt habe. Diese Deutung bedarf nach meiner im Übrigen völlig unerheblichen Meinung der gründlichen Bearbeitung!

Zur Untermauerung meiner Ansicht habe ich keine Mühe gescheut. Ich habe viele ausführliche Gespräche mit Mädchen und Frauen geführt, die Englisch sprechen und Chemie studieren und über die Wirkungsweise von Zementpumpen und die Tücken von Schneepflügen Bescheid wissen und dennoch auf Bettvorlegern knien müssen und Männer heiraten müssen, die sie nicht lieben, und ihnen Söhne gebären und den Befehlen ihrer Schwiegermütter gehorchen müssen, weil unsere Familien, was Mädchen und Frauen betrifft, immer noch nach der Weise des Konfuzius denken und nicht nach der Weise der Zeit, in der wir leben, und deshalb fühle ich mich berechtigt, Ihnen die folgende Alternative zur Deutung des Zeichens 女 *(nü)* zu unterbreiten: Die beiden von oben nach unten gezogenen Striche stellen den Körper eines Mädchens dar, das mit etwas zurückgebogenem Oberkörper in vorsichtiger Haltung ausschreitet. Der waagrechte Strich ist eine Balancierstange, die das Mädchen mit sich führt. Daraus wird klar ersichtlich, dass es sich um eine Luftakrobatin handelt, die sich auf einem Drahtseil vorwärtsbewegt!

Diese in aller Bescheidenheit und ohne jeden Anspruch auf Beachtung von mir vorgebrachte neue Deutung des Zeichens 女 *(nü)* trägt den modernen Lebensumständen auf korrekte Weisung Rechnung. Entschließen Sie sich, sie zu veröffentlichen, so wird der das Zeichen 女 *(nü)* schreibende Mensch künftig nicht länger Mitleid und Verachtung empfinden, sondern es werden Erkenntnisse in ihm geweckt! Er wird etwas von den Entbehrungen und Entsagungen, den zerreißenden Widersprüchen begreifen, unter denen unsere heutigen Mädchen und Frauen leiden, und gleichzeitig wird Respekt in ihm aufsteigen, Ehrerbietung für ihr hohes Können, die Kraftleistungen und Gleichgewichtskunststücke, die sie in ihren Familien und Arbeitseinheiten täglich im Stillen vollbringen.

Weiße und schwarze Katzen mögen – wie der allseits geliebte jüngst verstorbene Führer unseres Landes ausführte, dem wir die allseits begrüßte neue Richtung unserer Politik und unseres Denkens verdanken – gleichermaßen Mäuse fangen, aber wenn die Katze die Mäuse nicht fressen darf, die sie selber fängt, wird sie eines Tages ärgerlich! Es liegt mir, ich betone es nochmals, total fern, Ihrem unermüdlich zum Wohle unserer Sprache und Kultur sich abplagenden Autor ins Handwerk pfuschen zu wollen, aber wenn Sie daran interessiert sind, dass Ihr armseliges Machwerk der wissenschaftlichen Erkenntnis und dem revolutionären Fortschritt unseres Volkes dient und nicht nur dem Bau von Eselsbrücken für faule ausländische Sinologiestudenten, dann üben Sie Selbstkritik! Diskutieren Sie die Angelegenheit in Ihrem

Leitungskollektiv! Verhindern Sie den Druck der nächsten Auflage! Gestalten Sie die Seite 242 nach meinem Vorschlag neu!

Mögen alle Ihre Wünsche in Erfüllung gehen:

Eine Leserin.

ZEICHEN (2)

Was entgeht mir! Wie viel bleibt unbegriffen, missverstanden, deutungslos! Wie viel entgleitet der Aufmerksamkeit, bleibt auch dem sprachmächtigen Ausländer noch verborgen! Hat man es in der Sprache nicht mit Zeichen als Vertretern von Gegenständen zu tun? Wenn aber Gegenstände als Vertreter von sprachlichen Zeichen fungieren?

Der Fisch *(yu)*, den man zum Neujahrsfest isst, den Kinder als Laterne tragen und als Drachen steigen lassen, der Glückwunschkarten und Türetiketten schmückt, vertritt das gleichlautende, anders geschriebene Zeichen, das »übrig haben«, »Überfluss« bedeutet und mit dem der Wunsch nach Reichtum ausgedrückt wird.

Die Dattel *(zao)*, die von Braut und Bräutigam bei der Hochzeit verspeist wird, steht für ein gleichlautendes, anders geschriebenes Zeichen, das »früh«, in der Verdoppelung »so früh wie möglich« bedeutet und die Hoffnung auf baldigen Kindersegen enthält.

Den Neujahrskuchen aus Reismehl *(gao)* isst man deshalb, weil man durch das gleichlautende, anders geschriebene Zeichen »groß«, »hoch« den Wunsch nach beruflichem und gesellschaftlichem Vorwärtskommen andeutet.

Wie viele Dinge des täglichen Umgangs sind Bestandteile solcher gegenständlicher Wortspiele? Wie groß ist die Lust der Zeichen, aus ihrer glanzlosen Vertreterrolle auszubrechen, um im eigenen Interesse zu wirken! Wie leicht schaltet das Chinesische zwischen Begrifflichem und Handgreiflichem hin und her, den täppischen Fremden aufs Glatteis führend! Wie oft stößt man an sprachliche Grenzen und erfährt, dass es die Grenzen einer Welt sind!

ZIEHNUDELN

Das Lokal besteht aus zwei fensterlosen Räumen, beide zur Straße hin offen, Gastraum und Küche. Auf dem Bürgersteig ein Kästchen mit Schubladen, die Kasse. Außerdem ein dreibeiniger Dämpfer aus Blech und auf einem mit Kohle beheizten Ofen der große Kessel zum Kochen der Nudeln. Ein Mädchen, mürrisch, in kurzen Hosen und Plastikschlappen, mit schmuddeliger Bluse, fungiert als Kellnerin. Rechts an der Wand klebt ein Schild aus roter Pappe, darauf stehen, mit schwarzem Filzstift geschrieben, Gerichte und Preise. Zehn bis zwölf wacklige und von Essig und Sojasauce klebrige Campingtische mit Hockern füllen den Raum aus. Alle sind besetzt, zumeist von jungen Männern, Studenten der nahe gelegenen Universität und Arbeitern der umliegenden kleinen Autowerkstätten. An der hinteren Wand eine elektrische Uhr, darunter ein Farbfernseher. Es laufen Actionvideos aus Hongkong. Die Kellnerin schlurft im Gang zwischen den Tischen auf und ab und ruft die bestellten Gerichte aus. Sie hat Mühe, sie dort abzuliefern, wo sie bestellt wurden, denn gefesselt vom Lärm der Bilder, scheinen sich die Gäste der eigenen Wünsche bald kaum noch zu entsinnen.

Die Küche ist ebenso lang wie der Gastraum, aber nur etwa anderthalb Meter breit. Wände und Decke sind schwarz verräuchert. Säcke mit Mehl sind aufgestapelt. Zwei Männer bereiten die Speisen zu. Einer von ihnen hackt im dunklen hinteren Teil des Raumes Gemüse, das anschließend auf einem der Gaskocher mit zwei Flammen oder im Dämpfer gegart wird. Vorn wirkt der Nudelmacher, ein stämmiger Mann mit dunklem, schweißglänzendem Gesicht. Er trägt eine weiße Mütze, ein schmutzigweißes, verschwitztes ärmelloses Unterhemd. Auf dem Tisch vor ihm warten etliche Klumpen gelblichen, zähen Teigs. Er mehlt die Platte, nimmt einen Klumpen und walkt ihn mit beiden Fäusten. Er formt ihn zu einer Rolle, nimmt die Rolle in beide Hände und zieht sie, indem er sie kreisend durch die Luft schlägt, in die Länge. Er halbiert den langen Strang, indem er die Enden vom Handgelenk herabbaumeln und sich rasch umeinander ringeln lässt, längt ihn wieder, halbiert ihn, wirft ihn wieder klatschend auf den Tisch, um ihn mit Fäusten zu traktieren, mehlt die Platte, formt eine Rolle, die er in der Luft wieder mehrmals in die Länge zieht und halbiert. Endlich ist der Teig geschmeidig genug, die Rolle wird in mehrere kleinere Rollen geteilt, jede davon mit atemberaubender Schnelligkeit durch die Luft geschleudert und langgezogen. Diesmal jedoch entstehen bei dem Vorgang mit Hilfe aller Finger beider Hände die langen, sehr dünnen Nudeln, die sofort ins dampfende Wasser geworfen und gekocht werden.

Hier Blut und Eisen, Geschrei, Mord und Rache, dort der Tanz der Hände mit dem kreisenden und wirbelnden, sich widersetzenden, sich fügenden Teig. Dazwischen eine große braune Kakerlake, die ohne Eile die Wand hochklettert.

NACHWORT ZUR NEUAUFLAGE

Angeblich wird Geschichte von Siegern geschrieben und handelt von den Erfolgen derer, die sich am Ende – militärisch, politisch, ökonomisch – durchsetzen. So könnte man die Geschichte der Volksrepublik China als eine Kette von Fortschritten betrachten. Eine lange, strahlende Bahn führte von der Armut in den Reichtum, von der Unterdrückung zur Befreiung, von der primitiven, bäuerlichen Vergangenheit in die globale techno-kapitalistische Zukunft, von der Unterjochung durch Kaiser, Großgrundbesitzer und Imperialisten zur Herrschaft über die Welt. Die Propaganda der Macht nährt sich von dieser Lüge. Doch Erkenntnisse, die der geschichtlichen Wahrheit dienen, sollten dort gesucht werden, wo es nicht herrschaftlich zugeht, bei den Besiegten also, den Überholten und Zurückgelassen, die dem Fortschritt immer nur nachhinken und von dem erzählen, was bei Modernisierungen auf der Strecke bleibt, von Verlusten, aber auch von freudigen Anfängen und Hoffnungen und erstaunlichem Beharren, von dem vielfarbigen, vibrierenden Mischmasch also, aus dem zu jeder Zeit das gewöhnliche Leben besteht.

Das vorliegende Buch ist entstanden, als ich 1997/98 an einer Shanghaier Universität ein Jahr lang Deutsch unterrichtete. Es war eine janusköpfige Epoche; der gerade erst verstorbene Deng Xiaoping hatte den Auftakt zur »sozialistischen Marktwirtschaft« gegeben, und überall zeichnete sich schon die große technologische Umwälzung ab, die dazu führte, dass sich die diktatorischen Säuberungs- und Überwachungsmaßnahmen der späteren Zeit reibungslos durchsetzen ließen. Das Tian'anmen-Massaker war noch keine zehn Jahre her, doch unter den Studenten, mit denen ich Kontakt hatte, wurde dieses Ereignis nicht thematisiert. In unseren Diskussionen ging es fast ausschließlich um die Frage, wie man selbst, die Familie, das Land der Armut entkommen und mit den bewunderten hochentwickelten Nationen des Westens gleichziehen konnte. Die jungen Frauen und Männer, die mit erstaunlicher Hingabe und Disziplin westliche Sprachen lernten, träumten davon, im eigenen Auto durch ihre Stadt zu fahren, obwohl ihnen durchaus bewusst war, dass die Zunahme des motorisierten Individualverkehrs nicht nur die weitere Zerstörung der Natur, sondern auch die Beeinträchtigung ihrer eigenen Lebensqualität zur Folge haben würde. Die Propaganda des Konsums wirkte gerade unter denjenigen am stärksten, deren Familien unter den Entbehrungen der Kulturrevolution am meisten gelitten hatten. Doch es gab auch andere Stimmen. Ich lernte Kollegen kennen, die von einer Stadt schwärmten, in deren Straßen eine geradezu märchenhafte Stille geherrscht hatte, weil nur Fahrräder unterwegs waren. Ich sprach mit Professoren, die ihre besten Jahre als Zwangsverschickte unter armen Bauern verbracht hatten und voller Anerkennung das harte und für sie völlig fremdartige Leben in den Dörfern schilderten. Wie groß war der Abstand zwischen Bauern und Städtern inzwischen wieder geworden, ohne dass irgendjemand das zu kümmern schien! Ein erstaunlicher Optimismus begegnete mir, der sich ebenso sehr auf die private Lage wie auf die grundlegende Veränderung des ganzen Landes bezog. Junge Leute, die sich die Möglichkeit zu studieren oft unter größten Opfern erarbeitet hatten, glaubten, dass sich mit der bald zu erwartenden Verbesserung der materiellen Verhältnisse die politischen Probleme von selbst erledigten. Alle Repressalien und Ungerechtigkeiten, hieß es immer wieder, unter denen einzelne Gruppen heute noch litten, seien vorübergehende Fehler, sie würden bald korrigiert.

Das Emblem dieser naiven Zuversicht war Shanghai selbst, eine schon früh von den Engländern »geöffnete« Handelsmetropole, die sich damals innerhalb weniger Jahre in eine ultramoderne Boomcity verwandelte. Außer den kolonialen Prunkgebäuden am Bund blieb von der früheren Kernstadt, einem Gewirr aus zweistöckigen, von der ewigen Feuchtigkeit geprägten, erdfarbenen Wohngebäuden, schmalen Verbindungsstraßen, Märkten, Tempeln, nichts übrig. Das alte Campusgelände, auf dem wir »ausländischen Experten« untergebracht waren, bestand aus zugigen vierstöckigen Wohnblocks, die jedoch noch nicht so unbarmherzig mit dem Platz geizten, wie es die neuere Stadtplanung gebot. Abends war die dunstige Luft voller Fledermäuse, und nach jedem Regen hörte man das laute Quaken von Ochsenfröschen an den Pfützen unter den Bananenstauden. Wenige Jahre später war von alldem nichts mehr übrig. Die letzten verwilderten Gärtchen und unbetonierten Flächen wichen Autobahnen und spiegelnden Wohntürmen. Die neue Stadtstruktur ließ kaum noch Zwischenräume zu. Das vielfältige Kleingewerbe verschwand aus dem Stadtbild. Auch die wandernden Baumwollweber, Korbflechter, Spielzeugbastler, Osmanthusblütenverkäuferinnen und die vielen anderen, die sich mit irgendeiner besonderen, oft lange tradierten Fertigkeit in der täglich teurer werdenden Stadt zu behaupten suchten, verschwanden (oder wurden von der wachsenden Tourismusindustrie in Beschlag genommen). Die von Millionen elend lebender Wanderarbeiter erbaute neue Stadt war prächtig und gigantisch, sie war unzweifelhaft »modern« und bewies, dass China es mit Amerika aufnehmen konnte, sie versprach ihren Bewohnern reibungslose Funktionalität, Sicherheit und Komfort, und doch ging mit ihrem Aufstieg etwas Wesentliches verloren.

Es waren gerade die Relikte des alten Shanghai, die ich damals als so ungeheuer faszinierend empfand. Trotz aller Fremdheit schien etwas daran vertraut zu sein. Während ich abenteuerlustig die betriebsame Vielfalt in meiner chinesischen Nachbarschaft entdeckte, wurde mir klar, dass diese Vielfalt – in einer Zeit, in der man sich vom Ausmaß der Repressionen heutiger Machthaber noch keine Vorstellung machte – bedroht war von einer wachsenden Tendenz zum Aufräumen und Glätten, zum Vereinheitlichen, Bereinigen und Begradigen. Mir wurde aber auch bewusst, wie sehr mein eigenes Leben in der weit entfernten deutschen Stadt, aus der ich kam, einer ähnlichen, wenn auch weniger brutal anmutenden Entwicklung unterworfen war: So viele Dinge, die einst das städtische Dasein bestimmten, waren nach den Kahlschlägen der Globalisierung auch bei uns verschwunden. Ich blickte also durch den Schleier der Ferne in meine eigene Geschichte – und gewahrte zugleich den Umriss einer zukünftigen, post-globalisierten, gastlichen und menschenfreundlichen Traum-Stadt. Die Stadt, die ich mir vorstellte, sollte wieder konkret und irdisch sein. Es sollte ihr gelingen, die Verluste der Modernisierung durch die Wiedergewinnung von Lebensqualität auszugleichen. Wo auch immer gelegen, sollte sie, geprägt von den Kenntnissen, Kulturen und Herkünften ihrer Bürger, so vielfältig und widersprüchlich, so eigenartig und anziehend, so *bewohnbar* sein, wie man es sich angesichts der Verödung so vieler Nachbarschaften in heutigen Großstädten nur wünschen kann.

Der unauflösliche Riesenknoten Shanghai selbst generierte solche Gedanken. Er bot mir ein Übermaß an Eindrücken, denen ich schreibend versuchte, gerecht zu werden. Dabei ließ ich mich ausschließlich von den Wendungen und Sprüngen meines Interesses leiten, das von den Zufällen meines Aufenthalts, den Gesetzen meiner Stellung, der Lückenhaftigkeit meiner Kenntnisse nach allen Seiten hin beschränkt war. Die alphabetische Form gewährleistete innerhalb dieser Beschränkungen größtmögliche Freiheit, so dass nun Beobachtetes und Erlebtes, Gelesenes und Erdachtes gleichrangig und streitsam nebeneinander steht.

München, im Mai 2021

DANKSAGUNG

Während meines Aufenthalts in Shanghai lernte ich viele Leute kennen, die mich unterstützten und belehrten und mich auf manches aufmerksam machten, was ich, allein auf mich gestellt, nicht gesehen hätte. Es seien hier nur einige Namen genannt: Birgit Eckmann, Claudia Fecke, Nina Richter, Ursula Saarbeck, Tang Min, Yang Yihui, Zhang Qi. Wie viel ich ihnen verdanke, ist mir bewusst.

ZITIERT WURDE AUS FOLGENDEN WERKEN:

Wolfgang Bauer, *China und die Hoffnung auf Glück,* München 1971.

Vicki Baum, *Hotel Shanghai,* Köln, Berlin 1965.

Lu Xun, *Werke in sechs Bänden,* hg. von Wolfgang Kubin, Zürich 1994.

Jessica Rawson (Hg.), *The British Museum Book of Chinese Art,* New York 1993.

Tschuang-Tse, *Reden und Gleichnisse,* Zürich 1951.

Wu Cheng'en, *Journey to the West,* Peking 1990.

Susanne Röckel

Der Vogelgott

Roman

272 Seiten, btb 71871

Ein moderner Schauerroman voll dunkler Symbolik, betörend und verstörend.

Man kann sich seinen Gott nicht aussuchen. In Susanne Röckels unwiderstehlichem Roman entpuppt sich eine geheime Welt als unsere, eine Welt, in der die Natur ihre Freundschaft aufkündigt und wir ihrer Aggression und Düsternis gegenüberstehen: Die Welt des Vogelgottes, die, wie sich herausstellt, nicht nur ein Mythos ist.

»Susanne Röckel ist eine Sprach-Meisterin von höchsten Graden.«

Ö1 Ex Libris